Richard Lazarus was  .... Essex. He moved to Birming.... .... travelling extensively .... he returned to Engla.... ...... recently he has visite.... ...... East.

The author has a.... ...... plained' and he began researching ...... years ago. He is currently working on a new book about the existence of an afterlife.

Richard Lazarus lives with his wife in Essex.

UNNATURAL CAUSES

CAUSES

Richard Lazarus

Futura

In memory of my father

A Futura Book

First published in Great Britain in 1991 by Futura Publications
a Division of Macdonald & Co (Publishers) Ltd
London & Sydney

Reprinted 1991

Copyright © Geoff Viney 1991

The right of Geoff Viney to be identified as author of this
work has been asserted by him in accordance with the
Copyright, Designs and Patents Act 1988.

ISBN 0 7088 4936 9

Typeset by Leaper & Gard Limited, Great Britain
Printed and bound in Great Britain by
BPCC Hazell Books
Aylesbury, Bucks, England
Member of BPCC Ltd.

Futura Publications
A Division of
Macdonald & Co (Publishers) Ltd
165 Great Dover Street
London SE1 4YA

A member of Maxwell Macmillan Publishing Corporation

CONTENTS

'The known is finite, the unknown infinite;
intellectually we stand on an islet in the midst
of an illimitable ocean of inexplicability. Our
business in every generation is to reclaim a
little more land.'

T.H. Huxley (1825–95)

FOREWORD

It was inevitable that a book like this would be written sooner or later. The growing interest in astrology, spiritualism and other forms of occult lore, plus the mounting scientific evidence for ESP and telekinesis, have, during the past quarter-century, dramatically raised public consciousness towards the possibility of invisible influences active in our universe. As awareness of the unexplained has mushroomed, so the number of publications on the subject has turned into an avalanche. Yet curiously all but a few have chosen to ignore the most disturbing examples of paranormal phenomena – those in which the manifestation of mysterious forces results in the death or disappearance of human beings. It is these instances, the darkest and most disquieting aspect of the supernatural, that I choose to group together under the label, 'Unnatural Causes'.

Unnaturals come in many forms and are mysterious for a variety of reasons. In the least extraordinary examples, a series of odd events, omens or previsions may foreshadow an apparently normal fatality, strongly suggesting the involvement of an unseen hand or directing influence. In other cases, the actual physical destruction or literal disappearance of the deceased person runs so contrary to the accepted principles of science that one is forced to consider the preternatural. Examples of these impossible deaths are not hard to find. A cursory exploration of the daily newspapers in any given week will probably uncover at least one or two. In 1985, for instance, British tabloids reported upon the peculiar fate of one John Bennet, a fifty-six-year-old widower from Liverpool. What killed Mr Bennet we cannot say, for by the time the Liverpudlian's body was found lying face down on the sitting room floor of his tenement flat the corpse was decayed to a level of putrefaction suggesting that he had been dead for months. In fact Bennet had been seen alive and well by friends and family only the previous day. As one journalist pointed out, the bare facts of the case echo the gruesome fate of Edgar Allen Poe's Mr Valdemar whose bodily decomposition took only minutes, and whose still living flesh shrank and crumbled before the narrator's eyes until it became 'a nearly liquid mess of loathsome, detestable putridity'.

Certainly the parallel is clear, but with one important difference: the Liverpudlian was no literary creation, but a living, breathing human being. We shall never know the precise reason for his leaving this world, for so far advanced was his physical deterioration that Liverpool's police pathologist James Burns was unable to ascertain the likely cause of death.

Curious though the Bennet case might seem this particular piece of gothic horror is, if anything, among the least inexplicable of unnatural deaths. Among the multitude of oddities contained in the nine chapters of this book a simple case of advanced decomposition would be scarcely worthy of mention. In these pages we find truly incredible stories: of human beings exploding into shreds or vanishing into thin air; of men vaporised by glowing balls of fire and others crushed by hailstones the size of boulders; ordinary people from Brazil to Great Britain abducted, tortured or killed by aliens; USAF pilots lost in combat with UFOs over American airspace; the now-everyday occurrence of murders, massacres and suicides linked to black magic or possession; strange invisible entities which kill and mutilate for pleasure; weird animal forms which regularly slaughter livestock across three continents. These are just a handful of the deadly preternatural happenings recorded up to the present day. Taken individually they may seem unrelated; taken together they

2

appear to suggest the presence of unknown energies active in our material universe. Energies directed by intelligencies whose purpose can hardly be described as benevolent ...

Although it has taken just under four years to research and complete this study, my own fascination with the inexplicable began much earlier, in the summer of 1976. It was during my college holidays that I read a newspaper account of a teenage girl's mysterious death while dancing at a discotheque. The tragedy took place in Hornchurch, a London suburb in south-west Essex not far from my home. According to the story, printed in the *Sunday Mirror*, the girl had suddenly, and without apparent cause, burst into flames like a self-generating human torch. None of those present had been able to extinguish the blaze which burned with such intensity that the girl's body was reduced in seconds to a small pile of blackened ashes. Witnesses to the brief conflagration insisted that no naked flames had been present in the room and a spokesman for the local fire brigade could not offer any explanation. Unable to make sense of the logical contradictions presented by the witnesses' testimonies, the subsequent inquest recorded an open verdict and for a while afterwards the talk around one London suburb was of witchcraft.

This strange event intrigued me for some time. Knowing a little about the process of generating heat it seemed inconceivable to me that a girl could die from a fire that came from inside her, as some witnesss had implied.

And what of the fire's aftermath ... the claim that her entire body had been consumed to a point of near total carbonisation? Surely this was impossible.

Time passed. I went on with my degree studies and, as with all things, the Hornchurch enigma gradually slipped to the back of my mind. It was not until several years later, whilst rummaging through archive material for an article I was planning on Essex history, that I came across a faded forty-year-old newspaper cutting which bore uncanny resemblance to the account described above. Headlined

3

'Girl Burned in Ball Dress', it detailed the astonishing case of a Miss Phyliss Newcombe, who died of burns received during a dinner-dance at Chelmsford Shire Hall on 27 August 1938. Miss Newcombe, twenty-two years of age on the night of her immolation, had been dancing with her fiancé Henry McAusland when, at around midnight, her dress suddenly burst into flames. There was considerable panic, and by the time the fire was smothered with a tablecloth the unfortunate young woman had been reduced to a little more than a charred skeleton. The pre-war newspaper clipping went on to the report how county coroner, Mr L.F. Beccles, later described the incident as 'the most mysterious he had ever known'. In recording a verdict of accidental death, Beccles recognised that no natural explanation would account for the rapidity with which the flames consumed the woman's body. Yet he felt sure that a cigarette must have ignited her ball gown rather than believe the eyewitnesses who steadfastly maintained that it was Phyliss Newcombe herself, and not her garments, which were ablaze.

I was less convinced. Immediately upon discovering the report of the Chelmsford death I laid aside my planned research and set about instead to investigate these strange fatalities. Were there, I wondered, any more instances of young women bursting into fireballs whilst dancing? Over the next few days I spent hours in the local reference library checking through books on the occult and miscellaneous unusual happenings. Sure enough my labours were rewarded. In a book entitled simply *Strange Mysteries* by a Frenchman, Emile Schurmacher, there was recorded an eyewitness account of the dramatic conflagration of one Maybell Andrews, a nineteen-year-old London girl who met her doom in the public ballroom of a Soho nightclub. As the fiery visitation began, other dancing couples attested to seeing a fierce jet of blue flame burst forth from Miss Andrews' back, chest and shoulders, igniting her hair in the process. Her partner, William Clifford, was himself badly injured trying to extinguish the fire with his hands.

Afterwards Clifford expressed his solemn belief that his girlfriend's death was unnatural. It could hardly be otherwise, since the young woman had been reduced to a heap of glowing cinders. Yet there was one further detail which, if anything, was even harder to believe.

In the West End fire, Maybell Andrews' dress had not caught alight. Indeed Scotland Yard's forensic experts noticed with amazement that despite the obviously intense heat the inner material of the garment had not even been singed.

This, then, was the beginning of my interest in unnatural causes. Three girls burned to ashes in almost identical circumstances. Three deaths which defied any attempts at rational explanation. At the time I thought the examples I had uncovered were probably unique in the history of the world. Later I was to learn otherwise. In every year, from every corner of the globe, there will emerge a small but significant group of fire tragedies which do not fit into any recognised category. Often, because the circumstances surrounding these deaths are so bizarre, they remain unclassified, whilst in other cases the very fact of their existence is officially covered up. Incredibly, spontaneous human combustion is, if anything, one of the more common among unnatural fatalities, and each year brings a fresh crop of people who have ignited into a living funeral pyre. I have long since realised that not all are women and that dancing is not the only dangerous occupation. More importantly, I have discovered that 'SHC' is only one among many unnatural dangers which face mankind. It is but a single spectacular example of the presence of unseen forces beyond our capacity or willingness to comprehend.

Hard to believe? However then might we account for the German carpenter impaled by a twelve-foot-long ice spear that fell from a clear sky in 1953? Or the mystery of Zygmunt Adamski, a Polish immigrant whose body was discovered in 1981 covered in an unidentifiable corrosive liquid the same morning that members of the Yorkshire constabulary encountered alien beings on an adjacent housing estate? If we prefer to think of curses as superstitious nonsense how else can we explain the funerary procession of Earl Carnavon's archaeological team in the seven years following their defilement of Tutankhamen's tomb? Then again, if jinxes do not exist, how may we rationalise the legacy of carnage which passed on, without exception, to the owners of Archduke Ferdinand's Mercedes? As we shall see, all these and many more enigmas combine to confound the sceptic's disbelief.

Strange disappearances are also investigated. Oddities like that of David Laing, the Tennessee farmer who vanished before the eyes of his family in September 1880; or that of the first-fifth company of Norfolk fusiliers, a body of over a hundred men who marched into a bank of mist above Suvla Bay, Gallipoli, never to be seen again. Disappearances like that of Cambridgeshire stallion-keeper Donald Dent who went missing from his living room chair on a warm June evening in 1975, or that of Martin Cleghorn, a young Scot who dematerialised in front of his two brothers in a Glasgow street on the New Year's Eve of 1966.

Comprehensive details of all these and many even more bizarre happenings are included in the following chapters. The examples chosen are not the most sensational ones I have encountered, but those where a reliable level of documentary evidence exists to support the apparent facts. Therefore, wherever possible, dates, names and sources have been included so that the genuinely curious readers with time to spare can check the truth for themselves.

This book can be approached from whatever standpoint one wishes to choose. However, I feel it is necessary to emphasise one point to begin with. I am not a professional storyteller and *Unnatural Causes* is not simply a piece of morbid fiction. If one did have a macabre imagination there is plenty of material for a passable horror story to emerge from this particular cabinet of grim curiosities. Even so, that task must fall to another author. My own purpose is straightforward: to demonstrate that human beings are regularly dying, disappearing, or being driven to murder and madness through the direct intervention of supernatural agencies. I realise that is difficult for many people to believe and I do not ask readers to lay aside their natural scepticism. I ask only that cold facts should be faced soberly, no matter how far-fetched they may appear.

Realistically, I am aware that this will be impossible for some people. In today's society there is an inbred prejudice against that which science cannot account for. For those who are able to suspend disbelief for long enough to finish these chapters the evidence will seem eerily fantastic, and perhaps extremely frightening. At worst, it would appear that the human race is under general assault from a phalanx of strange and fearful entities; at the very least, we must recognise that there are forces in the universe beyond our control or comprehension. Either way, mysterious happenings lead us to question basic concepts upon which our view of the world is built. Where appropriate I have tentatively suggested possible directions for future study into the various enigmas, but I cannot pretend that this is very satisfactory. *Unnatural Causes* is not a book for people who prefer neat solutions to their mysteries. Some can only be explained in the most simplistic of terms whilst others remain as enigmatic as they are terrifying.

Even where jigsaw pieces are beginning to fit together, the pattern that is emerging appears to be profoundly unsettling. Whichever way we choose to look at it, there are still many more questions than answers.

THREE FINGERS OF FIRE

The small coastal town of Whitley Bay is typical of many traditional English seaside resorts. Quaint, narrow streets lead down to a promenade of whitewashed hotel façades, beyond which an unremarkable shingle beach is punctuated by timber breakwaters. Today few people spend their annual holidays at Whitley, but in the early years of the century it was a centre for middle-class recreation. A more unlikely spot to begin a study in supernatural powers is hard to imagine, yet it was here, in the spring of 1908 during the resort's Edwardian heyday, that a ghastly paranormal manifestation made headline news.

There was a gentle sea breeze that evening as retired schoolteacher Margaret Dewar walked up the front path of her home overlooking the bay. Her regular stroll had taken longer than usual, and with dusk already gathering she had expected to see a light burning in the drawing room. Even so, she was not unduly troubled by its absence, for her sister Wilhemina, a spinster like herself, often retired early. It was only when Margaret Dewar closed the door behind her and stood in the dark silence of the hallway that she began to realise something was wrong. The first thing she noticed was a dryness in the air, a heavy, choking atmosphere. Coupled with a sickly sweet aroma – a smell unlike anything she had encountered before – it sent a shiver down the old woman's spine. Trembling, alone in the oppressive shadows, Margaret called out several times to her sister; there was no reply.

For a while she continued to stand in the hallway

undecided on what to do. Eventually she lit a candle and, with mounting trepidation, ascended the stairway to Wilhemina's room. What she found in that room filled her with a horror so intense that she had no time to scream before she fainted.

It was small wonder. On the bed lay a sight unrecognisable as a human being: a congealed mess of bones, blood and ash which only hours before had been the living body of her relative.

Awful though it was, the grisly sight of her sister's remains was by no means the end of Margaret Dewar's ordeal by fire. Her grief and incomprehension at the sudden bereavement was compounded by the outright refusal of the Edwardian authorities to believe her story. Particularly suspicious were the police, who failed to see how a woman could burn so terribly on a bed which remained virtually untouched by the heat. Soon everyone began to doubt Margaret Dewar's story. Since the facts of the matter as she told them were clearly impossible, the facts could not be true. Thus, at the subsequent inquest the distraught spinster found her story ridiculed and her reputation slandered. It was the considered opinion of the Whitley constabulary that, at the time of the tragedy, both women must have been insensible with alcohol. Moreover, they were convinced that the fire had actually begun downstairs in the kitchen, and that only afterwards had Margaret carried her sister upstairs to her room, where the fire continued to consume her body until it was reduced to the appalling state in which it was found.

When the bewildered Margaret refused to accept this version of events, the coroner furiously suspended the proceedings and warned his witness of dire consequences if she continued to repeat such nonsense outside the court. In the weeks that followed, friends and neighbours urged her to heed the coroner's advice, whilst the local newspaper publicly castigated her for her stubbornness in holding to such a ludicrous tale. Finally, when the police threatened her with a charge of perjury, her will snapped.

Signing a pre-written statement, she admitted to having lied all along. Her sister, she now said, had really died after falling head first into the kitchen fire grate. With this wholly untenable version securely on record, the inquest into the death by fire of Wilhemina Dewar was swiftly reconvened and a verdict of accidental death returned. The principal witness was not required to attend but the coroner took time to congratulate her for her return to good, common sense. He also forgave her for having earlier wasted the court's time.

Over eighty years later the treatment of the Edwardian spinster seems unforgivable. Yet it was also entirely predictable and might very well be repeated even now. To understand why, one has to become aware of the near-universal denial by officialdom of the phenomenon which claimed the life of Wilhemina Dewar, a denial which persists to the present day. Spontaneous human combustion, the burning from within of living human bodies, is labelled as a myth by every official department that comes into contact with it. So deep is the determination to hide the fact of it, and so wide is the conspiracy that camouflages the evidence of its reality, that over the years doctors, scientists, pathologists, policemen, nurses, members of the fire brigade and ambulance services have all at various times been conscripted into an extraordinary web of deceit. Ostensibly, the cover-up exists to protect the general public from knowledge of a distressing and unpredictable form of 'natural' danger. The true reasons are rather more complex.

Spontaneous human combustion (SHC), apart from being among the most horrific forms of death, is actually impossible; impossible in the sense that its multifarious paradoxes defy virtually every physical law. 'A fact against nature' is how one doctor has aptly described it, and so great are its logical contradictions that most scientists remain inhibited from conducting experimental studies. Today, more than two centuries after the phenomenon was first identified by doctors, few medical figures are prepared to discuss it, and the vast majority of the population remain blissfully unaware of its deadly presence in our midst. Only the friends and relatives of its victims, or those witnesses who have experienced the awful effects at first hand, are any the wiser.

The official refusal to accept facts is saddening, since those left behind through such an unnatural bereavement often flounder in a morass of superstition and whispers of heavenly retribution, whilst at the same time are denied any hope of coming to terms with what they know. Some have been driven to madness or suicide as a result. Yet the policy of official silence on the subject remains as strong as ever.

Examples of the cover-up are easy to find. When in January 1979 the body of a Yorkshire widow was found burned entirely from the knees upwards, a police spokesman insisted that something must have fallen on to her from the open fire, despite the fact that the grate was empty. Similarly, the sudden inferno which engulfed another Yorkshire woman in May 1981 was blamed, laughably, on a lighted cigarette, even though the woman did not smoke.

Very occasionally, a member of the medical establishment may drop the inscrutable mask and allow sanity to prevail. On 3 April 1970 an inquest in Ireland was held into the death of an eighty-nine-year-old woman, Mrs Margaret Hogan, who had burst spontaneously into flames while standing at a bus stop outside her flat in Prussia Street, Dublin. Astonished bystanders attested to the peculiarity of the fire which destroyed Mrs Hogan. In summing up the odd circumstances of her death the Dublin city coroner Dr P. Bofin stated: 'She was ... reduced to a mere pile of ash. The circumstances of the burning are unusual, and would conform to what is called spontaneous combustion.'

Such candid statements from a figure of authority are rare. More often, any who might lend credence to the SHC theory are dissuaded in advance, or sternly reprimanded afterwards.

A typical example of the way this official censorship works is the experience of Dr Gavin Thurston, a London coroner whose decision to put his head over the parapet cost him dearly. In 1961 Thurston published an article in a leading medico-legal journal, which, whilst it did not explicitly support spontaneous combustion, failed to rule out the phenomenon entirely as a possible cause of mysterious fire deaths. 'There are undisputed instances,' wrote Thurston, 'where the body has burned in its own fuel substance without an external fuel, and in which there has been a remarkable absence of damage to surrounding inflammable objects.'

Cases Thurston cited from outside his own direct experience included the testimony of a New England physician, Dr B.H. Hartwell, who had witnessed the internal fire emanating from the stomach of a woman patient in May 1890 and subsequently wrote an account in a Boston medical journal, and the death of Mrs Mary Carpenter, a young mother who had burned in front of her husband and children whilst standing on the deck of their cabin cruiser during a holiday on the Norfolk Broads in July 1938.

Thurston went on to quote several cases he had personally dealt with, where human bodies were consumed beyond a point that might have been expected under normal conditions. Witnesses to these human conflagrations had spoken afterwards of an intense blaze which had enveloped the affected person within a matter of seconds. Attempts to douse the flames with water had proved unsuccessful in each instance. Thurston felt that the fires might have been generated through a similar stimulus and, although the exact descriptions of the deaths were not identical, he pointed to the fact that every fire was characterised by a strong, sweet pungent odour. Strangest of all were two instances where the immolation of the person's body failed to ignite the clothes they had been wearing.

To Thurston's disappointment, his article was not

considered interesting enough to be reported in the general press, nor did it provoke the sort of lively discussion he had anticipated within medical circles. It did not go unnoticed, however. Soon afterwards Thurston was rebuked by the medical council for submitting an 'unscientific' piece and warned about his future conduct. So strong were these threats of official censure that he felt impelled to perform a humiliating about-turn, writing an article the following year which included the words, 'No such phenomenon as spontaneous combustion exists or has ever existed.'

When officialdom refuses to recognise a phenomenon it is never easy to assess how widespread it actually is. Historical records of spontaneous human combustion are also difficult to uncover but we know for sure that the Romans were aware of it, calling it the 'Fire from Heaven', an evocative term borrowed by author Michael Harrison for the title of his 1976 study which remains the definitive work on the subject. In his book Harrison suggested that there may have been several hundred probable cases of SHC over the past two centuries, a figure he has since revised in the light of subsequent evidence. It would now seem that a more likely estimate for the same period runs to six figures. An article printed a couple of years ago in a pyschic publication quoted a British general practitioner as stating (incognito) that he expected to come across one combustion case every five years. Should this be an accurate guide, a country the size of the United Kingdom might well experience upwards of a hundred unnatural burnings every year.

The earliest detailed record we have of a spontaneous combustion death is an event which took place in the French city of Rheims in 1725. The preternatural burning occurred during the early hours of Whit Monday; the victim was one Madame Millet, wife of the proprietor of the Le Lion D'or inn. It was the innkeeper himself who discovered the tragedy after noticing a curious burning smell emanating from the cellar. Initially Jean Millet feared the building had caught fire and, shouting the alarm to his servants, rushed downstairs with a pail of water. There he found no ordinary blaze, but the charred form of his beloved wife Nicole, smouldering in her favourite leather armchair. There was no sign of any other damage to the room.

When the local gendarmes arrived they found Jean Miller too distressed to answer questions. Nor were any of his employees able to offer an explanation. Initially the captain of the guard suspected that the innkeeper had poured brandy over his wife and set her alight. However, the accusations of murder soon disappeared after a young surgeon, Dr Claude Nicholas le Cât, was called in to investigate the circumstances of the woman's death. From a brief inspection of the scene in the cellar, le Cât was quick to realise that no ordinary event had taken place in the Le Lion D'or. Madame Millet's body itself had been incinerated almost to a skeleton by the flames yet the leather chair upon which she sat was virtually untouched.

'Pray ask yourself,' le Cât declared to the President of the Assize Court, 'by what human agency could such a total combustion be effected?' Clearly there was no answer. The innkeeper was allowed to go free. Of his wife it was recorded that she had died 'by the visitation of God', a punishment some believed for her notoriously intemperate ways.

The mystery of Rheims caused a sensation not only in France but across the entire Continent. More interestingly from a researcher's viewpoint it provided a starting point for an early study into the SHC phenomenon, a study which culminated forty years later with the first publication on the subject: *De Incendis Corporis Humani Spontaneis* written by Frenchman Jonas Dupont. In it he mentions cases from Holland, Belgium and Germany as well as that of the French innkeeper's wife.

The preternatural death of Nicole Millet was not the only case of combustion to arouse interest during the eighteenth century. Scottish scientist Sir David Brewster quoted some equally convincing accounts in his book *Letters On Natural Magic*. Brewster's most detailed example was that of an Italian aristocrat, the Countess Cornelia De Bandi, who was found incinerated in her bedchamber in the year 1731. The remains of the countess, who was sixty-two at the time, were found by her maidservant. It must surely have been a gruesome sight for the young girl. A doctor's report detailed how the old woman had been turned to a thin film of blackened ashes, the only parts of her body remaining unconsumed being her head and feet. According to the maid's story a bluish flame had still been seen flickering from the cinders as she had entered her mistress's room. Though a more clear-cut case of un-natural death might be hard to imagine, the Italian physicians preferred a more down-to-earth explanation. It was well known, they said, that the Countess Cornelia occasionally rubbed alcohol into her skin before retiring to bed. Given that she used the same combustible substance on that tragic night, they reasoned that a naked flame from a candle ignited her, thereby engulfing the bed in flames. Thus was the mystery solved. Sir David Brewster, on the other hand, found this explanation unconvincing.

The implausible conclusion reached by the medical practitioners in Italy was not untypical of the period. Several English surgeons in the eighteenth century pronounced alcohol to be the real cause of SHC, though generally the theory referred to an excessive level in the bloodstream. The deaths of such notable alcoholics as Nicole Millet tended to uphold the idea. Around the same period, the demise of two English women after particularly heavy drinking sessions helped propagate the myth. On 9 April 1744, Grace Pett, a middle-aged fisherman's wife, turned into a human fireball in the East Anglian parish of St Clement's; five years later another resident of Suffolk, Mary Clewes, suffered a similar grisly fate in front of witnesses in a public house. Clewes was reputedly addicted to gin.

The belief that a saturation of alcohol in the body provoked an onslaught of 'Fire from Heaven' held sway for well over a hundred years until, by the mid-1860s, it became clear that alcohol poisons the bloodstream long before it could burn it. Even so, as late as a century ago hard drink was still being held up by Victorian temperance societies as a cause of spontaneous combustion. When, on the morning of 19 February 1888, the calcinated body of an anonymous vagrant was found in the loft of a house in Edinburgh, the local anti-drinking lobby lost no time in pointing out that an empty whisky bottle was found by his side.

In past centuries when many aspects of human biology remained mysterious, it is possible to forgive people for holding such superstitious beliefs. It is less easy to forgive modern sceptics who continue to put forward blatantly implausible explanations for an enigma which defies natural laws. Whilst the alcohol-factor theory may have passed out of fashion, there are still many even today who propagate the fallacy that SHC only takes place in the presence of a naked flame or that most victims die after falling into the grates of open fires. In his book *Fire From Heaven* British author Michael Harrison demonstrated conclusively that very few SHC cases could conceivably be accounted for in this way. Yet a decade and a half later scientists and medical figures hostile to SHC continue to put forward the long-since discredited myth. That a blanket denial of such an impressive body of documentary evidence should be deemed in the public interest may give a clearer impression of the real concern SHC causes to those above us.

Drinking, smoking or playing with matches may not increase the likelihood of being struck by the unnatural flames, but if there is one thing we can state with some degree of certainty, it is that spontaneous combustion is not wholly indifferent towards its victims. To begin with, it is an exclusively human enigma for the fire has never been seen destroying an animal. Secondly, it has adopted a strange sociological pattern, for there is a notable imbalance between the age, gender and status of typical SHC victims. According to research to date, the fire is more likely to consume older people rather than those in their prime. So far I have not personally come across a younger male combustion than eighteen, whilst I can find no evidence of a girl burning before the age of puberty. Statistical analysis also suggests that women in any age group are more likely to burn than their male counterparts: a ratio of over three to one. Class status also appears to play a part, although it is frankly inconceivable why this should be so.

Apart from the Italian countess there has been no other recognised example of SHC in the upper echelons of society, and certainly no deaths of famous people. If anything the history of SHC would seem to have included a disproportionate representation of the so-called 'lumpen-element' in society: criminal types, vagrants, low-life characters and others who might be rather unkindly labelled as no-hopers. Persons living on their own or those who suffer habitual depression also frequently appear as cases of combustion.

At various times researchers into the supernatural fire have conjectured as to the peculiarities of the fire's social distribution. In the nineteenth century, for example, it was assumed that only great wickedness might induce the onslaught of SHC, a belief reinforced by Charles Dickens who chose spontaneous combustion as a fitting end for his devilish creation Krook in *Bleak House*. Those who prefer this literal interpretation of the 'Fire from Heaven' syndrome – death by God's vengeance – might find comfort in the words of Job: 'By the blast of the Lord they perish. By the breath of his nostrils they are consumed.'

Sentiments such as these may be acceptable to religious fundamentalists but the idea that a fiery death is just reward for a life of moral degeneration has its weaknesses. To begin with, there is little evidence that many of those who have burned were genuinely wicked, whilst others seem to have led positively blameless lives. Moreover, there have been countless evil figures in history who conspicuously survived the Lord's fiery wrath. Although it would provide a neat answer to the mystery, there is little to conclude that SHC is the product of heavenly intervention. In any case, witnesses to a spontaneous combustion will soon tell you that the event has more in common with the diabolical than it does with the angelic.

Whatever peculiarities might arise from a sociological study of spontaneous combustion, the problems for scientists are more fundamental. Quite simply, the central contradiction of SHC break every rule in the book. According to the laws of physics there is no way that burning human tissue could generate the levels of immense heat necessary for the calcination of bone structure. Yet this effect is regularly observed in cases of SHC. Moreover, even if such extreme temperatures were created it is inconceivable that other highly combustible materials nearby could remain unaffected; nevertheless it is a common feature of SHC that victims incinerate inside undamaged clothing.

Such was the fate of one Mrs Euphemina Johnson, a sixty-eight-year-old widow who was found scorched from the inside out whilst she sat down to drink a cup of tea in her Sydenham home one morning in the summer of 1922. Found as a pile of bones and ash inside her flimsy yet untouched cotton dress, Mrs Johnson's fiery departure from mortal life had scarcely bubbled the varnish of the chair upon which she had been sitting. Similarly, the death of Waymon Wood, a twenty-two-year-old American from Grenville, South Carolina, failed to damage the interior of the automobile inside which he had ignited on the first day of March 1953 whilst driving along an inter-state highway.

Clearly the fire is an unnatural enigma, and seen in this light it is perhaps not too surprising that scientists have been unwilling to investigate something which defies all the known laws of physics. Even so, the perplexities

18

presented by spontaneous combustion cannot condone the dishonesty of many scientific figures who have deliberately set out to obliterate evidence of its existence. Occasionally these 'combustion debunkers' will attack directly those who dare to suggest the truth. In the last century one notable physician who was particularly intolerant of SHC stories was J.L. Caspar, a respected Victorian doctor whose handbook on the *Practice of Forensic Medicine* became a central plank in nineteenth-century medical progress. Caspar despised all mention of spiritualistic phenomena and derided psychic investigators as 'credulous busybodies'. Following a series of odd fatalities in France, he was moved to denounce the 'myth' of SHC in no uncertain terms: 'It is sad to think that in this Year of our Lord 1861 ... we must still treat of the fable of spontaneous combustion.'

As to the mysteries reported from across the Channel, Caspar was content to offer the opinion that the French were a 'backward race' and that the Gallic testimonies should therefore be considered as without value.

The Victorian physician's xenophobia may be idiosyncratic, but his deliberate refusal to take seriously the testimony of witnesses is absolutely typical of modern sceptics. It is an easy way out for our scientists, since if one refuses to consider the possibility of the existence of any phenomenon one is necessarily saved the problem of explaining it. This is of little value to those who experience the flames at first hand ... the emergency services, policemen, coroners who must find a logical reason for the tragedies, relatives and witnesses shocked with horror and incomprehension ... not to mention the victims themselves.

Throughout the nine decades of the twentieth century the medical and scientific research establishment has deliberately ignored spontaneous combustion of human beings. Very occasionally, though, an individual has had the courage to meet the challenge head on. One man to do so was Dr Wilton Krogman, an American forensic scientist of international repute, who became interested in the phenomenon after helping the FBI in their investigation of a woman's fire death in Florida.

It was in July 1951 that a neighbour noticed smoke drifting out of an open window in the apartment of Mrs Mary Reeser, a sixty-seven-year-old woman spending her retirement years in the East Coast resort. By the time the fire services had forced entry Mrs Reeser had been incinerated to a blackened circle of ashes, four feet in diameter. Only one piece of flesh remained unconsumed in the inferno – a small piece of liver attached to the vertebrae. Mrs Reeser's skull, though intact, had been shrunk to the size of an orange. The local police department also noticed other curious aspects to the incident. For one thing, the sofa on which Mrs Reeser had been sitting remained untouched, but the floor below was burnt through. Elsewhere in the room furniture and curtains did not show the usual signs of smoke damage, yet the walls were blackened with a greasy soot below the height of four feet. Strangest of all was the curiously selective nature of the heat, which had left highly combustible materials unaffected while melting metal objects including wall-mounted electrical wiring.

As soon as news of the enigma leaked out to the press the case of the 'Cinder Woman' became the chief topic of gossip in Miami. The American public, already stunned by Russia's acquisition of the A-Bomb, now began to turn their fears towards the possibility that 'Uncle Joe' Stalin had invested in a death ray. The official announcement in August, stating that Mrs Reeser died from accidental death caused by a dropped cigarette, did little to quell public unease. Few people believed it.

Dr Krogman also remained unsatisfied with the pathologist's report and persuaded the FBI to allow him to continue investigating the circumstances of the Miami widow's death. After several months, he came up with evidence that contradicted not only the police department's explanation, but also the very basis upon which modern science rests its case. Concentrating on the bizarre nature of the fire itself, Krogman experimented on other corpses to see whether they could be made to burn in the same way. The tests proved negative. On the contrary, Krogman found that even under a temperature of 3000 degrees Fahrenheit, applied continuously for twelve hours, human bones would not powder in the manner that Mrs Reeser's skeleton had done. Nor could a human body weighing eighty kilos be reduced to only five kilos of ash. As regards the shrunken skull, this too proved impossible to replicate in controlled conditions. For Krogman the whole incident was a scientific conundrum which beggared belief.

Years later, he wrote a full account of his studies of the Florida woman's death. It was, he said, 'The most amazing thing any of us ever saw. As I review it, the short hairs on the back of my neck bristle with a vague fear. Were I living in the Middles Ages I'd probably mutter something about black magic ...'

The federal pathologist need not have carried out his own corpse-burning experiments. A few words with an undertaker would have been enough to convince him of the difficulty of effecting total destruction upon the human cadavar. In early cremations operators frequently had to grind bones because the heat generated by the furnace was insufficient to complete the task of obliterating the human remains. The 'Fire from Heaven' clearly has no similar problems.

Given the enormous levels of heat present in outbreaks of unnatural fire, one might suppose that the effects are always fatal. However, this is not so. One man to survive the internal inferno was James Hamilton, a Nashville University professor who, on a fine morning in 1835, caught fire whilst strolling along a sidewalk. According to Hamilton's testimony the fire originally manifested itself as a small jet of bluish flame coming from the inside of his left trouser leg. With what must have been a tremendous presence of mind, the professor did not panic but successfully extinguished the blaze by covering the affected part of his skin with his hand, thereby denying it oxygen. The bewildered academic was left in much pain and limped to the nearest infirmary where his injuries – third degree burns on his calf – were treated.

Sometimes victims of SHC survive the initial onslaught of the flames but die subsequently, either through the shock or because of the burns themselves. Such was the fate of Englishwoman Madge Knight, who was found engulfed in flames in her bedroom in 1943. Rushed to hospital by her husband, Mrs Knight never regained consciousness but remained alive for two further weeks. Another instance of delayed death, this time from eighteenth-century Italy, surrounds the grisly fate of a priest, Father Bertholi. Dr Luigi Battaglia, the distinguished specialist who treated Bertholi, later wrote an article for a contemporary Florence journal in which he gave details of the strange injuries the priest suffered. Fire had consumed his patient's arm to the elbow and when Dr Battaglia examined the stump closely he immediately suspected spontaneous combustion since the burns seemed to have been generated from the inside outwards. No other part of Bertholi's anatomy was affected, yet a day after his peculiar ordeal by fire the clergyman fell into a coma and died.

Reminiscent of the Italian priest's fate, though somewhat less disastrous, were the injuries suffered by American Jack Angel in November 1974. Waking up after a night's sleep in his motor home in Savannah, Georgia, Angel found his right hand charred black. The bed clothes remained unscorched and there was no sign of fire damage elsewhere in the home. Fire authorities and insurance investigators could offer no clue to the strange event and Angel himself, who slept through the whole thing, remains dumbfounded by the episode to this day.

The American's reaction was typical. Partially combusted individuals who live long enough to describe their ordeal usually express only bewilderment. In December 1916 when Thomas Morphey, a hotel owner from Dover, New Jersey, found his housekeeper Lilian

Green smouldering on the floor of his living room she was still conscious, yet unable to account for the flames that had briefly engulfed her. In 1942 Aura Troyer, who was discovered burning inside the vault of the Illinois bank where he was employed, survived briefly and could only say that 'it had happened all of a sudden'. Jeanna Winchester was riding in the back seat of a car in Jacksonville, Florida, when she burst into a human torch on 9 October 1980. Remembering little of the incident when she regained consciousness in hospital, she nevertheless became convinced that she was not responsible: 'At first I thought there was a logical explanation, but I couldn't find any. I wasn't smoking. The seat didn't burn. I finally thought about spontaneous combustion when I couldn't find anything else.' Echoing Mrs Winchester's suspicions, investigating fire-officer T.G. Hendrix confirmed that no combustible substances nor heat-source had been found in the car's interior. He said that in his twelve years' service he had never seen anything like it.

Probably the most recent person to survive SHC was Paul Hayes, a nineteen-year-old Londoner who burst into flames whilst walking down a street in Stepney Green, London, in May 1985. Fortunately for Hayes the fire only lasted a few seconds and, although he suffered extensive burns, he was treated successfully for his injuries. In a report published in the London *Evening Standard* on 25 May, the victim described his experience as being similar to being thrust suddenly into a furnace. His arms had, he said, felt like red-hot pokers whilst his chest felt as though boiling water has been poured over it. Doctors treating Hayes were reluctant to discuss their patient's condition, though they admitted that his shirt had only been scorched on the inside. A spokesman for the London Fire Brigade agreed that the incident was baffling, but refused to comment further.

How some people survive spontaneous combustion is mysterious. Michael Harrison, the English author whose records of the phenomenon are more extensive than anyone else's, believes that men are more likely to suffer only partial burning whilst female fires generate rather more heat.

Harrison also believes that the flames of human combustion cannot be extinguished by water since the unnatural fire is itself a product of an extremely rapid process of oxidisation, in his opinion. (In this way the flames absorb oxygen from the body fluid leaving a hydrogen residue which in turn increases the rate of combustion. So, in fact, water merely aids the spread of the fire, rather than douses it.) Harrison's belief that water is an ineffective weapon against spontaneous combustion has been supported by eyewitness accounts. It was also the opinion of two Victorian writers, J.R. and J.B. Beck, who wrote in their massive tome, *Elements of Medical Jurisprudence* published in 1838, 'Water aggravates spontaneous combustion ... which has been recorded in all seasons and in both northern and southern countries.'

If one should fall victim to spontaneous combustion, one is well advised to follow the course of action employed by James Hamilton, the American professor who simply cupped his hands over the area of burning flesh. For the one property that SHC shares in common with natural fires would seem to be its dependence upon a supply of oxygen.

Combustion survivors may be unusual, but thankfully cases of multiple burnings are even more rare. In the whole recorded history of SHC there is only one positively confirmed case of two people dying from it in the same place simultaneously. This was in 1905, when a retired English couple, the Kileys of Buzzocks Heath, Surrey, were found as a pair of charred corpses sitting upright in their favourite armchairs. There was no other damage to the room, and the county coroner returned a verdict of accidental death – 'by what means we are unable to say'. A second example of a double tragedy resulting from SHC, though not of a twin fire consumption, was that of an Irish immigrant couple, the Rooneys of Seneca, Illinois, on the

Christmas Eve of 1885. Patrick Rooney had been last seen alive drinking with his wife in the kitchen of their tenement home. The following morning, Christmas Day, the Rooney children awoke to find their parents' corpses. Their mother was reduced to a calcinated skeleton; their father asphixiated by the foul greasy fumes which emanated from his wife's burning body.

If spontaneous combustion is a result of a single inexplicable cause then one might expect its effects to remain reasonably consistent. This is not always the case, however. Of those who have been unfortunate enough to witness the phenomenon, some speak of bluish flames, whilst others report yellow ones; many remember a sickly sweet smell, whereas an equal number report no aromatic recollections. As we have seen, the extent of the burn damage to the victims' bodies varies greatly, yet even in cases of people being completely consumed there are some marked variations. Whilst in most examples the subject's body is reduced to ashes, in a few instances the remains have been of a somewhat different nature – a substance likened to a repulsive glue or a sticky tar. Such oddities were first noticed by one parapsychologist investigating the burning of Dr John Irving Bentley, a retired physician from Coudersport, Pennsylvania, who fell victim to the fire on 5 December 1966. Found in the bathroom of his home, Bentley's entire torso had been liquefied, his remains dripping through a hole in the floorboards apparently created by the heat. Only Bentley's right foot remained untouched and it was estimated that a temperature in excess of 3000 degrees Fahrenheit had been created in the bathroom where the man died. On 13 December 1959 American teenager Billy Peterson was 'melted' into a 'sticky, loathsome mess' whilst sitting in the front seat of his garaged car in Detroit, Michigan. Forensic scientists investigating the incident noticed how the boy's underpants had remained untouched by the fire whilst the vehicle's sub-frame had been twisted entirely out of shape.

One factor that might be imagined essential for the phenomenon to take place is for the victim to be alive to begin with, but there has been at least one incident of combustion following death. In December 1973 the dead body of a Mrs Mary Satlow ignited spontaneously inside her coffin at the local chapel of rest in Hoquem, Oregon. She had passed away three days earlier. Upon opening the coffin, Police Chief Richard Barnes found the woman's corpse reduced to ashes below the hips. The remains of Mrs Satlow were then taken to Washington DC where they underwent a series of tests. A State Department spokesman later admitted that her body had been subjected to 'a force outside the laws of nature'.

The federal spokesman's comments were an unusually candid admission. Few official figures are willing to admit that such forces might really exist. In Britain, the medical authorities regularly deny that any inexplicable events of this kind have ever occurred. Typical was the attitude of forensic scientist Dr Keith Simpson who in 1972 was interviewed after he had investigated the horrific combustion of a woman named Edith Thompson. Thompson had turned into a ball of fire before the amazed eyes of several witnesses in an old people's home. However, ignoring the bizarre aspects of the woman's death, Dr Simpson simply denied any evidence for the phenomenon, claiming that in forty years of medical practice he had never once seen or heard of any fire death that could not otherwise be explained rationally.

In the years following Simpson's public negation of SHC the same story has been repeated time and again. Of the most recent British cover-ups, perhaps the one which defies logic most blatantly was the case of Jackie Fitz-simmon, a student at Halton College of Further Education, who burst into flames on 28 January 1985. After leaving her cookery class, the eighteen-year-old was walking along a corridor when a fellow student noticed a curious light form over her shoulder. Simultaneously, the girl herself began to panic and she shouted, 'It's gone down my neck, get it out!' But it was useless. Before the others could assist in any way, flames began sprouting from her back and shoulders. She died later in intensive care.

Due to its profound strangeness, the Fitzsimmon case provoked comment in the press, and it was swiftly recognised as a combustion death by paranormal investigators. To their credit, the Cheshire fire brigade were determined to solve the riddle and called in two forensic experts from the Shirley Institute in Manchester. A long and detailed report was subsequently issued, stating that the dead girl's clothes could not have conceivably been set alight by an earlier brush with a gas flame in the kitchen. On the contrary, the Manchester experts were convinced that this particular death should be considered as thoroughly inexplicable. Strangely, the thirty-page document compiled for the Cheshire fire services never appeared as evidence at the inquest on Jackie Fitzsimmon. Moreover, not a single member of the local fire brigade was called as a witness. Instead, a Home Office chemist was produced to confirm the coroner's suspicion that the girl's cookery smock must have caught alight at some moment earlier, smouldering unnoticed before catastrophically igniting in the corridor. Other evidence heard at the inquest was carefully selected beforehand so that the acceptable verdict of 'misadventure' would be reached. So determined was the coroner to tie up the case that he prefaced the proceedings by telling the jury to ignore anything they might have read in the newspapers of mysterious causes.

Having been put under such pressure it is not surprising that the jury returned the verdict they did. Even so, not everyone was satisfied with the outcome of the hearing. One witness to the original burning was said afterwards to have been 'disgusted' by the obvious bias shown by the coroner. Meanwhile, a paranormal researcher, Jenny Randles, who attended the hearing, merely expressed a resigned disappointment. Like so many who delve into the unimaginable, she had seen the truth distorted so often in the past that on this particular issue she had known what to expect.

Less clear were the feelings of the teenager's parents. Those close to victims of unnatural causes are often so upset or confused that they tend to accept any rational explanation foisted upon them, no matter how implausible it may seem. It needs a clear head and an open mind to see through the smokescreen of official denials and obfuscation. Yet even some committed sceptics become believers when they are faced with the full facts.

In 1986 English television journalist Steve Bradshaw investigated the spontaneous combustion phenomenon for the BBC's *Newsnight* programme. Originally intending to demolish the case for spontaneous combustion, Bradshaw soon came to realise the truth when evidence supporting the phenomenon's existence mounted. The reporter was particularly impressed by the testimony of a Welsh CID police officer, John Haymer, who in January 1980 discovered the remains of pensioner Henry Thomas in the front room of his Ebbw Vale cottage. Upon entering the house, Haymer remembered noticing a peculiar warmth, a heat that seemed to emanate from the very walls themselves. Plastic objects in the lounge were found to have been melted, as well as the light shade hanging from the ceiling. Yet there was otherwise little fire damage – except, that is, to the occupant himself. The stockinged feet of Henry Thomas lay unconsumed on the carpet, the only part of him still recognisable as human. The rest of the Welshman had become, in Haymer's words, an 'amorphous mass of ash and blood'. The CID man guessed that Thomas had died unnaturally since his death corresponded with the end of Krook in Dickens's *Bleak House*, which Haymer had read. Yet the officer was persuaded by his superiors from including this controversial opinion in his report.

As other reliable witnesses were interviewed, Steve Bradshaw realised that his original scepticism over SHC was misguided. When his *Newsnight* study appeared in

January 1986, it left no one in any doubt that spontaneous combustion might exist as a disturbing if rare occurrence. In the programme, a crematorium manager confirmed that pictures of SHC victims had been burnt from the inside, adding that the evidence was 'incredible ... terrifying'.

There have been some interesting suggestions regarding the nature of the energy source which fuels the human fireball. One theory that has gained ground amongst SHC experts is that the fire is a result of fluctuations in the earth's magnetic field. Global averages in magnetic field variations can show quite dramatic dips and surges during the periods of high solar activity and a comparison of this data with geographical patterns of SHC burnings was used constructively by Fortean writer Livingstone Gearhart in an article for the journal *Pursuit*, published in 1975. Gearhart drew up six charts showing how a period of intense solar activity correlated with several specific examples of spontaneous combustion in North America. Allied to this theory is the apparent connection between spontaneous combustion and sightings of ball lightning, a mysterious atmospheric phenomenon about which very little is known. Support for the ball lightning connection came in a 1969 study entitled *The Taming of the Thunderbolts* by American authors Maxwell Cade and Delphine Davis. In their book the two writers reviewed the theories of several physicists who believe that huge energies are involved in the formation of the lightning ball – energies that could also in turn manifest short radio waves of the kind used in microwave ovens.

Were this to be the case, then a lightning ball forming inside a human body might very well burn the person inside their skins, argued authors Cade and Davis. Obviously the hypothesis is difficult to prove; however, interestingly, a similar phenomenon was reported during the Second World War when farmers in the English Home Counties began finding hundreds of dead birds strewn across their fields, all apparently cooked inside their feathers. The mystery was subsequently cleared up when it was noted that the birds only suffered this fate after flying between the nearby radar towers. To SHC researchers, though, this held a vital clue: if the relatively weak energy emissions from radar stations killed wildfowl in such a way, might not a more powerful beam similarly burn humans? To take the argument a step further, if those beams were created by geomagnetic fluctuations, could they therefore manifest as extraordinarily powerful microwave diatherms?

It is just possible that answers to these questions hold the key to the SHC enigma. However, the magnetic field fluctuation theory has its drawbacks. To begin with, if spontaneous combustion was really caused by geomagnetic fluctuations it might be expected to affect a wider area than a specific individual yet, as we have seen, there is only one example recorded of a multiple burning. Secondly, the theory put forward by Livingstone Gearhart could in no way account for the curious sociological distribution displayed by the fire, nor does it account for the fact that it never consumes animals. Indeed, so bizarre are the anomalies inherent in SHC that many researchers have become convinced that only the presence of a directing influence could account for them.

Whilst researching different areas of paranormal phenomena, it has come to my attention that occasionally deaths from spontaneous combustion coincide with outbreaks of other unnatural happenings. Nor am I alone in my conclusions. In his classic study *Fire From Heaven* Michael Harrison devotes an entire chapter to theories linking SHC with other manifestations of psychic phenomena. In one example, a spate of mysterious cattle maimings across the American state of Oregon followed hard upon the corpse burning of Mrs Satlow mentioned earlier. The attacks upon cattle, which began the day after Mrs Satlow's body was consumed inside her coffin, were highly unpleasant. Many animals had their ears, testicles and even internal organs ripped away, while others were simply drained of blood. No one was ever caught attempting to butcher livestock in this way and after a few months the Oregon cattle killings ended as suddenly as they had begun. A similar instance from an earlier age was noted by veteran paranormal investigator Charles Fort. This time the incident came from Britain when, in the year 1905, the slaughter of more than two hundred and fifty chickens and geese on a Lincolnshire farm near Binbrook began the same week that a young farm girl burst into flames in a neighbouring district.

The fowl had each been slaughtered in the same hideous fashion: the skin around their necks being pulled off from head to breast and their windpipe drawn from its place and snapped. Could it be possible, thought Charles Fort, that some invisible entity, malevolent and sadistic of mind, had systematically destroyed the lives of the innocent girl and the defenceless animals, killing them in the most repulsive ways imaginable – by fire and slow strangulation respectively? In his book *Lo* Charles Fort makes clear his suspicion that a being of incendiary appetite really does exist: 'If we accept that, in Binbrook Farm, something was savagely killing chickens, we must accept also that whatever we mean by a being was there.' Of the girl herself Fort writes, '... unknown to her, something behind her was burning her, and she was unconscious of her own scorching flesh.'

Fort's idea of a causal link between the two phenomena may be no more than conjecture, yet I myself remember noticing how, in the early summer of 1976, the spontaneous combustion of a teenager in Essex synchronised curiously with a spate of odd events which were never fully explained. In April a farmer in nearby Upminster woke one morning to find his daughter's two Shetland ponies each with their heads quite literally bitten off. 'Wild dogs' were blamed for the carnage, though none was ever caught. Meanwhile, a 'phantom pyromaniac' was starting fires on a nearby council estate in Harold Hill. These incidents continued for a period of months during which time a total of more than forty fires was reported. Despite the considerable police time given over to solving the problem, no culprit was seen, let alone apprehended. The officer leading the investigation, Chief Inspector Geoffrey Kitchen, was quoted in the local press as saying that 'we have no idea who this person is or how he starts his fires despite intensive investigation from our forensic people'.

In fact the firestarter's reign of terror ended with the combustion of the unfortunate girl in Hornchurch. Following her death, there were no reports of unexplained fire damage to property in the area.

Invisible pyromaniacs or 'firespooks' have struck on many occasions around the world. In January 1922 an especially persistent one descended upon an isolated farmhouse in Nova Scotia, Canada. During one evening thirty-eight small fires started but were successfully extinguished by the farm's occupants. The next night saw the outbreak of a further thirty-one blazes, forcing the family to move out. According to witnesses of the incident, inanimate objects burst into flames even when previously soaked with water.

In the same year invalid Mrs Ona Smith of Alva, Oklahoma was terrorised by a firestarter. Fires seemed to start in the air, blue flames jumping and crackling above witnesses' heads. In a similar incident in 1932, air-born flames consumed furniture, curtains and carpets owned by Mrs Charles Williamson of Bladenboro, North Carolina, according to many witnesses including the local mayor. At a farm ten miles south of Maycomb, Illinois, fires began erupting on 7 August 1948. To begin with, the phenomenon was limited to small brown patches on wallpaper, but gradually the fires grew in intensity, eventually consuming the whole house and surrounding outbuildings.

Reports of phantom firestarters have continued in recent times. In August 1979, ninety mysterious fires which broke out on a farm near Hautes Pyrénées, France during a three-week period were only brought to an end when a priest held a ceremony of exorcism. Four years later a similar series of fires plagued residents of an old people's home in Kokstad, Cape Province, South Africa. The same year saw the fiery destruction of many homes in the West Virginia coal towns of Wharncliffe and Beech Creek; over two hundred separate outbreaks were reported yet no arsonist was caught.

The force behind poltergeists may be related to SHC, since the more bizarre activities of these noisy spirits of paranormal mayhem sometimes provoke the spontaneous combustion of inanimate objects. Habitually attaching themselves to children or adolescents, the poltergeist's mischievious presence is usually no more than annoying, yet amidst their standard repertoire of rappings, voices and levitations there are darker instances of vicious physical assaults. Their role as firestarters is no less disturbing, especially for those who become the unwilling focus of their attention.

During 1921 a thirteen-year-old boy in the Hungarian capital of Budapest found objects regularly lifted into the air around him; at night blue flames would flicker above his sleeping body. In 1929, on the Leeward Island of Antigua, a poor village girl found the clothes she was wearing regularly igniting into ashes yet leaving her skin unaffected; on several occasions even her mattress and bedclothes ignited although reports suggest she was never hurt. Less fortunate was the wife of an Indian police inspector who became the focus of a poltergeist in Lucknow during June 1975. After a series of preternatural events including the spontaneous combustion of wet clothes hanging on a washing line, the woman herself was found ablaze, screaming, 'The evil spirit is burning me!' Her son managed to extinguish the fire with a blanket but she died later the same day.

People continue to attract fire-starting poltergeists. Two incidents were reported in 1983 from the Mediterranean island of Elba and the island of Réunion in the Indian Ocean; and a further example occurred in

1984 in Rome where a young female typist was badly burned in an office. Curiously, however, the most recent example I have uncovered seems to have been motivated by benevolence.

On 3 February 1986, the London *Daily Express* carried the tale of Eddie Matthjits, a Belgian invalid who had been miraculously cured of his illness the same day that a plastic Madonna had burst into flames on the wall of his bedroom. Doctors were mystified by his recovery and Matthjits's wife was convinced that the Holy Virgin herself had interceded on his behalf. Her faith was apparently confirmed when in the following weeks an image of Christ appeared on the faded wallpaper of their room. Today the house has become a shrine and the couple are celebrities.

If the good Lord was responsible for the Belgian's cure, a similar compassion can hardly be directed at those who die so horribly from SHC. Yet clearly the strange events cannot be altogether separated. It is doubtful whether anyone would seriously suggest the two miracles in the Belgian's household – cure and fire – were wholly unrelated. However, if we accept this analysis then the likelihood of a similar directing agency behind spontaneous combustion itself grows stronger. The difference may be merely the difference between good and evil or Christ and the Devil.

In cases of spontaneous combustion, as with all strange deaths, really bizarre coincidences do regularly occur. One example which perhaps reveals the sick humour of fate was the death by fire of an English spinster named Edith Jones on 14 February 1972. Miss Jones's immolation came fifty years to the day after a woman who shared her name died on the London gallows for murdering her unfaithful husband. That a crime of passion should have been the cause of the earlier woman's downfall is ironic, since it was Valentine's Day when the second Edith Jones exploded into flames. Curiously the spinster died whilst attempting unsuccessfully to light a fire in the front room of her home.

Why was her wish so sadistically granted? We might wonder ...

If the cruel hand of fate occasionally uses spontaneous combustion to be the vehicle of its grim humour, then some outbreaks of SHC demonstrate a degree of simultaneity which can surely be no mere coincidence. The clearest example of this tendency is provided by the extraordinary events which took place on 7 March 1938, a day in which the fiery persecution struck three men in as many minutes, men who were hundreds of miles apart.

First to die was Willen Ten Bruik, an eighteen-year-old Dutchman who was driving in his car through the small town of Ubergan, near Nijmegan. The second, a middle-aged Englishman named George Turner, was driving a lorry along a bypass outside Chester. The fire's third victim, a seaman named John Greeley, was at the helm of the SS *Ulrich*, a steamer bound for Liverpool. The *Ulrich* was several hundred miles from her destination when the unnatural flames began and researchers have estimated that her position lay at a point exactly equidistant to that of the other victims. In other words, Greeley began to burn when he reached the apex of an enormous equilateral triangle, the others being at the base angles. Why such a factor of distance should matter to the force behind spontaneous combustion remains obscure, yet the fact can hardly be coincidental. It should also be noticed that each man was engaged in a markedly similar activity at his moment of death – steering a mode of transport, thereby echoing weird similarities between some other SHC deaths. (Remember once again the three girls who burned while dancing, mentioned in my introduction to this book.) The burnings of Greeley, Turner and Ten Bruik have fascinated paranormal researchers ever since they were first identified. In the words of journalist Frank Russell it was as if 'a galactic being of unimaginable size had probed the earth with a three-pronged fork ... three fingers of fire which burned only flesh'.

*

Historically, the factual existence of spontaneous combustion has been marked by suppression of evidence unequalled by that of any other unexplained phenomenon, apart from UFOs. Decades after the first scientific study of SHC was published in Europe, the distinguished English forensic doctor, J.L. Caspar, felt able to dismiss the idea summarily. It was, he wrote, 'a myth whose proof of existence rests upon the perfectly untrustworthy testimony of non-professionals'.

In 1873, thirty years and many cases of combustion later, another respected London physician, Dr Alfred Swain Taylor, was moved to write an even more damning condemnation: 'The hypothesis of such a mode of destruction is not only wholly unsupported by any credible facts, but is wholly inconsistent with all that science has revealed.'

Official prejudice against a phenomenon 'inconsistent with all that science has revealed' continues to the present day. In *Fire From Heaven* psychic researcher Michael Harrison describes how he saw with his own eyes the words 'spontaneous combustion' repeatedly written in the case files of the London Metropolitan Fire Brigade. Yet when it became clear what his real interest was, the press officer and other senior figures in the force denied that the phrase had ever been used, and Harrison was refused further access to their records. I myself have experienced a similar reluctance on the part of police and hospital authorities to release details of unusual fire deaths. Clearly, unless there is a more open policy from official circles serious scientific investigation of this bewildering and frightening phenomenon cannot hope to begin. As the twenty-first century approaches we know little more about the fire from heaven than did our Roman predecessors who first named it.

I have no doubt that many of those who hide evidence of spontaneous combustion do so because they genuinely wish to save the public unnecessary anxiety. One medical acquaintance, who characteristically did not want to be identified, put this side of the argument to me quite succinctly: 'We don't know why it happens or how and strictly speaking it can't. It isn't possible. So the general feeling is that it's best never to talk about it.' That is a view shared today by many dedicated and otherwise honest figures in the field of medical science.

Many people would probably agree with this policy. However, the conspiracy of silence on the subject has even included, at times, those whose business it is to investigate the unexplained.

Arthur C. Clarke's Mysterious World is a case in point. In the early 1980s Clarke, the world-famous science fiction writer, was commissioned by a British independent television channel to gather together material for a personal tour of the paranormal. Borrowing from contemporary UFO phraseology, Clarke labelled his phenomena 'Mysteries of the First, Second and Third Kinds'. Mysteries of the third kind, of which spontaneous combustion was considered to be one, were, according to the SF writer, completely inexplicable and therefore unworthy of investigation.

In this way one of the most disturbing of unnatural phenomena was neatly ignored whilst far less interesting mysteries were offered for the viewers' attention. Such a deliberate attempt to sanitise and trivialise the paranormal is typical of the British media's attitude, but it was most disappointing that the writer himself should have been party to the cover-up. To his credit, Clarke later changed his stance and admitted that spontaneous combustion gave him more 'unease' than any other mystery.

A similar attempt to sanitise the facts surrounding SHC was the BBC Television programme in the *Q.E.D.* series. Broadcast on the evening of 25 April 1989 the programme investigated the fiery phenomenon, concentrating on three British burnings from the previous eighteen months, but the widespread nature of spontaneous combustion was only briefly hinted at, and wholly natural explanations

37

offered for the three cases. Without ever coming close to proving their conclusion scientifically, the programme makers maintained that SHC did not exist, and sought support from David Halliday, a forensic scientist with the London Metropolitan Police. In the programme, Halliday confidently asserted that he had never come across a fire death which could not be explained naturally and offered a supposition that the human body might, under the right conditions, burn slowly, 'like a wick from one end of a candle to the other'. Given enough time, said Halliday, the corpse would be totally consumed to a state consistent with cases of apparent spontaneous combustion; the process would probably take over twelve hours. In those cases focused upon, it was suggested that the victims had died of heart failures, fallen on to naked flames and burned steadily overnight before their bodies were discovered the following morning. Thus was the riddle solved.

Needless to say I was one viewer who was less than convinced. Since there were no naked flames or indeed any heat source present in at least two of the *Q.E.D.* examples, the 'wick' theory seemed somewhat tenuously constructed. But there were far more serious inadequacies in the programme's investigations than a single over-sight.

For one thing, the *Q.E.D.* film never mentioned that spontaneous fire deaths have been witnessed on many occasions; that its progress was always described as being swift and intensive; that some victims of SHC had lived to tell the tale. The film did not dwell upon the most curious aspects of the fire – the fact that it produced more heat than a furnace yet sometimes left the victim's clothes undamaged. It did not interview parascientific researchers who had studied SHC in depth, nor did it refer to the growing body of literature devoted to the phenomenon. Most worryingly, by including only those cases which suited the programme's premise that SHC as such did not exist, and at the same time ignoring documentary evidence to the contrary (the vast bulk of known cases), the BBC was laying itself open to a charge of misrepresenting the truth.

In the month following the screening of the *Q.E.D.* film I managed to put a few of these points to its producer, Teresa Hunt. Though not unfriendly, she was immediately on the defensive. Why, I asked, was no attempt made to prove the wick theory by experiment – burning, say, the carcass of a pig? Hunt said that such a test might be regarded as distasteful by viewers. Why then, I asked, was no mention made of the numerous witnessed accounts, or of the fact that many SHC fires had taken place out of doors? The producer said she was unaware of such examples. (This was a disappointing response from a serious researcher. Michael Harrison's *Fire From Heaven* – which was never mentioned in the programme – contains dozens of witnessed examples. A Reader's Digest publication from the 1980s contains details of forty-two cases in one chapter alone.)

I pointed this out to Teresa Hunt. The conversation was ended.

After speaking to the BBC producer I decided to contact a few of the scientific experts and fire brigade officers interviewed in the film. Some refused to speak to me, but others were less reticent. One of those I spoke to was Roger Penny, an officer of the Hampshire fire brigade whose discovery of the charred corpse of Mr Alfred Ashton of Southampton was one of the three cases focused upon. Having heard the *Q.E.D.* documentary team's explanation, Penny admitted to be less than convinced. Like myself, the fireman was also surprised that no attempt had been made to interview witnesses to SHC fires. Another of those interviewed by *Q.E.D.* was even more outspoken in his criticism of the programme's 'safe' presentation. A senior lecturer at Kent University, and expert on atmospheric phenomena, Professor Roger Jennison described the programme's rationalist conclusions as 'incorrect and perhaps misleading'. It was impossible, he said, for the conventional generation of heat to be responsible for the total reduction of a human cadavar to ashes – let alone in a room where other highly combustible materials such as paper remained virtually untouched by the flames.

The opinions of the Kent University professor are difficult to argue with. Yet once again it was the official interpretation of SHC which was reinforced in the minds of millions of British TV viewers in April 1989.

As the deception goes on, the unnatural flames continue to claim lives.

Writing these lines in the December of 1989 I notice that an inquest into the burning of an Essex man has recorded a verdict of accidental death. The man had apparently collapsed on to an electric fire, lying there until his body was entirely consumed; or so we were led to believe.

In cases of spontaneous combustion there are always two victims, and the second is invariably the truth.

SINISTER ENCOUNTERS

On the afternoon of Thursday 22 October 1987 a British Aerospace Harrier GR5 jump-jet flown by test pilot Taylor Scott took off from Dunsford, Surrey on a low-level flight over Salisbury Plain. At exactly 17.06 hours radio contact with the Harrier was lost. Some time afterwards an American transport aircraft sighted the Harrier ninety miles south west of the Irish coast; its cockpit canopy was missing and it was obviously pilotless. After a further four hundred miles it ran out of fuel and crashed into the Atlantic Ocean. The next morning a search of farmland near Winterbourne Stoke discovered the body of Taylor Scott in a field of rye. Nearby two circles of scorched earth measuring twenty-five metres in diameter had appeared from nowhere. There was no apparent explanation for the circles nor for Taylor Scott's fatal ejection.

Four years later, the Harrier pilot's last moments remain a mystery. Few details of the incident were made public and the official report of the tragedy failed to mention the mysterious circles (or similar circles found in fields at Bratton, Chilcomb and Westbury during the previous three months). Not one British news journalist saw fit to link the Harrier's loss to reports of unidentified lights hovering over the area the previous night or to the numerous stories of strange objects landing all over Britain during the first nine months of 1987.

The omission of the 'unnatural angle' will come as little surprise to researchers of the UFO phenomenon, for so great is the secrecy surrounding the subject that even very firm evidence rarely reaches the public. On the few occasions when it does, it is usually discredited without delay by the contrary opinions of so-called experts. Blatant examples of the cover-up are numerous.

At approximately three a.m. on 30 December 1980, two mysterious objects landed in a wooded area outside Woodbridge NATO air base near Rendlesham, Suffolk. They were not aircraft of a human origin, and it remains unclear where they came from or what their purpose was. All we do know for certain is that they were there ... real, solid, metallic objects of a design unlike anything earthly science has so far produced.

In contrast to most sightings of unidentified flying objects the evidence for the Rendlesham landings was massive. Firstly, the UFOs did not arrive in Suffolk unheralded. Their descent to planet earth was tracked on radar, not only by staff at Woodbridge Base itself but also by RAF officers stationed near Norwich. Secondly, their appearance on the ground was investigated thoroughly by United States Air Force service personnel, several of whom have since testified to the facts after leaving the armed services. These witnesses could hardly be more reliable. Those who saw the objects at close quarters included an American wing commander, a lieutenant colonel, a British squadron leader, the Woodbridge Base commander, and a host of junior ranks. Furthermore, a report sent subsequently to the British Ministry of Defence (MOD) described the event in terms of the utmost clarity, speaking of 'structured metallic craft of triangular shape', even specifying dimensions. The report, which included details of marks left on the ground after the ships took off and spoke of unusually high levels of radiation in the location, concluded by suggesting that they were a pair of interplanetary craft from a civilisation beyond our solar system.

That two alien vessels could suddenly appear in rural England is astonishing enough. What is more astonishing, however, is that eleven years after the Rendlesham happening the overwhelming majority of the British people remain blissfully unaware of it. To begin with all details of the incident were officially suppressed. When the story finally broke in 1983, after the secret report of the MOD fell into the hands of a national tabloid newspaper, it made headlines for just one day before quietly slipping into the back pages and obscurity. Most of the 'serious' journals didn't touch it, whilst others like *The Times* openly ridiculed the tale, deliberately ignoring the calibre of the witnesses involved. One so-called expert suggested that what had apparently appeared outside the base had really been the flashing beacon of a lighthouse five miles distant. Thus yet another flying saucer mystery was neatly cleared up and only the cranks of the UFO lobby continued to believe in the little green men of Suffolk.

That such an impressive catalogue of evidence could become so comprehensively discredited is a vivid indication of the unwillingness of the press to take unnatural phenomena seriously. More importantly, however, the debunking of the Rendlesham enigma was a tribute to two seasoned misinformation bureaux: the United States Air Force (USAF) and the British Ministry of Defence, organisations who between them, through their manipulation of the Western media, have done more than any other official bodies to limit or deny evidence of alien presence in our skies. The truth is very different. For governments on both sides of the Atlantic UFOs pose a sinister menace that they are singularly unable to counter, a menace which has been responsible for the deaths and disappearances of an unquantifiable number of human beings during the last forty-five years. Just how significant that threat remains is only now beginning to come clear. Under the United Sates Freedom of Information Act, previously secret documents relating to UFO activity in the late 1940s and early 1950s are currently being declassified. At last the full story of the human race's battle against UFOs can begin to be told ...

It is a widely held misconception that the first wave of flying saucers arrived on earth during the summer of 1947, when an American pilot named Kenneth Arnold described strange objects he had seen above the Cascade Mountains of Washington State. They had flown, he said, 'like a saucer would skipping over water', thus coining the now familiar term. In fact, as many anthropolgists know, saucers have been around for much longer, perhaps as long as man himself. Granite carvings found in China's Hunan Province and dated as early as 45,000 BC show figures not unlike men in spacesuits, while above them fly cylindrical objects. At Font De Gaume in France, Cro-Magnon ancestors of a mere 15,000 years past painted pictures of discs on the walls of their caves alongside representations of mammoths, bison and reindeer. Ancient religious tracts also attest to the occasional visitation by aliens. Ezekiel, the Old Testament prophet, saw God arrive in a fiery wheel whilst his counterpart Elijah ascended to heaven in a fiery chariot. Among Hindu scriptures the Mahábhárata and the Ramayana mention 'flying castles of metal' from which strangers emerged.

Whether early American Indians also encountered strangers from the skies is open to question since none of their remnants depict saucer shapes. There can be no doubt, however, that the UFOs seen by Kenneth Arnold were not the first to invade the air space of North America.

On 18 November 1896 headlines in the *San Francisco Call* proclaimed the startling news that a huge flying shape had been seen by hundreds of people as it passed slowly over Sacramento the previous day. Several months later, on the morning of 19 April 1897 a Kansas cattle rancher named Alexander Hamilton watched in amazement as an airship hovering above his farm lowered a steel grab amongst his herd, picking up a two-year-old heifer and winching it kicking and bawling into the craft's underbelly. Two days later, a neighbouring rancher found the hind legs and head of the butchered animal on on his property. As the year 1897 wore on, strange tales similar to Hamilton's were repeated up and down the West Coast whilst elsewhere in the continent airships flew above the skies of Michigan,

Iowa, Missouri, Mississippi and Texas. Along with them came dark tales of men and women disappearing and a report from California of a horse roasted by a beam of light from an airship. In the most well witnessed example of all, a silvery ship floated low over the streets of Milwaukee and hovered for fifteen minutes while literally thousands watched in awe.

After Kenneth Arnold's saucer sighting in June 1947, the by-then long forgotten events of 1896 and 97 were resurrected and compared to the growing number of contemporary reports. To begin with the Washington government showed little interest in the phenomenon, a position shared by the USAF whose top brass, publicly at least, simply did not believe in any of it. However, an event was about to take place which would alter their assessment permanently.

The fateful day was 7 January 1948. The location – Godman Field Air Base, Kentucky.

At around one o'clock in the afternoon, the duty officer in charge of Godman control tower received a telephone call from the chief of state highway patrol. The police officer wished to clarify the reality of certain reports that had been coming in all morning of a huge glowing object shaped like a saucer, an object which, according to the same witnesses, measured over five hundred feet across its diameter. Could Godman confirm it was one of theirs? The duty officer was not amused. He curtly pointed out that a craft of such prodigious size was a physical impossibility; it was most probably the sun that motorists were seeing or some sort of reflection. In any event, the chief should know better than to waste valuable Air Force time. With the point firmly made the duty officer hung up. He had better things to do than investigate the hallucinations of some civilians who were most probably drunk. Besides, it was his lunch break.

The same man changed his mind a few minutes later when an urgent message verifying the aerial phenomenon was received from Army personnel guarding the nearby federal gold reserve at Fort Knox. A massive disc, unlike anything they had ever seen, was presently hovering over the area. With the menace now taken seriously the Godman Base commander, Colonel Guy Fix, ordered a flight of Mustang P-51 fighters to be scrambled. Within minutes they were in the air and had made visual contact with the UFO – 'a silvery metal disc of tremendous size', according to the radio commentary of flight leader Thomas Mantell, a World War II veteran. As the fighters closed in the other pilots corroborated his description. 'It's got a ring and a dome', said one. 'I can see rows of windows ...' claimed another. Listening in the control tower, Colonel Fix and his fellow officers were incredulous. Yet their amazement soon turned to horror. With the Mustangs now only a half a mile from their target, the flying monstrosity began to climb, demonstrating a manoeuvrability hard to believe. Lieutenant Mantell led his men in a chase, but at a height of 20,000 feet something suddenly went wrong. Mantell's fighter banked steeply and disappeared from view behind a cloud; simultaneously his radio went dead. Meanwhile the UFO had also vanished from sight.

The recovery of the flight leader's plane began that afternoon. Wreckage was scattered over an area of two miles, strongly suggesting the likelihood of a mid-air explosion. According to USAF sources Mantell's body was also found, although no civilians – not even the dead airman's parents – were allowed to see it. The three other pilots were debriefed and instructed to stay silent. An official explanation was issued the following day stating that Lieutenant Thomas Mantell had unfortunately been killed 'while trying to follow the planet Venus'. It was felt most likely that he had flown too high and fainted through lack of oxygen. Earlier stories of a flying saucer were, said the Air Force spokesman, without foundation and were probably the result of a similar misidentification of the planet. Meanwhile a full report was sent to the Pentagon.

For a number of people the official explanation defied

logic. Too many civilians had witnessed the UFO's slow passage over Kentucky that morning, and knew that the object they saw was most definitely not Venus. Others found it hard to believe that an experienced pilot, a veteran of the Pacific war, could possibly make such an elementary mistake. And what of the other pilots: why weren't they allowed to state their opinions? The widespread increase in public interest in UFOs across America made it difficult for the Air Force to blame the death of one of their men on such a flimsy story. So they changed it.

At the end of January, in response to the continuing interest in the Godman Base affair, the USAF announced that the object sighted above Fort Knox on 7 January had in fact been a skyhook reconnaissance balloon, the silvery surface of which had reflected sunlight.

For a while this new natural explanation served to allay public fears, but later that same year another ominous report reinforced the unease over the saucer situation. On 1 October 1948 Lieutenant George Gorman of the North Dakoka National Guard was buzzed by a bright glowing ball as he was about to land his F-51 fighter at Fargo Airport. Realising the craft was not a conventional plane, Gorman abandoned his landing and investigated it. However, after the highly manoeuvrable object made two more attack runs, the National Guardsman gave up and headed for the safety of earth. Details of this report, though classified, managed to leak out to the press, and the incident was immediately linked to the loss of the USAF plane nine months before. Once more the official explanation – that the object had been a small Piper Club training plane – did little to quell speculation.

For the Pentagon, whose task it was to protect the territory and air space of the United States of America, the increasingly threatening nature of UFO activity was as disturbing as it was baffling. The ability of these flying machines – if machines they were – to outfly any known terrestrial aircraft clearly had profound implications for national security. The flying saucers seemed to defy the most fundamental laws of aeronautics, even of gravity itself. There were a hundred questions and precious few answers.

The depth of the government's concern became clear in the autumn of 1948, when details of a report by a high-ranking officer fell inadvertently into the hands of the Washington press. In a memorandum to the Air Technical Intelligence Centre (ATIC) General N.F. Twining of Strategic Air Command described flying saucers as being 'interplanetary craft' and confirmed the recent wave of sightings were 'undoubtedly real'. The full report, which many believed to contain details of civilian air losses, was suppressed. When the storm broke over the leaked memorandum ATIC issued an immediate press statement denying that the opinions of General N.F. Twining in any way reflected an official viewpoint. These refutations have long since been shown to be a sham. Under the United States Freedom of Information Act, classified material may enter the public domain after a period of time has elapsed. The full text of General Twining's memorandum, which became available during the late 1970s, shows clearly that it was a widely held belief among senior Pentagon officials in 1947 and '48 that UFOs were manned space vehicles.

One letter, written to the then Supreme Commander of the Air Force, Brigadier General George Schlugen, states the case categorically: 'It is the position of this command that so-called flying disc phenomena is something real and not visionary ... operating characteristics such as extreme rates of climb; manoeuvrability and evasive action when contacted by human craft lend belief to the possibility that the objects are controlled ... (Twining).'

Significantly the full ATIC report has never reached the public domain. It was shredded in 1955.

In response to the wave of UFO sightings across America the USAF set up a special study group entitled 'Project Sign' whose job it was to investigate and monitor all information of sightings. Classified as a Grade A secret, and with headquarters at Wright-Patterson Base, one of Project Sign's first assignments was to investigate thoroughly the loss of the P-51 Mustang earlier that year. Testimonies of witnesses were collected under the most stringent security regulations and the press deliberately kept in the dark. When, in August 1949, a detailed preliminary report was sent to Air Force Chief of Staff, Hoyt S. Vandenburg, it concluded that the saucer had been real, almost certainly of extra-terrestrial origin, and potentially hostile. General Vandenburg, a fervent Cold War hardliner who had previously considered UFOs to be Soviet secret weapons, decided to burn the report. The following month, at a news conference arranged jointly with ATIC, a spokesman for Project Sign declared that it had been established absolutely that all stories of flying saucers could be explained in natural terms – as the misidentification of conventional aircraft or stars, a mild form of mass hysteria, plus the occasional hoax. It was their opinion that further studies into these reports were unwarranted. Nevertheless, unbeknown to the general public, Project Sign did continue to exist under a new title, Project Blue Book. It also had a new brief: now it was not only to investigate saucers but to systematically suppress evidence of UFO sightings, thereby limiting public awareness to a minimum. It was the start of a policy that has continued to the present day.

During the three years after the creation of Project Blue Book, saucer sightings decreased and what reports did appear in the American press arrived on the nation's breakfast tables in a highly sanitised version. However, Blue Book officers were receiving sightings every day from pilots buzzed by saucers, and those same pilots tended to get angry when they were told that the UFOs were sunspots or tricks of the light.

At the same time reporters were becoming impatient with transparently artificial explanations, and some sections of the press began to talk openly about a cover-up.

Occasionally details leaked out. Reluctantly in 1952 Air Force officials admitted that three F-94 jet fighters had intercepted more than a dozen unidentifieds over the capital city Washington DC. Then, in another embarrassment for Blue Book, the Secretary of State Dan Kimball made an off-the-cuff remark to the press, suggesting that he had personally witnessed two discs chase a naval plane during an exercise off Hawaii. Kimball's comments forced the authorities to stage a public relations exercise – the setting up of a Central Intelligence Agency (CIA) investigation panel headed by the distinguished Californian scientist H.P. Robertson. A noted sceptic about UFOs, Robertson was chosen deliberately to help debunk the rumours. Unfortunately for the CIA the plan went badly wrong when the team of experts concluded that UFOs were real. In the event, the Robertson report was ignored and its recommendations quashed.

Meanwhile, in the skies above America the saucer situation took another sinister turn. On 24 June 1953, a two man F-94C jet fighter was scrambled from Otis Base, Cape Cod, its mission to investigate a single unidentified radar blip picked up by ground control. As the interceptor closed on its target, a bright light hovering to the east at an altitude of 1500 feet, Captain James Suggs prepared himself for combat. But the battle was over before it had begun. The moment Suggs primed his cannon for firing the fighter suffered an immediate and total malfunction. Within seconds the plane was locked into a steep nose dive and Suggs had barely enough time to eject. His co-pilot Lieutenant Robert Barkoff was less fortunate: he was killed instantly as the jet exploded on impact with the earth below. The reason for the breakdown in the fighter's flight systems remained a mystery, though there were speculations among Blue Book officers that a malfunction of the type described by the surviving pilot Suggs might also have accounted for the death five years earlier of Lieutenant Mantell in Kentucky.

Whatever the cause of the Cape Cod tragedy, worse was

soon to follow. On 25 November, Lieutenant Felix Moncla and Radar Officer Robert Wilson took off from Kincross Air Base in their F-89 fighter to intercept a saucer spotted by Air Defense Command over the Canadian border. The object, which had appeared on radar screens as an erratically moving blip, turned out to be a large saucer-shaped craft hovering above Lake Superior at an altitude of 8000 feet. Moncla's description of the UFO recorded by fellow officers at Kincross turned out to be his last words.

Seconds after visual contact was made the impossible happened. Radar officers stared at their screens as the UFO began moving towards the jet at a velocity many times the speed of sound. Within moments the two blips had merged into one and the sound of the pilots' voices was replaced by the eerie crackle of static. What became of officers Moncla and Wilson was never discovered. A search of the Lake Superior area was carried out by a joint US and Canadian task force but revealed nothing. No wreckage or slick of oil was found upon the calm waters to suggest a clue to their fate. Though a mid-air collision seemed the most likely probability, radar controllers at Kincross were unable to shake off the nagging doubts that their comrades might have been space-napped – ensnared in some unimaginable way by creatures whose technology was already known to be far ahead of mankind's.

Whatever the private fears of junior ranks might have been the top brass quickly took steps to ensure that the incidents received little publicity. This time the Air Force line was that the radar controllers had mistaken the UFO for a C-47 flying boat of the Royal Canadian Air Force. When the Canadians disobligingly denied having any C-47 patrols in the vicinity, the Americans changed the story to 'freak atmospheric conditions'.

The USAF continued to lose planes throughout the next twelve months. On 1 July 1954, a strange signal appeared out of the blue on radar screens at Griffiths Base, New York State. An F-94C interceptor, of the same type that was lost in the June of the previous year, was scrambled to intercept it. After only twenty minutes the F-94C's two-man crew had confirmed the object to be of the now familiar saucer variety, a gleaming metallic vehicle with a diameter of over two hundred metres. The F-94C rose to fly alongside the craft as it glided serenely over the cloud banks and, doubtless mindful of the response of which UFOs had proved capable, the pilot chose to attempt radio contact rather than open fire. It was a gesture of friendship which proved futile. As soon as the airman began transmitting, he found his dials spinning wildly and his electrical systems malfunctioning. As if locked in a terrible vortex the jet spun out of control. On this occasion the airmen lived to tell the tale, both ejecting to safety before their fighter ploughed into a housing estate below. Less fortunate were four civilians who perished in the trail of devastation left in the aircraft's wake.

The early fifties were difficult times for the US Air Force high command. If the loss of their fighters to alien hostility was not enough, reports were beginning to come from civilian pilots suggesting that flying saucers were harassing airliners with increasing frequency and some were even being lost.

In March of the previous year, 1953, the pilot of a DC-6 en route from Wake Island in the Pacific to Los Angeles had radioed his destination to say that he was being attacked by three glowing balls. Seconds later his radio went dead and the plane disappeared along with twenty passengers and crew. Later that summer another DC-6 on an internal flight crashed after reporting interference from unidentified lights. People on the ground who witnessed the descent of the plane confirmed the involvement of UFOs. In this disaster a total of fifty-eight died; there were no survivors.

As the tally of saucer-related crashes grew longer Blue Book officers redoubled their efforts to hide the facts. In February 1955 a conference was organised in Seattle, in which officers from the military's air transport service intelligence division met the heads of America's major commercial airlines. The single item on the agenda was UFOs or, more specifically, the need to control the flow of information regarding them. Up until then, civilian pilots had reported sightings upon landing; now the Air Force wanted all reports sent directly to the Pentagon, a special channel being allocated solely for this purpose. A second change regarded the pilot's right to repeat stories of UFOs to others. Hitherto civil aviation personnel had been requested not to talk to the press, but now, following a special CIA directive, military style curbs were to be introduced to compel commercial aircrew to maintain strict silence. Air Force regulation AF-200-2, which had been drafted in 1948, stated that reporting UFOs could 'prejudice the security of the United States and its forces'. Originally intended to apply only to servicemen, the regulation was, in 1954, extended to include all those holding a pilot's licence. Anyone who did not maintain the level of secrecy required by the CIA was liable to ten years' imprisonment or a fine of ten thousand dollars. Naturally, these draconian measures provoked a backlash and by the late summer more than a hundred pilots had signed a petition against AF-200-2. However, it remained on the statute books, and with aircrews forbidden to release details of further incidents, the flow of UFO information to the press dried up.

For a time the policy worked. Serious newspapers, starved of hard evidence of UFOs, turned instead to the Cold War and other international crises, leaving only the less scrupulous press to indulge the fantasies of numerous cultists and pseudo-religious freaks by printing stories of their imaginary trips to Mars. With Hollywood churning out a plethora of saucer B-movies, the UFO phenomenon gradually diminished as an issue and entered instead the realm of science fiction. Only the tens of thousands who saw them continued to believe firmly in their reality.

When the situation changed, as it did in 1960, it was not an alien invasion that resurrected the UFO issue but, ironically, the treachery of one leading member of the conspiracy. Vice Admiral Robert Hillonkoetter was a recently retired head of the CIA when, in February 1960, he shocked former colleagues by releasing to the media photostat copies of a classified directive which warned senior officers in Bomber Command to regard UFOs as 'serious business'. Red-faced Air Force chiefs admitted issuing the order but insisted that the words had been taken out of context, being merely the small part of a much larger document.

However this time the explanation lacked credibility. The following month in the highly charged atmosphere of a press conference at Wright-Patterson Base, reporters repeatedly questioned USAF spokesmen about the existence of a cover-up policy, and the loss of Air Force planes in extraordinary circumstances. As usual the Air Force denied it but they were on the defensive. Across America millions of ordinary people began to wonder why the military should be so concerned about something they said did not exist. For the official debunkers in Project Blue Book, the misery was compounded when a team of distinguished scientists, astronomers and ex-military officers called NICAP (National Investigations Committee on Aerial Phenomena) published a 184-page review entitled *The UFO Evidence*, which not only stated unequivocally the fact that UFOs were dangerous but charged US official agencies with the deliberate falsification of evidence.

Recent publications have upheld that charge. In Timothy Good's *Above Top Secret*, a brilliantly researched exposé of the world-wide UFO cover-up that has operated for the past forty-five years, Captain Edward J. Ruppelt, former Chief of the US Air Technical Intelligence Centre in the 1950s, is directly quoted admitting that the CIA ordered the Air Force to 'debunk sightings and discredit witnesses'. According to Ruppelt, on occasions even USAF pilots suffered this demeaning treatment. An even more revealing statement contained in Good's book is that of General Benjamin Chidlaw, former Commanding

Officer of Air Defense Command, who said: 'The US Air Force lost many men and planes trying to intercept them (UFOs).' Chidlaw also revealed that the intelligence services had a standard practice of hiding details of these incidents.

In reality censorship may have been the least of their dirty tricks. In their determination to suppress evidence of sightings during the period the CIA resorted to methods incompatible with a free society, harassing witnesses whose only crime was a desire to tell the truth. In his book *The UFO Experience* Dr J. Allen Hyneck, director of the North Western University Observatory, detailed several cases in which those who reported seeing alien ships found themselves the subject of outrageous personal vendettas. Individuals hitherto considered respectable citizens were accused of deceit, insanity, hallucination or incompetence according to the particular official strategy at the time. Under the weight of official ridicule some found their marriages broken, their careers wrecked and their reputations ruined. CIA methods ranged from the threat of legal action to direct physical violence, and those who refused to respond to intimidation frequently disappeared.

One luckless American citizen who may have overstepped the mark was Dr Morris Jessup, an astrophysicist who became interested in UFOs after he first saw one himself over Cincinnati. Jessup made a name for himself as one of the leading opponents of the government's policy of official secrecy and appeared several times on television in the late 1950s to denounce Project Blue Book's role in the debunking of genuine reports. The astrophysicist's career as a rabble-rouser ended abruptly on 20 April 1959 when police found his lifeless body in a station wagon parked alongside a lonely Florida state highway. A tube led from the exhaust to the passenger compartment. The real story of Jessup's 'suicide' has never been ascertained, yet he was not alone among critics of the American authorities' excessive secrecy to die in mysterious circumstances. Dr James E. McDonald, a senior physicist with the Institute of

Atmospheric Physics at the University of Arizona, and Professor René Hardy, a leading authority in parapsychology, were both found dead with bullets in their brains and a gun at their sides. These men, like Jessup, had seemingly ended their own lives after driving alone to a deserted roadside place. Yet both had been highly critical of governmental policy, and Hardy's suicide came only two days before he was due to attend a press conference to release details of the CIA's suppression of UFO evidence. Following his death his files on the evidence disappeared.

As the 1960s wore on disquiet grew over the mounting number of aircraft lost for no apparent reason. One man who was not afraid to speak out – despite the pressure from above – was Dr Warren Lovell. Dr Lovell, a Seattle pathologist, conducted his own private study into a series of mid-air explosions for which there was seemingly no explanation. In all, he investigated over one hundred and fifty separate disasters from around the world, crashes which involved over two thousand deaths. He had first been alerted to the possibility of alien involvement after being called in to report on the destruction in 1964 of a Canadian Pacific DC-9 which had been torn apart by a force that had literally split the aircraft in half. Chemical examination of the wreckage could detect no traces of nitrates, thus ruling out the likelihood of a bomb. Yet there was no alternative theory. Intrigued by the mystery, Dr Warren Lovell found many other cases where the same pattern was repeated. On completion of his exhaustive research, the pathologist went on record to profess a belief that 'a force unknown to science' was responsible for the increase in air tragedies, adding that the force might well be from outer space. For his pains, Lovell was forced into early retirement and denied a government pension. Meanwhile, the hidden sky carnage continued unabated. Over the next five years eight DC-9s crashed in circumstances bearing an uncanny similarity to those identified by the Seattle pathologist.

All things must inevitably come to an end. For the CIA

and their allies at Project Blue Book the campaign to limit public awareness of flying saucers fell apart in the summer of 1965 when waves of unidentified objects arrived over the continent of North America in such numbers as to render previous saucer flaps inconsequential. The brilliant white objects which streaked across the skies of Pennsylvania on the night of 24 July were merely the beginning. The next morning, mysterious objects appeared on radar screens at a North Dakota air base while elsewhere jet interceptors chased objects over Duluth. More UFOs were engaged by fighters of Texas, New Mexico, Kansas and Illinois, and in August there came reports of saucers landing at Tinker Air Force Base in Oklahoma and Fairchild Base in Washington. By the end of the month over ten thousand separate sightings had been recorded across half the states of the Union. As the avalanche of reports grew, beleaguered Air Force spokesmen worked overtime to blame them on a wide variety of mistaken identifications: swamp gas, conventional aircraft, optical effects, smoke from factory chimneys, reflected starlight, parachutes, satellites, missiles, fireflies, shooting stars, meteorological balloons and the perennial favourite – mass hysteria. By now, however, the familiar tired explanations carried little weight and news editorials from Lincoln, Nebraska, to Richmond, Virginia, told them so. A leading article for the *Denver Post* was typical: 'Stars of summer nights don't appear in broad daylight or cause blips on the radar screens across a whole continent ... they can stop kidding us now about there being no such thing as flying saucers.'

They never have stopped kidding us about flying saucers. But 1965 marked a watershed in attitudes towards UFO sightings in America. Since then awareness has grown so fast that by 1987 a Gallup poll suggested that over half of the US population believes that aliens were regularly visiting our planet.

A recent British opinion survey similar to the one conducted in America suggests that belief in flying saucers on this side of the Atlantic is much less widespread. This may well be a tribute to the Westminster government's quieter, more subtle approach to dampening UFO speculation; yet there is also an inbuilt reluctance among serious journalists to lend credibility to any form of psychic phenomenon. The careful playing down of the afore-mentioned Rendlesham enigma is typical of the way newspapers sometimes conspire to devalue quite incontrovertible proof of an alien presence.

Although the story broke in the notoriously salacious Sunday tabloid the *News of The World*, its basis could hardly have been more reliable – a memorandum on USAF headed paper to the British Ministry of Defence dated 13 January 1981 and signed by a senior American officer, Colonel Charles Halt, which described in explicit detail the object's dimensions and appearance. That Sunday the midday ITV newscast gave the story prominence but then, unaccountably, ITN dropped the story from their early evening bulletin. The following morning the serious dailies attacked the story unmercifully. Adrian Berry, the *Daily Telegraph*'s scientific correspondent, wrote that only one person had seen something unusual, contradicting Colonel Halt's memorandum entirely. Likewise *The Times* failed to mention Halt's description, preferring to conjecture that the 'lights' in the forest were an optical illusion caused by light refractions from the Orford Ness lighthouse which was situated some miles away.

The cover-up continued in the weeks that followed. Every single copy of Halt's letter went missing and when journalists from Thames Television's *TV Eye* documentary series asked for tapes made at RAF Waxton – where radar officers had tracked the alien craft's descent – they were told that the tapes had been confiscated by USAF personnel. Thus, the full background to the affair has never reached the general public. With the story effectively debunked, few people are aware that Colonel Halt has stuck by his original account or that other senior officers present, including the former Base Commander Colonel Sam

Morgan, have since corroborated the Halt version of events.

Clearly newspaper editors continue to follow the MOD line on the subject of flying saucers – that any attempt to treat the subject seriously is contrary to the national interest.

British newspapers are not alone in showing unacceptable bias. The visual media's supine acceptance of government guidelines was evident four years previously in the BBC's refusal to screen an American-made documentary entitled 'UFOs Are Real'. Their alternative offering screened in 1976, supposedly espoused the case for UFOs, but in fact achieved the precise opposite. In the documentary the accounts of sensible witnesses were denigrated, while groups on the lunatic fringe of ufology were given full prominence alongside the sane voice of sceptics. Unbalanced to such a degree, the documentary had little difficulty in convincing neutral viewers that UFOs did not exist. If the British establishment was satisfied by the job done by their official broadcasting organ it was ironic, since the programme's screening coincided with a spate of landings on British soil and a sharp increase in the number of people who mysteriously disappeared.

On the morning of 4 February 1977 a glowing saucer, said to be roughly fifteen metres in diameter, landed in a field next to a rural county primary school in Broadhaven village, on the coast of Dyfed in Wales. The machine stayed on the ground for ten minutes and was seen by a total of fourteen children playing outside during a break in lessons. Meanwhile a strange looking spaceman, six foot tall and wearing a silver suit with helmet and breathing apparatus, was sighted by a teacher and two of the canteen staff, who also saw the object rise into the air. The 'Dyfed Enigma', as it was dubbed, quickly became the focus of attention in the British popular press, some of whom claimed it was the first positive landing of aliens on earth (which it most certainly was not) whilst others suggested that it was nothing more than the children's imagination. The controversy was further fuelled when another member of the school staff – Mrs Dorothy Cole, a school meals supervisor – admitted that she had herself seen a spaceship two months previously, whilst driving along a nearby lane. Up until the sighting of 4 February she had kept silent for fear of ridicule.

Whatever it was that visited the Welsh primary school on that cold winter morning, strange objects continued to appear all over Dyfed in the months that followed, with particularly frenetic saucer activity invariably leading to electromagnetic disturbances and regular breakdowns in the county's mains electricity supply. Predictably, not everybody believed these stories. One sceptic was Mrs Josephine Hewison, a farm manageress who had derided all talk of flying saucers until she found one parked outside her home one Saturday morning. Other disbelievers were the Coombes family of Ripperston Farm, who changed their minds when, in April, they not only had silver-suited beings running all over their property but lost several of their herd at the same time.

If the spiriting away of cattle brought a new hint of menace to the Dyfed phenomenon, a far more disturbing incident occurred a few weeks later, and cost the lives of five men. Ostensibly, the motorists who died on the A48 Carmarthen to Swansea road were the victims of a straightforward head-on collision. Yet the accident had occurred at precisely the same spot as an alien visitation in which, a few days previously, a couple of long distance lorry drivers had encountered two monstrous humanoids, an experience frightening enough to cause one to suffer a nervous breakdown. Had a similar vision caused the dead driver to swerve wildly into the path of the oncoming tanker, thus ending the lives of his friends and himself? Since the tanker driver also perished in the inferno the truth remains unknown.

As the reported sightings in Wales mounted, speculation grew as to their real cause. As usual, mass hysteria became the official explanation and naturally enough the one favoured by *The Times*, an organ guaranteed to support the British Establishment in periods of difficulty. Dutifully following the Ministry of Defence line, *The Thunderer* pointed out to readers that the Welsh sightings had all been confined to a small area, thus reinforcing the mass-psychosis theory. In fact nothing could be further from the truth, for reports had been drifting in steadily from across the British Isles. One such example came from Haverfordwest where a grounded saucer was seen by seven witnesses. Another report of a UFO on the ground came from housewives in Leigh, Greater Manchester, whilst in a small mining village in County Durham two women saw a UFO land on waste ground. Meanwhile, on the Winchester bypass near Chilcomb, Hampshire, a number of motorists interrupted their journey to observe a saucer taking off from a field. The best documented case of all came from two metropolitan policemen who investigated a UFO alert on the evening of 3 May 1977. Entering a park in the North London suburb of Hainault, the officers came across a conical object, glowing red and pulsating rythmically. As they approached it with mounting trepidation the object shot skyways accompanied by a deafening roar. In the spot where it had been a bush had been crushed and grass scorched in a circular pattern.

Around the same time that UFOs began landing in large numbers in the United Kingdom, people from around the world started to come forward claiming personal contact with aliens. Invariably, these experiences took the form of a physical abduction, in which the contactee was transported to the flying saucer itself and thereafter released. Difficult to believe though most of these tales were, even the most hardened sceptic had to admit the similarities between the stories.

In the archetypal abduction, a person or persons would probably be travelling along a quiet road at night. A flying saucer would descend in front of them or simply materialise out of nowhere, whereupon they would mysteriously lose consciousness. Usually the victims would then wake up aboard the craft, surrounded by aliens, variously described, who would either interrogate them or carry out some sort of medical examination. The process completed, the humans would then be returned to earth, usually (though not always) to the same vicinity from where they were taken. Whether or not abductees fully remembered their experiences varied between individuals but in almost all cases a time-lapse element would be involved – the time, that is, for the space-napping to have taken place.

Details of abductions sometimes bordered on the ridiculous. One Brazilian farmer named Antonio Boas claimed to have been forced to have intercourse with a female Martian, whilst kindly Venusians apparently gave a Wisconsin chicken farmer named Joe Simonton a pancake as proof of their visit. Yet for every absurd tale of people riding around the galaxy in eighty minutes, there were many more whose testimony suggested that abductions represented a major danger. Nor could many of these tales be easily explained away in terms of hoax or hallucination. For one thing, many abductees stuck to their stories even under deep hypnotic trances in which it is well-nigh impossible to lie, while others were subjected to polygraphic lie detectors with similarly conclusive results. Physical evidence was often found at the places where abductions were reported, along with inexplicably high levels of dangerous radiation. Marks found on the skin usually confirmed their stories including outbreaks of burns and weals consistent with radiation exposure. Most telling of all was the sheer consistency between the reported ordeals of abductees from different parts of the world.

In Britain one of the first abductions to receive serious consideration was the experience of an English family of five from Essex who claimed to have been collectively lifted, inside their car, into the sky one evening in the autumn of 1974. According to their tale John and Elaine Avis had been driving along country lanes near their home in Aveley, a small village on the north-eastern fringes of Greater London. Their three children Kevin, Karen and Stuart were also present, and it was Kevin who first noticed the UFO – a pale blue globe – apparently chasing their car. After a while the manifestation disappeared from view, but as John Avis rounded a curved corner their car hit a bank of thick green mist which spread across the road. Immediately the radio began to crackle and smoke and the engine died. There was a sudden bump, and the mist evaporated leaving the bemused family to continue their journey home apparently uninterrupted. Had this been the only oddity, the family might have put their experience down to tiredness or hallucination. However when they arrived home and found three hours missing from their lives, they knew it had been for real. Clocks in the Avis household registered one thirty a.m. yet when they had left Elaine's parents earlier that evening it had been ten o'clock. A journey that had seemed to them to take only the usual thirty minutes had in fact taken well over three hours. A quick check on the television channels showed that broadcasting had ceased thereby confirming this extraordinary loss of time.

To begin with, John and Elaine told only their close family of their experience. Yet when both husband and wife began to share strange, terrifying dreams about weird alien shapes they decided to contact an Essex based UFO investigator named Andrew Collins. Collins suggested they try to relive their experiences through regressive hypnotism and the couple, who were by now on the verge of nervous breakdowns, agreed. The regression was carried out under the supervision of an accredited practitioner, Dr Leonard Wilder. As both adult members went back in time each recalled how they had been taken aboard the alien ship, still inside their car, and dragged to an examination room by grotesque creatures with hairy, claw-like hands. After being given a full medical examination, strapped down to surgical-style tables, they were allowed to view their descent to earth through a holographic image.

Elaine vividly remembered seeing the outline of the Thames Estuary as the ship dropped lower. What was not clear was how they were actually returned to the road on which they had been travelling.

It was the opinion of Dr Wilder that behaviour under hypnosis by members of the Avis family suggested a genuine traumatic experience had been relived, and that therefore the events retold had probably occurred. A further regression of ten-year old Kevin served to re-inforce this conclusion. When the family's bizarre story finally hit the London newstands early in 1975, however, it was received by public incredulity. To most people the idea that an alien craft could swoop down and suck up a car full of people was the stuff of science fiction – and poor science fiction at that. But the tale of abduction told by the Essex family was merely the first of many to appear in the world press that year.

Another abduction uncannily similar to that of the Avis family focused upon the experience of a young Arizona forestry worker who was snatched away before the aston-ished eyes of his comrades. Travis Walton was among five men driving home after a day's work near their home town of Snowflake when, after seeing a light they first imagined to be the sun's reflection, they instead found themselves confronted by a glowing UFO. Walton left the truck's cab to investigate, and was struck down by a beam of light. His comrades drove off in a panic, but returned the following morning accompanied by a disbelieving sheriff. Of Travis Walton there was no sign, yet curious burn marks on trees and grass intrigued the policeman sufficiently to mount a more intensive search using dogs and helicopters. The search uncovered no further clues and fears for Walton's safety grew until on 10 November the young forestry worker was found wandering cold, hungry and exhausted along a highway outside the neighbouring town of Heber. He had been missing for five days.

Unlike the Avis family, who remembered their ordeal only after induced hypnotherapy, Travis Walton recorded his experience clearly. To a bemused audience of doctors, nurses, law men and press correspondents, Walton related how he had awoken on board the alien vessel, his ankles and wrists clamped securely to a table. The aliens themselves, creatures similar to those described by the Essex abductees, seemed interested in all aspects of Walton's bodily functions and conducted numerous tests taking blood and urine samples. While sceptics of Walton's story openly questioned his mental health, doctors in the Arizona State Hospital confirmed marks on his flesh were consistent with an enforced examination. A full psychiatric examination was subsequently carried out, not just by a doctor but by a whole team of specialists led by the distinguished analyst Howard Kandell. The doctors, most of whom had assumed that Walton and his fellow workers must have undergone a purely hallucinatory experience, changed their opinion after an eight-hour session of deep hypnosis reinforced Walton's original story. Risking their collective reputations Kandell and his team stated publicly their belief in the abduction.

Tired and half-starved though he may have been, Travis Walton emerged from his encounter in decidedly better condition than many. Typical physical afflictions of close contact with alien life include the effects of radiation poisoning – markings on the skin like second-degree burns, bleeding from the gums and the partial or complete loss of hair and teeth.

Such severe physical effects were noticed by doctors at a Texas hospital, who treated two women abducted by aliens from a state highway on 29 December 1980. The women had grown peculiar nodules on their skin which burst seeping a clear viscous fluid, and they were unable to sleep for weeks afterwards, suffering acute nausea and diarrhoea. One, Nickie Landrum, went temporarily blind, whilst the other, Betty Cash, developed breast cancer which required a mastectomy. Doctors were convinced that both afflictions were in some way connected to their close encounter. An even more unfortunate fate befell

Brazilian Inacio De Suza whose day-long abduction in 1967 was followed by an immediate onset of leukaemia, the spread of which was so rapid that he died only a month after his reported experience.

Sometimes death follows upon abduction even more swiftly. One of the oddest UFO stories of recent years seems linked to the mysterious death of Zygmunt Adamski, a Polish immigrant to Britain whose lifeless, mutilated body was found dumped on top of a coal-tip in June 1980. Adamski, who lived in the Leeds area, was last seen alive on 11 June, five days before the discovery of his corpse. According to his wife he had simply strolled down the road to buy some vegetables and never returned. How Adamski's body came to have ended up sprawled on the summit of a coal mound five days later remains a mystery, as does the precise cause of his death. What also puzzled the doctors who carried out the autopsy was not the reason for death itself, but the nature of an unidentifiable corrosive substance which had been carefully applied to the dead man's head. Altogether, the fate of Zygmunt Adamski was an enigma, and in summing up the evidence at the subsequent inquiry Yorkshire coroner James Turnbull described it as 'quite the most mysterious death' he had ever investigated. An open verdict was recorded.

Yet Adamski's fate was even more strange than the coroner suggested. For, unbeknown to James Turnbull, the Yorkshire Constabulary had obtained further evidence that indicated the likelihood of UFO involvement, evidence that the British Ministry of Defence had advised them not to submit. The truth behind the Adamski affair only became known when two journalists from the London tabloid, the *Daily Mirror*, stumbled upon the fact that three officers from the Yorkshire Constabulary had reported seeing a flying cigar UFO on the morning of the sixteenth, the day that Adamski's body was found. One officer, PC Alan Godfrey, had actually been transported aboard the ship as it hovered above the Todmorden council estate, an area adjacent to the tip where Adamski's corpse lay.

After his experience PC Godfrey had initially been reluctant to tell his superiors, yet the discovery of the missing man and the realisation that other colleagues had also reported the alien craft made him change his mind. To his surprise and relief, police headquarters believed the story, and arranged for him to undergo a hypnotic regression with the department's own criminal psychologist in order to see if he could recall any further details. Reliving his abduction, Godfrey described the ship's occupants as a nightmarish parade of grotesque forms with heads like lamps. When he became hysterical the police psychoanalyst ended the session to save him further distress.

When the *Daily Mirror* broke their astonishing exclusive in August, they printed the full text of PC Godfrey's recollections. What the luckless Zygmunt Adamski might have remembered is anyone's guess.

Many abductees never return at all. The missing persons' files from around the world contain numerous names for whom direct UFO contact has coincided with their permanent disappearance from the face of our planet. This unenviable fate would seem to have befallen an illiterate Brazilian peasant named Rivalino Da Silva who was snatched from outside his shanty house on the outskirts of Rio de Janeiro on the morning of 20 August 1962. Initially the only witness to the incident was Rivalino's eleven-year-old son Raimundo, who rushed immediately to the local police station to raise the alarm. Through the flood of hysterical sobbing the boy told how the silver men had come and put his father in a 'big ball'. Apparently mesmerised, Rivalino had assented to the abduction. Afterwards the ball rose slowly into the sky. To begin with the police were understandably sceptical, but their curiosity was aroused by an odd set of markings outside the Da Silva home where dust and sand had been blasted away. After several neighbours came forward to corroborate young Raimundo's story the police began to appreciate the truth of the mysterious happening. Two weeks later a glowing object glided slowly over the rooftops of the Brazilian capital and this marked the beginning of a spate of abductions in which victims never returned. Lieutenant Wilson Laboa, the officer who headed the inquiry into these mysteries, ordered a full psychiatric examination to be made upon the young Da Silva orphan. The psychiatrist responsible, Dr João Atunes De Oliveria, stated in his report that as far as he was concerned, Raimundo was no liar.

Until very recently, stories concerning abductions by alien beings were treated with almost universal disbelief. Even committed UFO researchers tended to avoid them because many seemed too incredible to be taken seriously. But the stories do not go away, indeed they increase in number as the years go by. By the early 1980s it had become apparent that abductions presented a new and perhaps more disquieting menace than any UFO threat yet identified. Just what aliens might hope to learn from our civilisation can only be guessed at, but ufologists are now convinced that UFO occupants are abducting humans as part of an extensive investigation into human society.

One American ufologist, Budd Hopkins, has a particularly novel theory. Whilst studying a group of adult abductees, Hopkins noticed that all had suffered a similarly mysterious injury during their childhood. Tracing the facts of each incident the ufologist discovered that the wounds – scars to the right knee – had appeared without apparent reason in the victim's seventh year. Coincidentally, the UFO abductees had been born in the year 1943 and suffered their accidents in the summer of 1950. Through regression Hopkins was able to establish that these injuries had been created surgically – on the operating tables of an alien ship. In all these cases the abductees' descriptions of the craft tallied closely, both to the separate adult experiences as well as to each other's testimony. It was Hopkins' belief that some sort of implant had been induced into the human guinea pigs, though no evidence existed to support the theory. In any case the purpose behind such surgery remained obscure. Whatever aliens might be learning about us, it is a sad fact that we still know very little about them. Despite the multitude of close encounters now on record, we are really none the wiser on even the most basic questions. No concrete information has emerged to explain how these space ships are powered, or how they defy gravity and conventional aerodynamic laws. In reality, we do not even know positively that they come from outer space at all.

Many ufologists prefer the theory that UFOs exist all around us hidden from view on an unseen dimension beyond our sensory perception, while a diminishing band see their worldly home as being in the centre of the earth. Neither theory is remotely satisfactory and if one wished to be cynical one could say that we understand less about UFOs now than our Paleolithic ancestors who first drew their shapes on the walls of their cave homes.

Nevertheless, the one thing that we do know for certain is that they are there. Hundreds of thousands, perhaps millions of human beings have now seen alien ships. Contrary to popular belief the typical UFO sighter is not a drunk, an attention seeker or a drug addict, but a normal, sane, probably very ordinary individual. UFO spotters are not cranks, nor are they likely to be out to earn money or fame. Whilst a few abductees have made money from books based on their adventures, the vast majority get nothing whatsoever and many have lost much in terms of reputation. There is little to benefit a distinguished judge, a chief constable, a school headmistress, a government minister or a senior civil servant by admitting to a close encounter with creatures from another planet. Yet these are among the many respected members of society who have claimed to have come face to face with the impossible.

Sightings of saucers cannot be put down to misidentification of conventional aircraft or satellites simply because, as we have seen, UFOs predate the beginnings of powered flight. When one takes away the ninety per cent which can be put down to fraud, hoax or hysteria, we remain left with a body of human testimony the size of which the combined governments of the world cannot bury. Add to that the physical evidence – the radar blips, the still photographs, the cine-footage, not to mention the radiation, blast areas and other damage caused by alien landings – and the case for UFOs is proven beyond question.

Occasionally acceptance of that fact comes from surprisingly significant directions. Before his death, former Air Chief Marshall Lord Dowding, Commander-in-Chief of Fighter Command during the Battle of Britain, registered his absolute conviction that UFOs were real in a since-published letter to Italian diplomat Alberto Perego. From Timothy Good's *Above Top Secret* it emerges that the same belief was held by Lord Louis Mountbatten during his time as British Chief of Defence Staff (1958–65). Impressively Good's book is prefaced by no less a personage than Lord Hill-Norton, a former Admiral of The Fleet and also Chief of Defence Staff (1971–3). In his introduction Hill-Norton makes plain his personal belief in UFOs and his suspicions of a high level cover-up.

Incredibly, official agencies on both sides of the Atlantic remain determined to limit public awareness of UFOs. Nor is this obsessive secrecy likely to change. In November 1987, John Hurley, chairman of a UFO study group in Birmingham, England, asked the MOD to grant access to records which should have become declassified under the thirty-year rule which restricts recent secret information. To his disappointment, though not altogether his surprise, Hurley was told that all documents relating to UFOs before 1957 had been inadvertently destroyed. Afterwards, in an angry letter to the press, Hurley denounced the Ministry as undemocratic and claimed that the public were only being told as much as the government wanted them to know. Predictably, the MOD refused to comment further.

The British security organisations are not always content to simply dead-bat inquisitive ufologists. In *Above*

Top Secret, author Timothy Good cites several examples where Military Intelligence officers have warned contactees against talking to the press. Good himself incurred official wrath when he discovered the whereabouts of the RAF's secret UFO research unit at Rudloe Manor, Wiltshire. Arrested whilst trying to take photographs of the building he was twice interrogated, first by the military officers and then by Special Branch. He later described the experience as a 'salutary lesson'.

Similar allegations of cover-ups have been levelled against governments across the world, especially in cases involving the loss of civilian aircraft. Occasionally, damning evidence does emerge of aircraft lost to alien activity. One such example concerns the strange disappearance on 27 October 1978 of Frederick Valentich, an Australian pilot who vanished while flying his single engine Cessna 182 from Melbourne to King Island in the Pacific. Valentich had only been airborne for about fifteen minutes when he radioed Melbourne air traffic control to report how he was being followed by four brilliant orange lights. For the next two minutes radar screens at Melbourne recorded the unidentifieds close in and finally merge with the Cessna. As they did so contact with Valentich was lost. The following morning rescue planes scoured the area of the Bass Straits where the Cessna was presumed to have gone down. Nothing was found. The true fate of the Australian pilot might never have seen the light of day had it not been for the determination of his family and the sharp investigative journalism of one courageous Antipodean newspaper editor.

In the weeks following the Cessna's disappearance the Australian Bureau of Air Safety attempted to play down rumours of a UFO link to the mystery, even though six other reports of strange lights had been reported the night of 27 October. When one newspaper editor tried to obtain a recording of Valentich's last words, he was told that the tape had been erased. What the newspaperman did discover however, was that the area of the Cessna's last reported position had seen more than its fair share of enigmas in the past.

As early as 1920 odd lights in the sky accompanied the loss of the *SS Amelia* as well as the search vessel sent to find her. Reports of strange flying shapes over the Bass Straits persisted during the next three decades, a period which saw the vanishment of no less than seventeen aircraft in circumstances uncannily reminiscent of Frederick Valentich's last flight.

Another incident which almost did not become public was the narrow escape of a charter jet carrying 109 German and Austrian tourists in November 1979.

The airliner was attacked by two saucers soon after it took off from Majorca en route to the Canary Islands. As the two unidentified objects dived and swooped around the aircraft the pilot, Captain Javier Lerdo-Tejeda, radioed Barcelona airport for assistance which quickly arrived in the form of two French-built Mirage fighters. For once the intervention of terrestrial war planes was decisive and the discs flew off at the first burst of the Mirages' cannons. Afterwards, having made an unscheduled landing at Valencia, shaken passengers and air crew described their encounter to astonished officials. Initially the Spanish authorities played down talk of UFOs, yet after a maverick newspaper published a series of eyewitness accounts, Sanchez Teran, Spain's Minster for Transport and Communications, went on record as admitting the truth behind the bizarre episode. Nor was the minister's admission the only concession to the UFO lobby. In a highly unusual gesture of openness a reporter from a Madrid newspaper, Juan Jose Benitez was given access to the UFO files of the Spanish Air Ministry; writing afterwards, Benitez told readers 'It became definitely and categorically clear that UFOs exist and, quite evidently, are a matter of the deepest concern to governments of the whole planet.'

The passengers and crew of the Spanish charter craft had a lucky escape. Less fortunate travellers earlier that year were the five men aboard a private Learjet lost over the Sahara Desert on 11 August during a trip from Athens to Jeddah. Following a call mentioning a strange ship flying alongside, the Learjet disappeared from radar screens. When it was found the fuselage was still intact, yet inside the men's bodies had been reduced to piles of thin powder. Examining samples of the remains at London's St Thomas' Hospital, Osteologist Professor Michael Day was certain that no natural circumstances – neither wild animals nor the desert's extreme temperatures – could have produced such change in bone structure. A force outside the laws of science was responsible.

Will the governments of our planet ever admit that flying saucers are a menace? Interestingly, the new atmosphere of glasnost in Russia has led Soviet military sources to become far more open in discussing UFO contacts – even where the encounters have led to tragedy. Specific incidents from the past that have only recently come to light include a MiG fighter brought down by a UFO over Basunchak on 16 June 1948, a laser beam attack by a UFO hovering over the headquarters of the Tactical Missile Command at Sverdlovsk in the spring of 1958, and the loss of passengers and crew aboard an Antanov AN-2P mail plane which crash-landed whilst en route to Kurgan in 1961. In this incident a circle of scorched grass was found close to the aircraft but no bodies were found and none of the people on board were seen again.

Russian close encounters show no sign of drying up. In October 1989 a series of bizarre reports began to emanate from Tass, the official Soviet news agency. According to the stories a large spaceship, shaped like a flattened sphere, had landed in a heavily populated area of Russia on three consecutive days during the previous month.

The centre of this mystery was Voronezh, a city of one million inhabitants situated some three hundred miles from Moscow. In the most widely reported incident, the object was said to have landed in the city's central park in broad daylight. As hundreds of witnesses later described, two aliens and a robot emerged from the craft and afterwards Soviet scientists found curious unidentifiable rock samples at the site of the landing. Publicly, few Western journalists took the Voronezh occurrence seriously, preferring instead to treat the whole thing as a joke. Nevertheless Tass stuck to their story, pointing out that they were not in the business of humour. Speaking on British television, veteran Moscow correspondent Joe Adamov indicated the lack of discrepancy in the numerous verified testimonies to the landings and added that a similar phenomenon had appeared above the skies of another Russian city, Petrovozavodsk, in 1977, using a laser beam to start fires and cause widespread structural damage.

It is hard to believe that the British or American governments could be so candid in their attitude, but events may force our political masters to change their stance since, at the present time of writing, UFOs are appearing in the skies in greater numbers than ever before.

As sightings multiply, reports of abductions by strange flying objects continue unabated from as far apart as Vietnam and Venezuela. During 1989 a French maintenance worker described how a strange object sucked up his wife and two children, whilst in Britain a thirty-nine-year-old woman from Warrington, Cheshire, disappeared the day after she reported that she had had an encounter with aliens. Throughout the following year similar reports have come from almost every continent around the world. According to Mike Birdsall, editor of the British UFO Journal *Quest*, 'Something very strange is happening; we have never received so many reports in such a short space of time. They have come from the public, police, RAF officers and astronomers.'

Certainly something strange is happening. But it is nothing new. The menace of UFOs has been with mankind since the dawn of time, yet only now is that danger becoming so dreadfully apparent.

DARK SHADOWS

There was a time when everyone believed in the Devil. In the Middle Ages it was universally accepted that Lucifer was a real being, Lord of the Nether Realm and served by an army of spirits whose purpose was to overthrow God's creation. To resist these insidious forces medieval man needed to be constantly on his guard; Satan was public enemy number one.

Today we think very differently. In an age of computer science and space-age technology, few still fear the old images of hell fire and the Devil has long since been consigned to the level of religious symbolism. But the Devil has not gone away and neither have his followers.

For many Americans the events of the night of 8 August 1969 were a stark introduction to the excess of evil-worship. It was on that night in the twilight hours of the swinging decade that a group of youngsters known as the 'Family', hippy followers of Charles Manson, entered the California home of Sharon Tate and ritually butchered the movie star and her guests. Five died in a charnel house of horror, beaten, strangled, stabbed and mutilated beyond recognition. The following night the clan repeated their performance at the Hollywood home of the La Bianca family, owners of a supermarket chain.

Few crimes have caused greater publicity. The sheer mindless brutality of the Tate–La Bianca killings shocked the entire West Coast community, yet it was only following their arrests, when Manson's faithful disciples boasted openly of their part in the orgy of bloodletting, that the American public began to learn the full depth of the 'Family's' depravity. Even after the murderers were safely confined to the state penitentiary for life terms, one question continued to trouble criminologists. How was it that Manson, a former petty thief of small stature and unremarkable appearance, had been able to exercise his grip upon these young men and women, a hold so powerful that they had obeyed any instruction without hesitation, no matter how degrading or dangerous that order might be? Manson's personal history held one small clue: a nondescript individual, he began reading books on the occult during a short spell in MacNeill Island Federal Penitentiary, books which apparently gave him the idea of setting up his own cult to the demon-god Satan. Sure enough, on his release from jail in June 1966, he set himself up as a messianic figure whose religion taught that evil was the sublimest form of joy, and that blood lust was the supreme sexual pleasure. Transformed almost magically into a personality of magnetic attraction, he had little difficulty in persuading hordes of young people to join him in regular orgies of sadism at his rented Death Valley ranch. Under his now expert tutelage they came to think of themselves as 'Satan's Slaves' and it was to do the Devil's work that they were despatched on the night of 8 August.

Was Manson's Diabolism real or imaginary? Some doctors claimed at the trials that the cult leader's mesmeric power was induced by LSD, but others could not help but notice how deeply the Family had become involved in black magic. The testimony of his disciples demonstrated how the strength of Manson's mind alone bound them so securely to his will. One of their number, Paul Watkins, described it as being like 'mental thought transference'. Another told of Manson's ability to place cult members in a form of suspended animation, rendering them completely immobile for days on end. In reality, it seemed that the disciples' subservience to his will was total; they were little more than puppets he could manipulate as actors in his dark drama. As for Manson himself, he remained proud of the association of his destiny with that of the Devil and confident of the final victory of evil. Conducting his own defence at the trial he described those whom he had controlled as his children who had done well. Eyes burning at the jury, he ended his address with an ominous warning: 'There are many more coming in the same direction; they are running in the streets and they are coming right at you!'

At the time most people assumed that he was talking of those remnants of the Manson Family still at large. Only later did it become clear that the cult leader was speaking of something quite different – the spirit of evil itself, a discarnate entity made manifest in the minds and actions of living people, human beings driven by unnatural urges to commit crimes of unspeakable barbarity. Was this prophecy merely the claptrap of a tortured and demented fanatic? Or had Manson's dabbling in the occult led him to become possessed by invisible forces – forces which manipulated him with the same intensity that he controlled his numerous followers?

Certainly those who Manson claimed to be his children are still with us. In April 1989 student Mark Kilroy was the last of thirteen youngsters picked up at random and used as human sacrifices by Satanists operating in the Rio Grande Valley, New Mexico. Once kidnapped, the young people were drugged, tortured and murdered at a remote ranch. Unsuspecting police assumed that the missing teenagers had simply run away. It was only when a cult member turned informer that the horrific truth was discovered. The Rio Grande murders followed a pattern formerly seen in other states. On 26 March 1985 a nineteen-year-old girl named Jacqueline Martella was abducted from a street in Oceanside, Long Island. Raped and butchered by cultists, her naked body was found along with satanic insignia in a wood close to her home. Another cult victim that spring was sixteen-year-old Theresa Fusco, whose mutilated corpse was found beside railroad tracks in nearby Lynbrook. A satanic pentagram had been drawn on her body with a magic marker and a note left containing the cryptic words, 'Sex ... virgin ... devil.' Police believed both girls had been used as sacrifices. Yet another victim of cult fanatics that year was Eigil Vesti, a Norwegian immigrant whose corpse was found with its heart cut out. Forensic tests carried out at the scene led police to believe that Vesti's blood had been drained and drunk by his killers. The three East Coast murders from 1985 may or may not be connected. In truth we cannot say, for in contemporary America such horror stories make everyday news.

In the years since Charles Manson received a life sentence, crimes like the Tate–La Bianca massacres have become almost commonplace. Indeed, on the very day that I began researching material for this chapter, in July 1986, I noticed a newspaper report describing the carnage found in a mansion in Lynchburg, Virginia, where two middle-aged wealthy Americans had been ritually slaughtered in what appears to have been a ceremony of Devil worship. Detectives discovered blood smeared upon the floor in the shape of a triangle and the figure 666 – the biblical number of the Beast – carved into the floor. Footprints showed where the group of killers had danced in the blood which flowed freely from their victims' gaping throats. If the Lynchburg murders bear the distinctive hallmarks of the Evil One they are far from unusual. One might casually pick up a newspaper in any US state on any week at random and read of similar atrocities committed somewhere in the community. Nor are these weird black magic cults the exclusive preserve of America.

In July 1988 a British Conservative MP caused a sensation when he stood up in the House of Commons and gravely pronounced that the country was living through a period of unprecedented evil, marked by a resurgence in the practice of witchcraft, black magic and satanic rituals. The Rt. Hon. Geoffrey Dickens, member for the Yorkshire constituency of Littleborough and Saddleworth, was no stranger to controversy. A colourful northerner, he had often been prepared to say the sort of things his political masters preferred not to hear. Yet the speech in 1988 was extraordinary even by his standards, since, in alleging that Diabolism was sweeping the country, he also implied that covens were regularly abusing, and on occasions even sacrificing children to the Evil One. To many, such suggestions beggared belief. Yet Dickens's case was not lacking in proof. Nor was he without supporters ready to corroborate his bizarre claims.

By 1988 many experts in the Catholic church, including Benedictine exorcist Dom Robert Petitpierre, were estimating that some forty thousand self-proclaimed witches were practising their diabolical art across the United Kingdom. At the same time, the Reverend Robert Law, the Church of England's senior adviser to the Bishop of Cornwall and a specialist in occult matters, stated in a newspaper article that 'satanic worship takes place all over Britain'. Another respected church figure to issue a similar warning was John Burgan, a Pentecostal pastor from Sussex, who claimed to have personally saved several children from Devil groups practising in the Home Counties. In assessing the extent of Satanism in Britain, all three men pointed out that almost half of Britain's churches had been broken into during the previous two years, often to be desecrated by the unmistakable hallmarks of the Beast's disciples: crucifixes broken or stolen; gravestones smeared with goats' blood; hexagrams and other insignia daubed upon walls. Even so, to many it seemed entirely incredible that the council estates and sedate chalet bungalows of English suburbia could be concealing so widespread and dark a secret. Yet by 1988 it was not merely committed defenders of the Christian faith who were beginning to take the threat of Satanism seriously.

Addressing a conference of police officers, psychiatrists and social workers at the Royal College of Medicine, consultant child psychologist Dr David McDonald professed his own concern that satanic rituals were on the increase. Quoting information he had gleaned through various case studies of disturbed children, McDonald made it clear that he was not alone among his peers in believing that these rituals not only left scars on the mind, but at their most extreme involved violence and, in some instances, sacrificial death to those who were drawn into the web of evil.

Dianne Core, national organiser of Childwatch, a charity for the monitoring of abused children, also believed that children were regularly being used as sacrifices in witch-craft ceremonies all over Britain. Interviewed for the women's magazine *She* in October 1988, Core spoke of saving three children from a celebration of the Feast of Beltane, a key satanic ritual. During the feast the children, having been previously drugged, were forced to drink blood and urine before being tied upside down upon a cross and raped. In the same magazine article a former black witch described how seventeen years earlier she had witnessed a thirteen-year-old girl being raped violently over a black temple altar and then put to death with a ceremonial knife. The ex-Satanist went on to describe how witches often hid signs of pregnancy so that they might give their own children as offerings to the Prince of Darkness. In one ceremony, in which she had personally taken part, members of her coven cut the throat and drank the blood of a nine-day-old baby girl, who belonged to their high priestess. Since the birth had never been registered, and the body buried in secret, no murder investigation could follow.

Six months after the *She* article appeared, a detailed report was published by the tabloid *Sunday Mirror* news-paper, alleging that Diabolism was even more widespread than Dianne Core had feared. *Mirror* journalists claimed to have uncovered proof that girls as young as eleven were being raped and later forced to undergo abortions to provide foetuses for black magic ceremonies. The exposé, which appeared in May 1989, suggested that as many as four thousand of these 'Brood Mares', as they were termed, were currently under the influence of secret groups across the country. Interviewing two schoolgirls who admitted to having had thirteen forced abortions. between them, the *Mirror*'s men alleged that the foetuses had been eaten.

Also quoted was a senior police officer, Detective Inspector Charles Horn, whose eighteen-month investigation into the girls' allegations ended in an Old Bailey trial. Plainly believing the 'Brood Mares' stories, Horn described the investigation as being the most disturbing case he had come across in eighteen years of police work.

As 1989 wore on other equally disturbing cases were coming to light. The following month Mrs Maureen Davies, a director of the 'Reach Out' Christian Group, claimed in a national newspaper to have helped deliver several children from becoming Brood Mares. According to Davies one girl had even been made to sacrifice her own aborted offspring and eat part of its remains. Backing up Davies's allegations was Jackie Balodes, a former black witch turned Christian, who said she had visited black masses in which flesh had been stripped slowly from the bodies of young children. Others were nailed upside down and left to bleed to death. A similar story emerged from a television documentary, *The Cook Report*, broadcast in September, in which one ex-Satanist named Audrey Harper claimed she had evidence that over thirty human sacrifices a year were carried out in the single county of Surrey.

Claims and counter-claims began to turn into police convictions. In a case that summer making legal history, thirty-six members of the same West Midlands family were handed sentences for paedophile-related crimes which had been performed in honour of the Devil. Over a period of years a total of twenty-three children had been regularly abused, sodomised and had their young bodies smeared with the blood of slaughtered animals. One teenager had been subjected to three incestuous rituals a day for ten years. No less repulsive were the practices of warlock Peter

McKenzie, a self-styled black magician from Hertford-shire, whose career of satanic debauchery involving some thirteen children aged from six to fifteen was ended finally by a long prison sentence handed down the following August. The cases of McKenzie and the Coventry paedo-phile ring were just two amongst more than twenty serious crimes to come to light in the first six months of 1989, all of which shared links with the diabolic.

The involvement of so many children in these obscene practices is unsurprising for anyone who understands the motivation behind Satanism. To drink a child's blood is not only pleasurable to a dedicated disciple of Hell, it is also believed to be power enhancing. For black magicians, infants provide the best sacrifices since Satan seeks to defile the pure in spirit. If children can be induced to commit atrocities upon one another, thus endangering their souls, then so much the better. Police forces across Great Britain, long doubtful about many of these stories, now believe that subtle forms of mind control are being used upon young children in order to manipulate them into taking part in ritual abuse.

If these consciously satanic child-abuse rings were the worst threat posed by the Devil it would be serious enough, but they may not be. Some believe there is an even greater menace facing society from the forces of darkness – a menace represented by the growing numbers of motiveless murders that remain unsolved each year. Murders which appear to have nothing in common, except perhaps for the killer's fascination with psychic evil ...

On Wednesday 5 June 1986, at Leicester Crown Court, England, a nineteen-year-old youth named Paul Bostock pleaded guilty to the savage murder of two young women. The following day newspapers described his outrages under lurid headlines such as 'Face of Evil' and 'Day of the Beast'. For once the press was not exaggerating. Bostock had indeed played the part of a beast, cruelly enjoying the sufferings of those he had killed. In passing sentence, the judge, Anthony Smith QC, said the most frightening thing about the case was that doctors had been unable to discover why he had committed such unspeakable crimes. Yet in fact it was an obsession with evil – and the occult forms evil took – which had led the youth down his murderous path.

Bostock's first victim was Caroline Osborne, a twenty-nine-year-old secretary who was assaulted while she exercised her dog in a park. Tying her up first, Bostock plunged a long knife into her heart seven times in a ritualistic sacrifice to Satan. Afterwards police found black magic symbols carved into trees near the body. In the two years following the attack Bostock regularly visited the cemetery where Caroline Osborne was buried to gloat over her grave, and chant incantations promising her soul to Hell. It was after one of these macabre visits that he killed his second victim, Amanda Weedon, a twenty-one-year-old nurse. Once more the stabbing had the hallmarks of demonic sacrifice. During intensive police investigations Paul Bostock was interviewed several times. On each occasion he claimed a perfect alibi but his odd manner made officers suspicious until at last he broke down during interrogation and admitted his foul deeds. Later, before his trial, Bostock wrote a long and remorseful letter to his girlfriend in which he could not account for his behaviour. Neither, indeed, could anyone else. Psychiatric reports detailed that Bostock had an unhealthy obsession with horror and the occult, but nevertheless pronounced him sane. After the trial the father of Bostock's second victim, Horace Weedon, said bitterly: 'There are people who are mad and there people who are bad. There is no evidence that this man has psychiatric problems. He is just evil.'

But was the evil always within Bostock, or had it entered him from the outside ...?

Another person to be denounced by an English court as evil that same summer was Mirella Beechook, a twenty-six-year-old Mauritius-born mother who became obsessed with witchcraft. Like Bostock, the obsession ended in two savage deaths. On Tuesday 1 July 1986, at the

Old Bailey, Beechook was found guilty of the voodoo murder of two young children. Earlier the court had heard how she had strangled, in a single violent afternoon, four-year-old Stacey Kavanagh with a wire flex, and then murdered her own seven-year-old daughter Tina. The police found the two small bodies in the Beechook flat, which was covered in occult insignia. Like Bostock, Mirella Beechook was never able to account for her actions. Only her estranged husband Ravi, a thirty-eight-year-old factory worker, offered a clue to her extraordinary behaviour. After his ex-wife was handed two terms of life imprisonment, Ravi Beechook told the press: 'She may have been possessed. She had violent dreams and strange hallucinations. She would wake up screaming about blood. At the end I think witchcraft just took over her life.'

Oddly, Mirella Beechook had been known as a devoted mother by her friends and neighbours. Yet the double homicide which condemned her to a life inside prison was not the first time she had behaved irrationally. Six years earlier, Southwark social services had taken the other Beechook child, Sabrina, into care because Mirella had attacked her with a broken needle. Psychiatrists interviewing the woman at the time could find no reason for it. The mother herself talked of strange forces which directed her. Doubtless it was the same forces which returned to compel her, six years later, to strangle the two children. The two double murders involving black magic, Diabolism and the occult which appeared in newspapers during the course of less than a month in the summer of 1986 were no remarkable coincidence. It is increasingly common for murders to have overtones of the black arts and some detectives now firmly believe that invisible psychic forces may be responsible for turning ordinary, balanced, law-abiding citizens into crazed killers obsessed by cruelty and evil. If this hunch is correct many people convicted of murders may now be languishing in jails for crimes that strictly speaking they did not commit. Quite simply, they killed because they were possessed, possessed by an alien intelligence which controlled their minds and bodies, manipulating their will and corrupting their soul. Could the wave of violent crimes currently sweeping the Western world really be the product of an unseen cause? The evidence is chilling ...

'These entities are real, make no mistake about that. They are what the Bible calls demons. The trouble is the church today thinks itself too sophisticated to admit that they exist.' (English Cleric 1984.)

In contemporary Britain both the Roman Catholic Church and the Church of England continue to recognise officially as a reality the phenomenon of possession and its remedy through exorcism. Just as Christ cast out the devils into the bodies of the Gadarene swine, so modern-day exorcists perform regular ceremonies to cleanse Christians in their flock who are beset by evil spirits. In the past twenty years two Archbishops of Canterbury, the Most Reverend Michael Ramsey and his successor Dr Donald Coggan, have gone on record as supporting the need for exorcism. In the late 1960s the Rev. Ramsey said, 'I believe there is a genuine demonic possession and a genuine exorcism', whilst his successor was quoted in April 1975 as also recognising the reality of 'invisible intelligences', adding that 'these forces of evil are very great'.

However, it is not only from among the clergy that a belief in the dark powers has been professed. In 1981, Dr David Gill, a consultant psychiatrist at Mapperly Hospital, Nottingham, made a specialised study in possession-related cases of mental illness and severe depression. Later the *Catholic Herald* quoted Gill as being critical of the medical profession's unwillingness to recognise the possibility of outside influences in cases of psychiatric disorders. Said Gill: 'Unfortunately, our medical schools do not teach doctors except along conditioned, programmed, logical trains of thought. There should be more training in parapsychology ... the doctor should not dismiss occult phenomena.'

Gill is not alone in his conclusions. In Britain many doctors do occasionally refer particularly difficult cases to exorcists, at least if one believes the detailed case studies contained in author Leslie Watkins 1982 book entitled *The Real Exorcists*. In his book, which is a defence of the practice of exorcism and fundamentalist religious beliefs, Watkins quotes many practising Christian ministers who are also exorcists. One, Father Ian Hazlewood, is the Church of England's official exorcist in the diocese of Gloucester. Hazlewood pointed out that many spirits often manifest themselves in the guise of more acceptable psychological disorders such as hysteria or severe depression, conditions which allow it to continue its possession undetected. Hazlewood maintained that more and more doctors were beginning to refer patients to parish priests, and he himself averaged one or two cleansing services per week.

Another Church of England exorcist prepared to speak to Leslie Watkins was the Rev. David MacInnes of Birmingham Cathedral. In *The Real Exorcists* MacInnes described how he was regularly confronted by evil generated by the witches of Britan's second largest city. He cited one example of a girl invaded by baleful spirits conjured up by a group of Midland Satanists, a girl whose sanity was only restored after MacInnes ordered the demons to leave her body. Exorcists like Hazlewood and MacInnes believe they are regularly attacked by the elementals they do battle with. MacInnes explained how he often experienced the grip of the emissaries of Satan upon his physical frame. Hazlewood, on the other hand, told the story of a singularly powerful demon he encountered in the body of a former Coldstream Guardsman. Performing the exorcism in the vicarage of St Mary's Church, Prestbury, Hazlewood became aware of an unpleasant smell emanating from the skin of the afflicted man. It was the stench of death – a sickly-sweet rotting smell of putridity, as from a corpse. At the same time the temperature inside the room dropped to below freezing and as the ceremony progressed visions of evil manifested themselves on damp patches in the wall. Meanwhile holy water sprinkled on the possessed man's head began to sizzle as if on a hot plate. Although terrified by these supernatural manifestations, Hazlewood and his helpers wrestled for two hours with the demonic spirit, ordering it to leave and confronting it with the message of God and the power of prayer. In a climactic frenzy of hate the possessed ex-soldier crawled around the room making the most awful guttural noises. Soon after the spell was broken and the man became still and quiet. The evil had left him for good.

How much credence should be attached to the testimony of these ministers of God? Certainly they believed what they saw and few would question their integrity. Still, it is perfectly possible for hysteria and mental illness to produce bizarre behaviour patterns to mirror the symptoms of possession, and if we ignore the other inexplicable evidence it would certainly not be impossible to discount the phenomenon of possession altogether in these two specific incidents. These are not isolated examples, though: they are two from among literally hundreds of cases dealt with by the pair of exorcists. Moreover, experiences like the ones described above have been reported for generations by holy men of all religious denominations across the globe. Too numerous to detail, they have often been witnessed by sane, rational people with no motive for deceit or exaggeration. Perhaps the most startling evidence of possession is the growing number of medical figures prepared to countenance the possibility that actual possession might lie at the root of many of the more serious cases of mental illness. One of those to articulate this belief was Dr Richard MacKarness, a Hampshire psychiatrist, who wrote in a 1974 edition of the *Practitioner* that demonosis was in his opinion the true reason for the condition of many patients regularly diagnosed as schizophrenics. Dr MacKarness went on to reveal how he personally referred six seriously disordered patients to exorcists, with full recovery in each case.

'I am certain,' wrote the psychiatrist, 'that good and evil

forces exist, that people can become possessed, and that sometimes the only effective treatment is exorcism.' If the opinion of Dr Richard MacKarness is valid it would certainly go some way to explain the many thousands of mental patients currently languishing in asylums across Europe and America – patients for whom no diagnosable reason for madness is apparent. Many of these could have been perfectly sane individuals who committed out-of-character crimes while possessed by demons. Since their condition has not been recognised, the trigger which set their irrational actions in motion has remained undetected. Thus they are condemned to stay inside secure institutions, whilst actually sane.

The theory of possession also ties in with cases of motiveless murderers, a breed of criminal noticeably on the increase.

The criminal career of Graham Young is a case in point. An English schoolboy of a well-balanced disposition, Young became one of the most callous poisoners of the century after he developed an interest in black magic. In 1962, at the age of fifteen, he pleaded guilty at the Old Bailey to the poisoning of four people, including his father and stepmother. Sentenced to fifteen years in Broadmoor, England's maximum security prison for the mentally disturbed, Young never once showed a trace of his pathological tendency, and was released as cured of his previous insanity in 1971. Immediately he resumed his career as a motiveless poisoner, and a year later he appeared at St Albans Crown Court to plead guilty to the poisoning of eight more people, two of whom died. He received a life sentence for murder.

Clearly, medical science failed to detect the real cause of Young's murderous behaviour, but his sister, Winnifred Young, was convinced that her brother was directed by an unseen force to commit crimes against his will. She described how as a teenager he would regularly recite the Lord's Prayer backwards, praying in front of a crucifix hung upside down. Often there would be a cold, chilling atmosphere in his presence, as if evil itself was attached to him. Held in police custody, even the officers interrogating him became convinced that they were dealing with something unnatural.

Whilst the idea of evil attaching itself to a person might seem a fantastical theory, it is regarded seriously by many criminal psychologists and police detectives from homicide squads. One reason is that it goes a long way to explain many apparently senseless crimes, including some child murders, for which the usual mental sickness of paedophilia does not readily apply. A journalist friend of mine, a chief crime reporter on a British tabloid newspaper, explained to me the criminologists' dilemma:

'The traditional child killer is male, with an established record of child abuse. With paedophiles, the majority probably never intended to kill but did so through panic when their victims screamed or struggled, as they feared being caught. However, there is a second more worrying group emerging and growing fast. These criminals torture, murder or mutilate kids according to plan. When apprehended they often turn out to be respectable citizens, upstanding members of the community even. They invariably have a clean record, and even impeccable moral standards. It would be quite wrong to imagine them as typically violent or aggressive, nor are they mad.'

Obviously such unlikely suspects are difficult to catch and psychiatrists have not come to terms with this irrational behaviour pattern. They are not really lunatics in the conventional sense of the word. They simply have an occasional compulsion to kill. It is in this area that the possession theory is gaining ground – it would explain an awful lot if these murderers were driven to kill by an outside intelligence. The increasing number of killings linked to the occult during the past decade also ties in neatly with the same idea.

My journalist friend cited the British mass murderer Peter Sutcliffe as a possible case in point. Sutcliffe was jailed in 1981 for the sadistic murders of thirteen women over the previous five years. His reign of terror earned him the nickname 'Yorkshire Ripper', after the infamous London murderer of the nineteenth century. Yet his prolific tally of women victims was not the only similarity. Like his Victorian counterpart, Sutcliffe mutilated his victims in the most horrible way – disembowelling them and carving out their genital organs. Clearly such a monster must have been mad, thought the shocked British public, yet when finally arrested Sutcliffe turned out to be quite sane. Sane but obsessed with evil, according to the psychiatrist's report. Not all were surprised by this controversial conclusion. Earlier, whilst the killer was still at large, the chief constable of Yorkshire had described the mystery assailant as 'a man who carried evil around him like a cloak'. This same shroud of psychic darkness may have helped Sutcliffe evade arrest, according to the spiritualist mediums the northern constabulary brought in to help trace their man.

Whether right or wrong in their assessment, the mind of Peter Sutcliffe remains an anomaly in the annals of standard criminal psychology.

Another mass murderer whose compulsion to kill savagely was never fully explained was Richard Speck, an American who on 14 July 1966 massacred eight nurses in a hostel for the South Chicago Community Hospital. Like Sutcliffe, Speck's compulsion drove him to butcher and mutilate his female victims. Yet unlike Sutcliffe whose savage reign of terror lasted years, Speck's orgy of violence lasted less than half an hour. Commander Francis Flanagan of Chicago's homicide bureau, whose grim task it was to investigate thoroughly the contorted bodies of the girls lying in pools of congealed blood, went on record as saying that in his opinion the murderer was possessed by an evil spirit, for only something inhuman, he maintained, could conceive and carry out such an atrocity. An unprofessional remark, perhaps, coming from a man who had seen so many murders over the years, but like the Yorkshire Ripper, Richard Speck was found to be quite sane, a fact which earned him a life sentence and the loathing of an entire city. Only Speck's previous interest in the occult gave a clue to his later homicidal tendency.

Serial killers are another variety of murderer whose links with the unnatural are becoming increasingly apparent. Serial killers take their name from the fact that the circumstances of each murder remain consistent. In America, where the plague of these ghouls is reaching epidemic proportions, over one hundred serial killers have been jailed or executed, but another fifty are believed to remain on the loose. Many of these characters give up their regular employment and move from state to state, earning a living doing odd jobs. Yet their real motive is to keep one step ahead of the law and stay free to kill the innocent. Like the devotees of the Thugee cult, the Indian religious fanatics who strangled thousands across the subcontinent in the last century, serial killers are truly dedicated murderers. The sole purpose of their lives is to kill and torture mercilessly. It is hardly surprising, therefore, that black magic is often found to be responsible for their sudden personality transformations. The occult connection has troubled police departments and criminal psychologists across the USA. What is even more disturbing is the way the evil behind serial killers refuses to go away. When one is caught or executed, another person simply takes their place and continues the line of murders. According to one American criminologist it is 'as if the evil spirit that drove them simply goes away to infect a fresh soul. We cannot stop it'. The idea of the serial spirit forms the concept of W. Blatty's book *Legion*, a sequel to his earlier *Exorcist*. In the novels a discarnate entity drifts across a city infecting a succession of human minds to commit acts of homicidal violence. Only as time goes by do the police authorities begin to realise the impossibility of the task facing them.

Though a work of fiction, Blatty's story is not so far away from the theories of another contemporary American author whose realm is very much factual. One recent publication which attempts to draw a link between serial killers and evil incarnate is *The Ultimate Evil* by journalist Maury Terry, an examination of the circumstances surrounding the infamous 'Son of Sam' killings that terrorized New York during the 1970s. Originally believed to be the work of a single motiveless assassin, the 'Son of Sam' murders began with a series of random gun assaults dating from July 1976. Victims were invariably young persons or couples and the killer showed no mercy; by the time a suspect, a twenty-four-year-old postal worker named David Berkowitz, was apprehended, thirteen people had been shot. With Berkowitz owning up to all the slayings the homicide squad naturally felt satisfied they had their man, but investigative journalist Terry became alerted to the possibility that a conspiracy was behind the attacks after finding that a series of letters had been sent to the police department containing words and phrases with explicitly occult connotations. Other letters found in Berkowitz's apartment also contained numerous references to blood, Hell and Satan. One talked of the 'twenty-two Disciples of Hell'; another detailed plans for a further one hundred killings. When police identikit pictures of the reported killer remained inconclusive, and as Berkowitz's testimony of total guilt began to reveal flaws, Maury Terry became convinced that the police suspect was only a single member of a larger organisation dedicated to satanic slayings. He was right. In a face-to-face interview following his conviction Berkowitz admitted that there were indeed 'other sons out there'. At the same time, after a copy-cat 'Son of Sam' murder, the New York Police Department received a note saying simply: 'I am still here – like a spirit roaming the night.' More atrocities followed.

Maury Terry's own investigations turned up the probability that Berkowitz had been a member of a bizarre religious cult named 'The Process Church of Final Judgement' whose creed taught that followers should prepare for Satan's domination of planet earth. The Process Church was known to use German Shepherd dogs for ritual sacrifice, and since the twelve-month period from October 1976 to October 1977 saw the discovery of eighty-five skinned carcasses of these animals in New York there can be little doubt that the cult was in business. But the Process did not stop at canine sacrifice, nor did it confine its operations to the Big Apple. October 1974 had seen the vicious murder of Arlis Perry, a nineteen-year-old student whose body was found on the altar of the Stanford University Memorial Church. With an icepick through her skull and an altar candle rammed crudely into her vagina, the killing might have been the work of a sex maniac. In fact, as Maury Terry discovered, it was one amongst many carried out by Process members, whose network of hate spread across the country. Arlis Perry's only crime had been that she was a born-again Christian.

According to Terry's book, a meticulously documented tome of some six hundred pages, David Berkowitz lied to protect the security of his serial killer accomplices.

Other members of the network died involuntarily for the same reason. One, a fellow postal worker, had his head blown off with a shotgun barely a month after Berkowitz's arrest. Two more, husband and wife Richard and Shirley Hirshman, were found slashed, stabbed and strangled on the same night – but sixty miles apart. Other deaths followed. On 16 February 1978 a chief Process suspect named John Carr was found dead in a motel room. Blasted in the face by a rifle, Carr's body exhibited the number of the Beast – 666 – written in his blood. Soon afterwards Carr's brother Michael met a similarly sudden death. The remaining months of 1978 saw the murders of several more suspected Process members culminating in the ritual killings of self-proclaimed witches Howard Green and Carol Marrow whose bodies were discovered drained of blood in their New York apartment. None of these murders had any motive save the satanic connection; none was ever solved.

Long before *The Ultimate Evil* was published in 1987 the

New York Police Department had admitted they no longer believed that David Berkowitz had acted alone. Yet no one else has been caught. The intervening years have seen similar outbreaks of violence across the fifty states of the Union, and there has been much evidence· of Process groups as far apart as Florida, North Dakota, Massachusetts, Connecticut and California. One FBI source has described them as 'spores that drift on an evil wind'. It is an apt description.

The terrible threat posed by the serial killer phenomenon is presently on the increase. In 1966 only 5.9 per cent of all US homicides were considered 'random and senseless'; figures for the same murders today represent 18 per cent of a much higher total. Can it be mere coincidence that a disproportionately high number of these motiveless murders occur around the time of occult festivals like Lammas Day, All Hallows Eve and Walpurgis Night?

Of course, there are stranger compulsions than the desire to simply kill people. If possession be a fact it may well explain many of the more bizarre perversions in the annals of criminal history. Vampirism is an obvious example. True vampires may not exist in their legendary Dracula form, but medical vampirism – a condition known as haematomania – is all too real. Such individuals, literally bloodthirsty, become compelled to drink human blood and are driven to kill in order to satisfy their lust. A typical haematomaniac was Fritz Harrman, the notorious Hanover Vampire, who in the 1920s invited a succession of young men to tea in his flat and subsequently murdered them, tearing out their throats with his teeth. In December 1924, having been caught when police found a head hidden in his kitchen, the Hanover Vampire admitted to a total of twenty-eight killings. Found to be sane, he was decapitated and his brain preserved for medical research. But others who knew Harrman believed his interest in witchcraft to be at the bottom of his bestial behaviour. Meanwhile, unbeknown to the German police, a similar compulsion to Harrman's was driving another of their countrymen towards a career of horror. Peter Kurten, the so-called Dusseldorf Monster, killed at least sixty young girls between 1924 and 1930. In each instance he strangled and then slit the throat of his victim, sucking the blood from the gaping wound. Unbelievably, Kurten even found the cruelty occasionally to write to the parents of his victims, detailing with sadistic relish his disgusting treatment of their offspring. In 1930, when Kurten was finally apprehended, police were amazed to find the monster to be a calm, rational, somewhat unremarkable individual, a mild-mannered person for whom violence was distasteful. Kurten was equally calm when outlining his inhumanities in the witness box and, like Harrman, Kurten faced the headsman with his sanity pronounced intact.

Whilst medical vampirism has a name, it lacks an explanation. The inhuman beings described above may have turned to their disgusting practices through a warped mind, but the reasons for such an abnormal manifestation of human nature remains an enigma criminal psychologists have yet to unravel. It is certainly curious that mental illness was not diagnosed in either of the German vampire killers. Could men of sound mind really behave in such a way? Or were they led towards their inhuman deeds by a force they were powerless to control, a force we have long since ceased to believe in?

Probably the most repulsive of sexual perversions is necrophilia – the desire to have sexual intercourse with a dead person. Closely allied to this strange fetish is necrophagia – the compulsion to eat human corpses. Sometimes in cases of demonic possession the two go hand in hand. One notable example of corpse cannibalism was the strange story of one Sergeant Bertrand, a Napoleonic soldier who was apprehended in the Montparnasse Cemetery in Paris. Bertrand was caught one night whilst performing a series of desecrations and abominations that had outraged the French capital in 1801. Afterwards, when questioned, the bemused soldier explained how he would feel a sudden irresistible urge to find and mutilate corpses. He described how in a trance-like state he would enter the graveyard and exhume the bodies of women. Lying with them for a while, he would afterwards slice open their stomachs and consume their entrails. When brought to trial the astonished Paris court believed Bertrand's story that he was unable to control these compelling urges because of an outside intelligence and in a remarkable act of leniency sentenced the soldier to only one year's penal servitude.

If demonic possession by spirits leads to a sudden and overwhelming compulsion to eat human flesh it may also be at the root of lycanthropy. Among the many hundreds of cases of Europeans wrongly executed for being werewolves during the Middle Ages, there are some where the evidence for their prosecution appears conclusive. Giles Garnier, who was burned alive in 1573, clearly did kill and eat several children in the French village of Dôle. Later that century, Peter Stubbe, a German woodcutter from Bedburg, was found on all fours snapping and snarling like a ferocious beast with the partly eaten body of a child nearby. After admitting to twenty other similar killings, he was publicly tortured to death in front of a crowd of more than four thousand. Today we may no longer believe in werewolves, yet sudden urges to commit unthinkable atrocities are by no means a thing of the past. The British *Daily Telegraph* reported on 12 November 1985 the trial of one James Dean, aged twenty, an itinerant burglar who raped a girl on Dartmoor before stripping himself naked and killing a sheep by ripping out its throat with his teeth. The erstwhile petty thief, who was adjudged to be perfectly sane, described to police afterwards that he had been directed to rape the girl. Of the sheep, he added that he had suddenly felt the need to kill a totally defenceless animal. Drinking its blood afterwards simply made him feel better, he said. In handing down a long prison sentence to Dean the judge posed the question: 'What on earth could possess a man to revert to such bestial behaviour?' Certainly the metaphorical use of the word 'possess' may hide a truth more profound and fearful than the judge imagined.

Perhaps nothing on earth was responsible ... at least nothing visible. As more than one parascientific investigator has since pointed out it must not be forgotten that prior to his bestial behaviour Dean had become intrigued by the occult.

Mass killers who spontaneously kill or maim victims in motiveless orgies of violence often claim afterwards that an overpowering compulsion controlled them – forcing them to act against their will. Another type of crime on the increase are the filial massacres. In these incidents – which are growing increasingly common – whole families are wiped out as one member of the family, usually the father, goes suddenly berserk. Because these massacres usually end in suicide, there is seldom a full explanation for the carnage. Sometimes mental illness, depression or family problems have been known to lead to one of the tragedies. However, in other cases, no logical motive exists for the killings of happy, prosperous, families by a well-balanced, considerate, loving parent who has no record of instability or violence. What force is it that turns a perfect father into a homicidal killer who blasts, axes or strangles his wife and children to oblivion? The question is without answer. Yet so regular have these inexplicable massacres become that it is almost pointless to single out an individual example. Nevertheless two notable cases to hit the headlines recently in Britain were sadly typical of this type of slaying.

The first concerned champion speedway rider Kenny Carter, who on 20 May 1986 blasted his young wife with a shotgun before blowing his own head off. Friends on the speedway circuit were shocked by the tragedy, to which none could imagine an explanation. No note was left to provide an answer, and no evidence existed to suggest that Carter was jealous of his wife or depressed. Certainly he had no financial worries. In the words of another speedway ace, Kenny Carter was a young, famous and successful man who had everything to live for. But for some reason he chose to die, and took his pretty young wife with him. Could the rumours of the couple playing with an Ouija board earlier that evening have any bearing on the mystery?

Another headline-making massacre was carried out by Colin Gill, a senior superintendent registrar from Redruth, Cornwall, who shot his wife Linda and four children on 22 November 1986 before turning his gun on himself. Neighbours were staggered by the killings, since Gill, an ex-magistrate, was a popular and respected member of the community. He was notably a nonviolent, happy character who had in the words of the local vicar 'no enemies and no problems' in life. He was known to love his children and adore his wife, yet suddenly and for no apparent reason he woke up one morning and condemned each of them to an early grave.

Once more the question was 'why?'. No one could be certain, but some older residents of Redruth seemed to remember that the Gill home had once been haunted. Was this nothing more than coincidence?

Ironically, the growing trend in family massacres was used by one black magic fanatic to provide cover for a crime of pure avarice. In 1986 in one of the most famous murder inquiries of recent years, Englishman Jeremy Bamber was jailed for the murder of five relatives: his father, mother, sister and her two young children. His intention had been to pass the guilt on to his sister, a known drug addict and schizophrenic. His motive was money – his father's considerable estate. The plan very nearly worked.

Police were horrified to find the shotgun-blasted bodies of the five family members lying in various rooms in the Bambers' £500,000 Essex farmhouse. A suicide note, apparently written by Jeremy Bamber's sister Bambi Caeffel, described how she planned to destroy her family.

The last to die, a shotgun was found beside her stiffened corpse. Since Bambi, a former model, had a broken marriage, a cocaine habit and a history of mental illness behind her, the police readily believed the evidence. Yet one person remained suspicious. Bamber's fiancée, Sabina, knew that her boyfriend had dabbled in the occult. Moreover Bambi, who herself believed she was psychic, once told Sabina that her brother was controlled by the Devil and that he would in some way harm her and her children. Initially Bamber's fiancée had put the warning down to Bambi's paranoia, but after the orgy of bloodshed she was not so sure.

A month after the family's funeral, Sabina asked Jeremy Bamber point blank whether he had committed the shotgun killings. Believing her to be loyal he calmly admitted to the murders. The next day she informed the police. At the subsequent trial Jeremy Bamber was given a term of life imprisonment on five counts of unlawful killing. In passing sentence, the judge at Essex Assizes described him as evil beyond belief. If money is the root of all evil then Bamber's avaricious impulse to own his father's fortune may serve as an adequate motive for his incredible deeds. But others, Sabina amongst them, could not help wondering whether his heart of darkness had not previously been poisoned by his earlier interest in Diabolism.

If some medical figures are right, murders are not the only deaths resulting from the influence of evil spirits. In the late 1960s a British child psychiatrist, Dr Arthur Guirdham, voiced a controversial theory that a number of suicides he had investigated in the West Country city of Bristol might be linked to a form of spirit of depression which inhabited certain houses. These invisible intelligences were, wrote Guirdham, the end result of a succession of human inhabitants dying and leaving their negative thought patterns imprinted upon the physical bricks and mortar of the tenement blocks. The next person to occupy the living space was destined to have his own thought waves disrupted just as surely as a man might inhale an influenza germ and catch the illness. If Guirdham's ideas have any truth they may account for some suicide massacres; even so, in most cases the sudden changes in personality and behaviour point towards a violent possession by an entirely separate intelligence rather than a slow suffusion of negative emotions into their human consciousness.

One of the most bizarre ideas to emerge in the past decade is the opinion of the Rev. Donald Omand, an Anglican exorcist who has produced evidence linking road accidents in particular places to odd compulsions on the part of motorists. His theory, outlined in his book *Experiences of a Present Day Exorcist*, holds that latent demonic influences in particular stretches of road sometimes possess drivers to deliberately commit suicide by impulsively swerving into the path of oncoming vehicles. A weird concept, it is in fact supported by, among others, a leading Austrian psychiatrist. Donald Omand originally became alerted to the phenomenon after a nurse reported the strange story of a dying motor crash victim. According to the death-bed testimony, the man was driving along a clear stretch of road when he began to see white spots coming towards him. Suddenly, without reason, he felt an irresistible urge to steer his car straight towards an oncoming truck. The nurse's curiosity became heightened when the truck driver, who suffered only minor injuries, also spoke of feeling a similar compulsion. His curiosity aroused, the British priest made a study of several hundred cases of head-on collisions, visiting hospitals and convalescent homes to talk to survivors of road accidents as well as checking police records. The odd sensations to commit suicide were apparent in a small but significant minority. These oddities Omand attributed to possession, and noticing that particular stretches of roads were mentioned repeatedly, he personally visited them and conducted exorcisms on each black spot.

In fact Donald Omand was not the first to notice the

curious clustering of traffic accidents at an apparently safe point on a road. In 1929, a new German highway between Bremen and Bremerhaven became the focus of an extraordinary catalogue of carnage. Within a year of the road opening, more than one hundred cars had crashed – in nearly every case at a straight stretch of carriageway near a kilometre stone marker, number 239. When questioned afterwards by police, surviving motorists would recall how they felt the car being guided off the road by an invisible force. On a single day, 7 September 1930, nine cars left the road at the jinxed marker. Some German scientists believed that a powerful electromagnetic force underground was the source of the problem, but the theory lacked evidence. Only after stone marker 239 was showered with holy water did the accidents cease.

Not all attempts at exorcism lead to the desired results though. More than a few have ended in tragedy.

In July 1976, David Weilbacher, a three-year-old boy, died in Yakima, Washington, after a long and brutal exorcism. The ceremony had taken place in a building used by a small group of religious fundamentalists who believed among other things that a reincarnated John F. Kennedy would return as the Antichrist. The luckless David Weilbacher was suspected of being controlled by evil spirits after his mother, a member of the sect, noticed him acting abnormally. She reported his behaviour to the sect's high priest, a fat, balding Oklahoman named George Cunningham, who told her of a quotation from the Book of Proverbs which read, 'If thou beatest a child he shall not die. Thou shalt deliver his soul from hell.'

Taking this maxim as a literal truth, Cunningham and Debra Weilbacher beat the young David with heavy sticks in a series of ritual thrashings. It was after one of these savage beatings that the child died from internal injuries. Even then the sect did not lose faith but kept the boy's decomposing carcass in his bedroom for two months, believing that he would eventually be returned to life purged of the Devil. Eventually the body was found by police and in December 1976 the unrepentant killers received long jail terms for manslaughter.

Another victim of fundamentalist fanaticism was four-year-old Stephanie Hall whose mother, Goldie, was a member of an Arkansas cult named 'The Church of God in Christ'. In September 1978 a jury heard how Goldie Hall watched approvingly as her daughter was cleansed of Satan – a ritual exorcism which included severe beatings and burnings over an open fire. A final essential part of the ceremony involved shooting the child eight times through the heart. Five members of the church were subsequently jailed for murder.

Disastrous exorcisms are not always carried out by small, weird sects. In 1976 two Roman Catholic priests in Germany conducted one of the most horrifying officially sanctioned exorcisms and were jailed for their mishandling of it. The subject in this case was a young woman named Anneliese Michel of Klingenbuerg, Bavaria. By 1976 Anneliese had already had a long history of psychological problems: in 1969, she began to suffer fits and spells of deep depression; then in 1973 she began seeing and talking to invisible entities. Taken by her parents to a priest, she became violent, ripping her rosary apart and cursing the padre in guttural voices. After two more years, with psychiatrists unable to cure her, her parents gave up seeking medical help. In 1975 they put their trust instead in two exorcists who began what was to become a marathon battle against the demons possessing Anneliese Michel. Permanently imprisoned in her room, she began by screaming blasphemies at the sight of a Bible or a crucifix, and hysterically claiming that she was the spirit of Adolf Hitler, yelling 'Heil' for hours upon end. When approached she would claw viciously at the faces of the exorcists. After several months without a sign of recovery, the girl became totally demented and refused to eat or drink. She died of malnutrition and exhaustion on 1 July 1976, weighing just five stone. The priests received sentences of six months in prison, remaining convinced that the girl had genuinely been possessed and that their course of action had been correct.

In Britain, one of the most horrendous exorcisms to go wrong involved Michael Taylor, a member of a Christian fellowship group in Ossett, near Barnsley.

Described by a neighbour as a devoted father and a loving husband, Taylor had no record either of mental illness or strange compulsive behaviour patterns prior to his possession in September 1974. It began the morning Taylor experienced at first hand an exorcism ceremony at his local church. At the ceremony Taylor began spontaneously uttering glossolalia, what the Bible calls the gift of tongues. This manifestation was rapidly followed by a marked change in his personality. Becoming aggressive, Taylor abused his wife Christine both physically and verbally and made crude sexual advances to a friend's wife. Later that day Taylor spoke to his mother, telling her that he had seen the Devil and that the Devil had told him he must kill himself. Another member of the family who witnessed Taylor's metamorphosis later described his facial expression as bestial.

Hearing of Michael Taylor's changed personality, and attributing it to satanic powers, the Christian fellowship group contacted other religious bodies for advice. One of those to heed their plea was the Rev. Raymond Smith, a local Methodist minister and practising exorcist. Together with an Anglican vicar the Rev. Peter Vincent and a lay preacher, Donald James, Smith counselled Taylor and his wife. Possession was diagnosed and an exorcism arranged for the following evening. In the event the ceremony, which took place in the vestry of a nearby church, lasted the entire night. During the exorcism, dozens of evil spirits were expelled one by one from Taylor's body. Yet one remained tragically undetected within him.

The next morning, less than four hours after the cleansing ceremony was over, Taylor returned home from work and killed his wife Christine in the most horrific way imaginable. He gouged out her eyes, ripped out her tongue and clawed away part of her face. Afterwards, he choked to death their pet poodle. Taylor was found by police, naked, running along an Ossett street covered in blood. In a statement to detectives he was quoted saying that something inside him made him kill. 'I was compelled by the force within me which they could not get rid of,' he said. 'I felt compelled to destroy everything within the house.'

The detectives who found the mutilated body of Christine Taylor had no doubt that the beast who killed her was mad. Yet expert medical opinion soon proved otherwise. Consultant psychiatrist, Dr Hugo Milne, who gave evidence at the trial, reported that he had found Taylor to be both 'clinically and legally sane'. Moreover, another consultant psychologist called to give evidence described the accused man as a 'stable, intelligent, hard working young man with no signs of mental illness' prior to his sudden onset of demoniac delusions.

Despite the expert medical evidence a verdict of 'not guilty of murder by reason of insanity' was returned and Michael Taylor was committed to Broadmoor criminal asylum. Three years later he was released on special recommendation from the Home Secretary after Broadmoor doctors insisted that there was little point in holding a man who was clearly sane and did not present a threat to society. Today Taylor lives a quiet and peaceful existence untroubled by the spirits which once forced him to take the life of his young wife.

The case of Michael Taylor remains an anomaly in the criminology of homicide. If Taylor really was a sane man when he committed his terrible crimes, what compulsion was it that dramatically altered his personality and finally led him to sadistically murder and mutilate the person who meant most to him? The Rev. Peter Vincent, who took part in the abortive exorcism, continued to believe afterwards that Taylor had been possessed by demoniac forces and that a prolonged exorcism had been the right course to follow. At the same time many others felt that the exorcism itself turned the mind of Michael Taylor into a lunatic, and not the influence of the unseen. They may be right. However the Rev. Peter Vincent and his followers should not be criticised too hastily, for if some attempts at spiritual cleansing have gone disastrously wrong there are many more examples where exorcism might have saved lives.

In Britain the trial in 1987 of twenty-year-old Andrew Newell of Telford, Shropshire, is typical of such circumstances. When Newell's father was first told that his son needed exorcism by a priest he laughed off the idea that his boy could be involved in black magic, but he was totally wrong. In reality his offspring was heavily involved in the occult, so much so that he was spending his nights sleeping in an open grave in a nearby churchyard to ready himself for a sacrifice. The victim chosen by the powers of darkness was Newell's best friend, Philip Booth. The unsuspecting youth was lured into his friend's home, rendered insensible by alcohol, and then butchered with a ceremonial daggar. When police found the body its head lay on a makeshift altar with candles at either side and four puncture marks arranged around the heart in a neat pattern. Nearby a homily to the Evil One had been written in the dead man's blood.

Whether or not one believes that exorcism might have stopped Newell from committing his awful crimes depends upon one's opinion of the reality of demonic possession. Can such ideas really be given credence in the last decade of the twentieth century? Modern society may consider itself to be too sophisticated to believe in the supernatural, yet a belief in the existence of objective forces of evil has its roots in most of the myths and legends of the major world faiths which in turn form the foundation stones of our present civilisations.

Islamic tradition holds that demons, or Djinn, were created out of the primeval substance before man walked on earth and that the same spirits will remain after mankind is no more. Usually invisible, Djinn can appear as animals or ghosts, and can take possession of whole communities as well as individual human souls. Jewish belief in demons, or Dybukim, is enshrined in the cabala – the philosophy handed down from their earliest prophets – and possession by invisible forces is denoted by the Hebrew phrase 'Dybbuck M'Ruach Raa', which means 'attachment'. For their part Christians have always recognised the reality of the spirit world. In the Old Testament King Solomon banished the spirits he had summoned into the Red Sea where they were drowned. Jesus performed a similar act by sending the legion of spirits over the cliffs clothed in the bodies of the Gadarene Swine, and was himself tempted by Satan in the desert. The Gospels chronicle several separate incidents in which the Messiah cleansed the demon-possessed, and the early Christian church was clearly in no doubt that the forces of evil existed in a literal sense, with Lucifer at their head. These forces occasionally manifested themselves visibly as little devils of nonhuman appearance whose minds were evil and whose purpose was to lead virtuous men away from the paths of righteousness. The apostle Saul of Tarsus reminded Christians to beware these entities in his letter to the Ephesians (Ch 6, V 12): 'Our fight is not against human foes, but against the cosmic powers, against the authorities and potentates of this dark world, against the superhuman forces of evil in the heavens.'

Throughout the Middle Ages such fundamentalist beliefs in the objective reality of evil spirits continued to exist beside those of the ghosts, werewolves and witchcraft. Indeed, it is only in the last hundred and fifty years that the intellectual and religious establishment has begun to prefer a more enlightened approach to the subject. Nowadays, whilst many religious figures continue to believe in the objective reality of evil, others pass off biblical reference to evil spirits as psychological constructs and the manifestation of possession as a product of mental disorders.

Meanwhile, some faiths have moved in the opposite

direction. Spiritualism, a religion which has prospered alongside the age of scientific enlightenment, recognises the dangers presented by communicating with undesirable intelligences. Mediums, while attempting to contact the spirits of dead relatives still living on the mortal plane, must at all times be careful not to be deceived by earth-bound spirits, ghosts or, worse, those whose souls have descended into depravity.

According to the spiritualistic theory, there exists around our world many levels of consciousness, the lowest of which is a sort of psychic no-man's-land or criminal belt, a plane of being which contains the most pitiful creatures – souls devoid of truth or conscience. Strange misshapen entities walk these borderlands of the dead – the distorted products of their deranged and corrupted thought patterns. Experienced mediums point out that nature has chosen to put a curtain between us and the afterlife, and that only those trained in the relevant discipline should attempt to cross the barrier that separates our world and the next. Hence in 1987, the British Spiritualist Association called upon the government to ban the sale of the board game known as Ouija, which can enable ordinary non-psychic persons to join together and summon up spirits into their living rooms. This practice, spiritualists agree, is an extremely risky one since it greatly enhances the risk of psychic possession.

Spiritualists, along with religious fundamentalists of any denomination, might be accused of putting forward only the evidence which suits their particular belief system. In this way opinions which are disquieting to society's perceived view of the universe are usually dismissed. However, as we have seen it is not merely religious figures who are becoming convinced by the evidence of centuries that invisible spirits are real. The opinion of sane, rational figures like David Gill, consultant psychiatrist at Nottingham hospital, or Dr Richard MacKarness, the Hampshire psychiatrist mentioned earlier, cannot simply be dismissed as blind fanaticism. Such men have nothing to gain and potentially much to lose by expressing their belief in the invisible forces of evil.

Another medical figure prepared to risk his reputation is Dr Walter Franklin Prince, a Boston doctor who uses exorcism to cure patients referred to him as suffering from paranoia. Prince defends his controversial method with a high success rate and by maintaining that mental illness can sometimes be better handled by suggesting that imagined spirits might be actual ones. This follows the now well-proven principle that a person's mind can make him sick or well. Yet really the Boston physician genuinely believes that these purported entities are real – what he describes as 'fragments of psychic evil' – from a source outside the patient's consciousness.

A similar view has been expressed by another American psychiatrist, Dr Wilson Van Dusen of the Mendocino State Hospital in California. In a book entitled *The Presence of Other Worlds* Van Dusen concludes that voices heard by schizophrenics might really be communications with invisible intelligences. More recently, two other American specialists, Adam Crabtree and Ralph Allison have written books supporting Van Dusen's theory.

In France, a former policeman turned psychic investigator named Emile Tizane holds the same opinion. Whilst a detective in the Paris homicide squad during the 1960s, Tizane became convinced that a small but significant proportion of motiveless killings could not be solved by conventional police practice. These bizarre killings were, he felt, the result of a whole variety of unseen invading forces, manifesting in a wide range of psychic phenomena from poltergeists to possessions. Sometimes these energies could merge totally and become one with the consciousness of the victim; in other cases the entity would only occasionally penetrate the host's psyche. Either way the individual affected would eventually go mad. As we have seen, since Emile Tizane first formulated his disturbing conclusions there has been a dramatic increase in crimes identified as being connected with demons.

Nowhere is this more so than in present-day Britain, where each week seems to bring forward a fresh example. Jailed for life in September 1989, twenty-two-year-old James Arkwright was a petty criminal until he began to dabble in the occult. Days after attending a black magic ceremony in his home town of Rotherham, he embarked on an orgy of violence which left four dead and a community in shock. Wearing only his underpants and a devil mask, Arkwright broke into the house of a neighbour, Raymond Ford. Ford was stabbed five hundred times and his body disembowelled. The next victim was Arkwright's own grandfather, axed down whilst working on his allotment. Another neighbour, a cripple, was butchered in his wheelchair; his body was found by police along with the mutilated corpse of his housekeeper. Afterwards the killer gloated over his handiwork to detectives, yet criminal psychoanalysts were at a loss to explain his transformation from man to monster. Was his involvement in the occult ceremony the previous week to blame? Only those who had then been present with Arkwright knew for certain and, unsurprisingly, none came forward.

Some occultists are more helpful. The late Dion Fortune, the well-known British occult practitioner, had no doubt about the reality of incarnate evil and constantly warned against the threat it posed. Stressing that evil forces can be summoned up either by magicians or by spontaneous manifestation, Fortune hit out at the increasing use of magic in party games, as well as the growth of unlicensed covens. The occultist identified two potential sources of danger; firstly the negative quipoleth, demonic forces proper; secondly the seraphia, the quipoleth's positive counterparts, which comprise the disembodied souls of the depraved or insane. According to occult law both these varieties of undesirable entity can materialise in many forms, and the quipoleth, a particularly unpleasant specimen, is reputed to hover ghoul-like over graves and the corpses of the newly dead to feed upon their fading life substance or aura. Whilst occult lore recognises that the quipoleth and seraphia have a permanent reality and must be called upon rather than created, there is another quite separate variety of spirit which can literally be born – brought to life through the manipulation of the ether or astral substance that occultists believe surrounds and permeates the universe. These tangible thought forms can be either ugly or beautiful, good or evil, depending upon the mind which creates them, yet once they are brought into existence they are difficult to control. Perhaps the best description of this type of creature appears in the book *Magic and Mystery in Tibet* by French authoress Alexandra David-Neel.

In her book David-Neel described a thought form she created after learning a special technique of mental visualisation from the Lamas of the Himalayas. Using a form of super-concentration which took months of practice to master, the authoress was able to see and finally produce a 'tolpa', an animated thought form of a Buddhist monk. The three-dimensional figure, which was a few inches high, was visible not only to her but to her companions as well. In its originally conceived form the monk had a jolly and likable expression, but it gradually assumed a sly, malevolent smile and a mischievous temperament to match. David-Neel tried consciously to dissolve it and succeeded only after six months, so hard did the spirit hold on to life.

One wonders what trouble might have been caused by the Tibetan phantom had it not been destroyed by its creator. Such spirits, if not strictly disciplined, can go on to enjoy a free and autonomous existence according to Tibetan belief. Moreover, if the mind that gives them life in the first instance is itself evil, then it is easy to imagine how such tolpas could become dangerous. As we shall see in a subsequent chapter strange entities which materialise for malevolent reasons are not uncommon and it is not altogether improbable that the manifestations of yesterday's witches were not buried with the bones of their creators.

*

The sprites described by traditional occultists are by no means the most terrifying possibilities we have to face when confronted by the enigma of the invisible entities. In a best-selling book entitled *The Dark Gods* published in 1978, English authors Anthony Roberts and Geoffrey Gilbertson put forward an elaborate and disturbingly well-constructed theory that mankind has been under perpetual threat since the dawn of time from multifarious unseen forces of evil. These intelligences, interpreted in past ages as ghosts, goblins, dragons and a veritable host of super-natural phenomena, have, according to Roberts and Gilbertson, recently returned in the guise of UFOs and aliens in silver suits. Nevertheless, these visible entities are merely a small and barely significant part of the cosmic conspiracy. At the head of the forces of darkness are a phalanx of malevolent multi-dimensional creatures of enormous size and intelligence, satanic majesties which the authors label as ultraterrestrials because their powers have no earthly or heavenly limits. These ultraterrestrials (or UTs for short) are invisible yet real in the most objective sense, for their emissaries lurk on the fringes of human consciousness awaiting the chance to enter and gain a foothold. These vast mutated elemental beings are in fact the collective spirits of long-dead civilisations whose corruption was brought about through vice, avarice and the widespread practice of black magic. Long before Atlantis fell into the sea theirs was an empire which ruled the planet. These dark gods, having lost dominion over the earth, quickly became disenchanted with their half-life existence in an unseen plane and merged to create a new unnatural form of life. From their immortal fortress in the ether they conspire to overthrow the current guardians of material existence – the human race. When the time is ripe the British authors foresee a full-scale psychic invasion, a final conflict between good and evil like that envisaged in the biblical Book of Revelation.

On the face of it the apocalyptic fears of Roberts and Gilbertson might seem ludicrously far-fetched. Yet the two

British authors point out that psychic evil has already manifested itself through the destiny of dictators, political parties and even nations in our own century – the rise of Adolf Hitler's Nazi party and the spread of Fascism throughout Europe in the 1930s being cited as a notable example of an evil cause which very nearly destroyed the world. Was Hitler the Devil's man? Many might feel that the endless list of atrocities which culminated in the systematic extermination of millions of Jews is proof enough of the Führer's Satanism. Yet a close examination of the background to Hitler's rise to power demonstrates clearly that the German leader consciously used black magic to initiate his vile success.

Michael Fitzgerald's occult history of World War Two entitled *The Storm Troopers of Satan* describes how Hitler's associations with dark forces began as early as 1908 when, as a struggling painter in Vienna, he first caught sight of the Spear of Destiny, a first century artifact said to be the weapon which pierced Christ's side during his crucifixion. Believed by some to possess magical powers the spearhead was reputed to hold the key to the future of the world. Seeing it for the first time in a Vienna museum the young Hitler became convinced that he was destined to inherit both the Spear and its power. Soon afterwards he joined a group of Satanists, known as the Thules, who practised sadism, ritual rape and other perverted ceremonies. Hitler sought their help in contacting the cosmic powers of darkness. They in turn saw that the young man had a unique potential for cruelty – the perfect human chalice for the Antichrist. They were not to be disappointed. Years later as Reichsführer, Hitler was to take the Spear for himself and use its supreme power to plunge the world into an unprecedented maelstrom of chaos and bloodshed. The author of *Storm Troopers of Satan* believes that the German leader deliberately chose to accept the mantle of a Black Messiah. Other writers agree.

In his 1977 study entitled *Gods and Beasts*, Canadian historian Dusty Sklar details the influence occultism played in the planning of the Nazi high command from the 1930s onwards. In reaching the conclusion that Hitler was controlled by objective forces of evil, Sklar noted that the German leader exerted a superhuman will over his subordinates, a will so strong that in 1945 Rudolf Hoess, commandant of Auschwitz, declared that he would have happily gassed his wife and children had his master so desired it. Sklar goes on to point out that the black magicians' most basic hunger is the hunger for power, and that Hitler's achievement in holding a measure of supreme power in Germany made him something of a Kabbalistic god. (Appropriately, according to Kabbalistic numerology, even the dictator's name hinted at Diabolism, adding up to 666 – the fabled number of the Beast.)

Evidence of black arts in the Reichstag goes much further than speculation, though. The Library of Congress in Washington DC contains thousands of books from Hitler's personal collection which was seized after the Allied occupation of Germany. Several hundred of these texts are concerned with various aspects of eastern mysticism (the Swastika itself was an ancient Indian occult symbol deliberately reversed to honour Satan) whilst dozens more mixed pseudo-religious philosophies with Hitler's favoured concept of Aryan racial purity. Hitler's own writings also throw light upon the occult link. Like his adversary Churchill, Hitler believed passionately in destiny and in *Mein Kampf*, the autobiography of his early life, the future dictator describes a moment of transcendental insight he experienced after attending a Wagner opera. This was, he wrote, a moment when the spirit of the German race itself overshadowed him: 'I stood alone and trembling before the hovering form of the Superman – a spirit sublime and fearful, a countenance intrepid and cruel. I offered my soul as a vessel of His Will.' Could it perhaps have been the spirit of a much older race which possessed him at that moment?

Whatever the source, Hitler's personal magnetism was truly superhuman, those in his presence being dominated by the sheer force of his personality. According to one Nazi leader, Albert Speer, his generals were 'all under his spell, blindly obedient and with no will of their own.' Later several commentators made similar observations whilst attending the massive Nazi rallies. The dictator would go into a trance-like state before delivering mediumistic platform performances of hypnotic proportions, speeches in which his emotions and beliefs would spread to his audience almost like a psycho-osmosis. It was, wrote one American journalist, mass hysteria on a grand scale. Yet this was hysteria born of a hideous purpose. Hitler's intention was to corrupt the collective mind of an entire nation – and lead that nation down the primrose path to Hell and damnation.

Hitler's obsession with the occult was shared by his deputies. Rudolf Hess, Hitler's second in command until 1941, was fascinated by astrology, homeopathy and witchcraft; Luftwaffe chief Hermann Goering regularly consulted clairvoyants before launching an offensive. Heinrich Himmler, head of the SS, studied the occult after becoming convinced that he was the reincarnation of a tenth-century German king, Heinrich I. Every year, on the anniversary of Heinrich I's death, Himmler would hold a midnight ritual sacrifice in the dank crypt of the castle where the monarch's remains were entombed.

Like his master Himmler was a true disciple of evil. In his book *Gods and Beasts* Dusty Sklar mentions that Himmler had a profound belief in evil spirits and developed the SS along the lines of an occult society rather than a military regiment. It was through a deliberate and systematic suppression of human decency by occult means, rather than by straightforward political indoctrination, that the inhuman tyrannies of the SS brigades would later be put into practice. If Sklar is right it might go some way to explain how more than a million men were transformed within a few years from ordinary citizens to sadistic butchers. As part of their basic training these SS recruits were put through a series of rituals loosely modelled upon the Catholic Jesuit order. They had to take vows of poverty, chastity and obedience. After a further year of brainwashing Himmler's black guards would go through a secret mystical ceremony in the presence of their Führer. In the torchlight of the Nazi shrine in Munich, the legion of hell would take their sacred oath of allegiance. From that moment on any failure to carry out an order, no matter how bestial, would result in their death and the destruction of their entire family. Not subject to national German regulations but tried by their own internal military courts, the SS were effectively a law unto themselves. With this order of disciples Hitler held the German nation in an iron grip of fear. The thirteen highest ranking members of the SS – initiates as they now knew themselves to be – regularly met in a remote Westphalian monastery, the Wewelsburg, which Hitler had converted into a black magic fortress for the purpose of contacting higher spirits. Their especially promising officers would be sent and ordered to undertake the most unspeakable barbarities upon defenceless prisoners or animals in an effort to crush the last remnants of pity from their hearts. Any show of emotion or remorse for their cruelty would invariably result in instant death.

On nights of special occult significance Himmler would join the other members of his personal black coven in a small airless room known as the 'Realm of the Dead'. On these occasions blood sacrifices – often Jewish children – would be offered and the Spear of Destiny used to inflict the fatal wound.

If all this is not evidence enough of Hitler's Diabolism, the opinion of one contemporary, prominent anti-Nazi politician seems conclusive. Herman Rauschning, a leader of the Danzig Senate, fled Germany in 1940. Years later, in his history of pre-war Nazism entitled *The Voice of Destruction*, Rauschning wrote of the Führer's astonishing transformation:

'... Everyone who came into touch with Hitler was bound to feel – Hitler was abandoning himself to forces which were carrying him away – forces of dark and destructive violence. He imagined he still had the freedom of choice, but he had long been in bondage to a magic which might well have been described not in metaphor but in literal fact – as that of evil spirits ... we witnessed the development of a man possessed, the helpless prey of powers of darkness.' Hitler's role as puppet of the dark gods had been planned decades before. Shortly before his death in pre-Nazi Germany, Thulist high priest Karl Eckart wrote to a fellow initiate, offering some astonishingly prophetic advice: 'Follow Hitler. He will dance but it is I who called the tune. We have given him the means of communication with Them.' It is not hard to guess who Eckart meant by 'Them'.

When Hitler finally killed himself on Walpurgis Night, 30 April 1945, he was offering his own life as a final sacrifice to his unseen masters, completing his pact with the Devil made decades before. He had sold his soul to Hell and we all paid the price.

Doubtless Hitler chose the path of black magic at the outset, allowing those possessing entities to corrupt his mind in order to fulfil his ultimate destiny. When the Allied forces found occult symbols on the floors and walls of the torture chambers of the Westphalian monastery they began to have some idea of the real enemy they had been fighting for six long years. Even now we cannot be certain how much of their success the Nazis owed to the unseen forces of evil. Yet few can reasonably doubt that if invisible forces of darkness exist, be they quipoleth, ultraterrestrials or demonic powers, then those forces became manifest in the minds and actions of Adolf Hitler and his henchmen. Their cosmology was magical, their symbolism negative, their philosophy hatred, their purpose the advancement of evil. As English historian Michael Fitzgerald wrote: 'Probably at no time in recent history has the world come closer to falling under the domination of a group of initiates serving consciously Satanic ends.'

Perhaps the most eloquent testimony of all is contained

in a few lines written in 1934 by the German poet–magician Karl Houshoffer. Certainly they are striking in the appropriateness of their prophecy.

> In father life, the die is cast
> once it was in the power of his will
> to push the demon back into his cell,
> My father held the seal and broke it,
> He did not sense the breath of evil
> and let out into the world the devil.

For many people the objective reality of evil spirits remains a fantasy. For many more the evidence could hardly be more conclusive. Those reading this book must decide for themselves. Every day we read in our newspapers of a fresh crop of murders linked to black magic or see on our television screens the latest batch of suicides where the only explanation appears to be the subject's interest in the occult.

Church leaders warn that Satanism is practised on a wider scale than it was in the Middle Ages, while psychiatrists, police detectives and politicians are coming around to the disturbing conclusion that evil is truly in our midst.

Given the most recent evidence to emerge from the United Kingdom, they could hardly believe otherwise.

In March 1990 the tragic story emerged of Caroline Marchant whose initiation into Devil worship ended in her suicide at the age of twenty-three. As a teenager Marchant had been taken to a ceremony in a Norfolk graveyard where she was hung upside down and forced to watch her lover being sacrificed. Later – by then entirely under the group's influence – she put her own newly born infant to the knife. Following her suicide, the woman's solicitor offered proof to the police that her stories were not fantasies, and alerted a national newspaper to signed statements from twelve other girls whose experiences of satanic rites included drinking blood mixed with urine, the exhumation of bodies and the eating of human flesh.

At the same time as Caroline Marchant's story hit the headlines, the *Independent* published an interview with a twenty-year-old Brood Mare who recalled rituals in which babies were drained of blood and aborted foetuses frozen for future consumption. One infant was allegedly cooked alive in a microwave oven, its body fat melted down for candle wax and its bones ground to powder as an aphrodisiac. Confirming the report's accuracy, a spokesman for the National Childrens' Home Organisation said that children as young as ten had taken part in cult killings. It was, he said, the greatest threat facing society that he had ever known.

As the year wore on the true extent of that threat became shockingly apparent. In May a high level source for the National Society for the Prevention of Cruelty to Children (NSPCC) reported that seven of its regional watchdog teams were working on cases of ritual abuse. In July the BBC's *Heart of the Matter* programme revealed that large-scale networks of Satanists currently being investigated by the London Metropolitan Police were believed to be linked to at least twelve child murders.

More evidence soon followed. In September child abuse consultant Norma Howes told journalists that she knew of eighteen Devil-worship cases involving thirty-three children in the South-East of England. Quoted in the same article, Peter Biddy, Assistant Director of Social Services in an inner London borough, revealed the discovery by police of fifty occult networks in the Home Counties involving the abuse of several hundred children.

Elsewhere in Britain the now familiar story emerged. During the autumn came news of cults in Nottinghamshire, Cheshire, Leeds, Manchester and Rochdale where over one hundred children were made wards of court to protect them. In Humberside a council report showed that an investigation into Satanism identified 288 children as probable victims of abuse; a parallel investigation in Ashby, near Scunthorpe, had uncovered the abuse of some fifty-two youngsters. In October a Channel 4 Television

Dispatches programme focusing upon twenty-seven known child-abuse cases in Nottingham, found a network of secret tunnels leading to a sacrificial altar underneath the city's Rock Cemetery where graves had been desecrated throughout the previous year.

If dark forces do exist among us and sometimes inside us, then not all murderers can be held responsible for their crimes and not all insanities can be cured by the disciples of Freud. But how far has this psychic invasion progressed, and how much more dangerous could it potentially become? In *The Dark Gods*, authors Anthony Roberts and Geoffrey Gilbertson put forward the theory that the so-called powers of evil were the disembodied group souls of some lost civilisation of antiquity. These entities, which they called ultraterrestrials, lurked in the borderlands of human consciousness waiting for the right conditions to move in upon the minds of individual homo sapiens. A bizarre theory, it suggested that the ultimate goal of the UTs was world domination through possession. If the authors' theory is true and ultimate domination of our species is the aliens' goal, then how near are they to succeeding? Certainly they must be making progress since exorcists are having to work harder than ever. At the same time, the vast majority of mortal minds remain free of possession, or at least they appear to. Can we really feel safe? Consider the unnerving possibility that the UTs have already developed a subtle form of mass mind control: an astral espionage technique through which subliminal messages are gradually fed into the collective unconscious of millions of pre-selected humans. By such a systematic use of subliminal conditioning the unnatural aggressive and insane behaviour patterns might be induced but kept in the back of a victim's subconscious. Only when a hypnotic trigger was applied would the sleeper become activated. At some future moment, then, we might wake up to find that half the world had suddenly gone stark raving mad. Hardly a recipe for a peaceful future ... especially if the possessed ones included a few who happened to be the operators of nuclear missile silos.

Perhaps the real battle between mankind and his old enemies – those creatures St Paul described as 'the super-human forces of evil in the heavens' – is only just beginning.

GRIM REAPERS

In the late summer of 1939 a fate of almost unimaginable horror befell the thirteen-member crew of a US military transport aircraft minutes after it had taken off from San Diego Marine Naval Station on a routine flight to Honolulu. None of the men survived and the incident remained shrouded in secrecy for many years. However, details that have emerged since that time leave little room for a natural explanation.

Ground control personnel first became aware of trouble when the aircraft's pilot sent a frantic distress signal. 'Something', he said, was on board; he did not elaborate. Shortly afterwards the plane made an emergency landing at San Diego. When a rescue team entered they found only one man – the co-pilot who presumably landed the aircraft – still alive, and he died within minutes.

Precisely how the tragedy had occurred was unclear, but it was not so much the men's deaths as the nature of their injuries which horrified their rescuers. The scene inside the fuselage was one of absolute carnage with the blood of the dead men splattered everywhere; incredibly the gaping wounds each corpse exhibited appeared to have been made from the inside, as if their flesh had been forced outwards. There were no other signs of a struggle, though a quantity of used .45 cartridges suggested that the aircrew had spent their last moments trying to defend themselves with their automatic pistols. The plane was otherwise empty, the 'something' spoken of by the pilot was gone. Only a foul sulphuric odour remained as a clue to its diabolical identity.

Speaking fifteen years later, a member of the ground crew who boarded the stricken transporter described the atmosphere at the San Diego Base afterwards as 'chilling'. 'We all of us knew in our hearts that the thing which killed those boys wasn't from this world', he said. Air Force top brass felt the same, clamping a lid down on discussion and informing the airmen's families of a conventional crash.

'Not of this world' is a title more commonly associated with popular science fiction than real events. Given the circumstances of the in-flight massacre the witness quoted above may be right about the 'something' which came to be aboard the transporter. But there is another possibility: that our world really does contain such things. Creatures whose existence owes nothing to the natural selection of species....

Throughout recorded history mankind has been visited by creatures from other dimensions. From the dragons, fairies and goblins of medieval times down to the silver-suited spacemen of the twentieth century, reports continue to come in from across the globe of strange entities stalking our mortal plane. Rarely do these extraordinary occurrences cause more than a ripple of interest. As always, faced with evidence both disturbing and irrational, the natural human inclination is to dismiss it from our minds. Surely, we say to ourselves, these stories cannot be true. After all the people of the Middle Ages were a superstitious bunch, and as for today's visionaries, most of them are probably mentally unstable. Like Macbeth's view of life, we consider such visions to be 'A tale told by an idiot ... signifying nothing'. In truth, a more apt quotation would be Hamlet's: 'There are more things in heaven and earth ... than are dreamt of in your philosophy.'

For the tales do not go away. Indeed they are growing in number. In Europe this century there have been more visions of the Holy Virgin than ever before but twice as many of the Devil. Across every continent reports of phantom creatures are on the increase despite the creeping influence of our technological ideology. None of these impossible stories can easily be explained in terms of purely natural causes. Nor is the presence of these creatures merely hallucinatory. In many cases the objective reality of their evil is borne out by marks upon the corpses of their victims.

One of the most interesting and commonly reported creatures from the realms of psychic phenomena are the black dogs of rural England and Wales. Black dogs have their roots deep in the heart of British folklore and are known by a variety of names, including black shuck, shriker and shag-dog. In some areas of the countryside these enigmatic animals have actually been known to be benevolent and there are numerous tales of lost travellers being guided to their destinations by supernatural canines. Elsewhere, black dogs are seen as malevolent spirits, or manifestations from Hell intent upon human destruction. Counties in which black dogs serve as an omen of death include Lancashire, Yorkshire, Derbyshire, Suffolk and Norfolk. However, by far the most sinister of all reports of black dogs are those where the animals appear to have been directly responsible for human death through some unknown and inexplicable process. Incredible though such materialisations may be, they are too frequent and well-witnessed to be dismissed as mythical.

Among the most striking of black dog appearances is the one which occurred in the Suffolk village of Bungay, on Sunday 4 August 1577, a full account of which was recorded by a witness, Abraham Fleming, under the title of 'A Strange and Terrible Wonder'.

Being a Sunday, the religious folk of Bungay were at church whilst the sky above grew dark and a thunderstorm raged. According to Fleming's account the sky continued to darken until it reached a pitch of preternatural blackness, whereupon a bolt of lightning struck the church steeple. At the moment of impact, a fearful prodigy appeared before the church's high altar ... a huge black dog with glowing eyes like oriflammes of fire, a creature surrounded by a shining aura of gold. Clearly visible to all among the terrified assembly, the monster let out a single hideous bark before rushing headlong through the worshippers. As it passed down the aisle between the two sides of the congregation it brushed aside two men kneeling in prayer: there was a flash and the men fell dead. Another man touched by the vision was scorched 'like leather in a hot fire' and subsequently paralysed. When the dog reached the end of the church it disappeared in a violent flash.

Those who saw the phantasm of Bungay are long since turned to dust, yet even today physical evidence remains of the creature's visitation. Inside the church the stone floor still bears the deep scratch marks made by the animal's claws, while the spire's clock mechanism remains buckled and melted in the tower, marking forever the exact moment of the supernatural event.

Astonishingly the Bungay incident was not unique. Suffolk county records for the year 1577 described a similar manifestation which appeared in another church at precisely the same moment seventeen miles away. Again, in this incident, in the parish of Blythburgh, two people were killed and evidence of the unnatural visitor can still be seen scorched deep into the thick wooden door of the village church.

What can be made of accounts so fantastic? Contemporary records are considered reliable on other matters, yet our natural inclination is to treat stories like these with extreme scepticism. We should be aware of our own prejudice, for reports of black dogs have appeared with remarkable consistency even up to the present day. Indeed, the last time a black dog was seen in the graveyard of Bungay church was as recently as 1973.

The truth is that these creatures would seem to have a tangible reality. In typical sightings, black dogs are described as much larger than the normal canine variety, sometimes as big as a calf. Always the eyes of the manifestations are huge and glowing, as if the fires of Hell burn inside them. One man who encountered such a fearful vision, and lived to tell the tale, was author Stephen Jenkins. Jenkins saw the giant dog baying and slavering on a road near his Devon farmhouse in July 1950, the day before his brother passed away. Another omen was seen in 1928 by a student from Trinity College, Dublin, who was visiting England at the time. In this instance, the dog's appearance would seem to have indicated the demise of the Irishman's father, who was gravely ill.

Similar twentieth-century examples of black dogs presaging death have come from Buxton Lamas, in Norfolk, and the Isle of Man. In the most recent case of a fatal encounter, which I found in Janet and Colin Bord's *Modern Mysteries of Britain*, a couple who in 1978 saw a canine spectre on a road near the village of Exford, Somerset, found their family to be plagued by death and misfortune for months afterwards. Further details from sightings reinforce the essentially supernatural nature of the phenomenon. A dog seen by a girl in Bredon, Worcestershire, during World War II was said to have had eyes like coals, which lit up inside, whilst in 1907 a Somerset woman was menaced by a dog she saw near Budsleigh Hill, an animal of prodigious size with eyes like saucers. In both these cases the creature disappeared in a flash of fire, having signalled the impending doom of a close friend of the witness. It is doubtful whether anyone who sees a black dog could forget the experience. An omen seen by a man near Leeds in 1925 was said to have emitted a sulphurous vapour as it barked, whilst a similar vision which jumped out at a Norfolk woman during the same year had a hot breath of 'noxious' odour. In 1972 a pony-sized black dog visited a Dartmoor farmhouse causing damage to the building's wall, roof and electrical circuits. Understandably the occupants were terrified.

Black dogs can appear and disappear at will. When Irishwoman Margo Ryan encountered one in County Wicklow on 12 June 1952 she attempted to stroke it, only to find thin air. The next day saw the death of her mother. A similar dematerialisation, though apparently not ominous, was the one witnessed by coastguard Graham Grant at his Gorleston Rescue HQ on the morning of 19 April 1972. Grant saw the animal, 'like an Alsation but bigger', running across the beach before it vanished in a brilliant flash of light. On yet another occasion, a motorist ran over – or through – a ghost dog which then exploded on a road between the Norfolk villages of Little and Great Snoring in 1963. In this instance the driver was shaken but unhurt. He may have been fortunate, for in a similar incident in the late nineteenth century a wagoner near Hatfield Peverel, Essex, who attempted to drive over a black dog was apparently reduced to ashes along with his cart. Again in the last century, a case is recorded of a Somerset farmer being left paralysed after encountering a strange black dog with red eyes whilst more recently, in 1970, a similar fate befell a man who was confronted by one of the beasts whilst walking alone along a road near Woolpit, Suffolk. The examples listed above are merely a handful amongst hundreds of sightings of British black dogs recorded over the past two hundred years. They show no sign of abating, for 31 October 1984 saw the manifestation of a black dog in the village of Yeo Mill, Devon. Its appearance coincided with the mysterious slaughter the previous night of several hundred chickens in the nearby village of Yelverton.

There are other legends of omens of doom going back much further. For more than five centuries foxes have provided the messengers which stalk the deathbeds of the old Irish family, Gormanston. Indeed so famous is the phenomenon that the fox is incorporated into the family's coat of arms. According to ancient tradition foxes are seen to gather in large numbers around the time of the demise of a Gormanston male. This is no mere folk legend. Examples of the phenomenon have been witnessed on three occasions this century. The most celebrated occurrence took place on 8 October 1907, when more than a dozen of the creatures gathered to bay and cry a lament below the walls of the Gormanstons' castle home. Inside the fortress walls the fourteenth viscount was slowly slipping away from the mortal plane. Later, an even larger group of foxes was seen again lurking for several hours in broad daylight in the castle gardens, and on the day before the viscount's funeral a similar sight befell mourners who arrived at the chapel where the Irishman's body lay. Even after the service the vigil continued, for a solitary vixen was seen to sit beside the viscount's grave for more than a week after the burial.

Clearly such behaviour on the part of ordinary foxes would be highly unusual, since the animals do not gather in large numbers, nor are they habitually prepared to hunt as a pack in broad daylight. Yet the Gormanston foxes were stranger still, for they entered the castle grounds through an unknown route, disappearing and reappearing without warning or explanation. According to one report from a local farmhand, they were seen to pass a flock of geese without attempting to attack them, the very opposite of the animals' natural behaviour pattern.

Omens of doom often appear on the wing. The most famous English family retainer of supernatural folklore is the white bird of the Oxenhams. The origin of this omen is, like the Irish Gormanstons', lost in the mists of medieval history. One tale holds that a past Oxenham stabbed his bride-to-be in a jealous rage after being jilted, and that as a punishment God sent a white bird to mark the deaths of him and his descendants. Another legend has it that an Oxenham once became involved with Diabolism and sold his soul to the Devil who sent his own messenger of Hell to haunt the family down the generations. Whatever the origin of the omen, we do know that by the beginning of the seventeenth century the vision had been seen on several occasions and was well known to the family.

A particularly striking series of white bird appearances began on 12 September 1618, a day which saw the death of Grace Oxenham, a widow, though only in her late thirties at the time. Twenty years later her son James published a lengthy tract which detailed in chillingly matter-of-fact terms the reappearance of the omen on no less than four subsequent occasions in his lifetime, each time materialising above the deathbeds of members of the family.

First to die was James Oxenham's infant son, John, two days after the small white bird, described as being like a glowing chaffinch, was seen by witnesses hovering for several seconds above the child's cot. Among those who witnessed the phenomenon, no one saw the creature enter or leave the bed chamber and the windows were apparently closed. Five days after the boy was buried, James Oxenham's wife, Thomasine, fell ill of a fever and died within hours. On the day prior to her sudden illness, the same bird was discovered fluttering above her head. Next to die was their teenage daughter Rebecca, who expired after apparently contracting the same illness which accounted for her mother. Once more the white bird appeared, this time at the precise moment of her last breath. Finally, James Oxenham's misery was complete when his only remaining child Grace was killed in an accident the following month. As before, the winged vision was seen, although this time not until after her death – on the day of the girl's funeral.

Whatever terrors this particular horror may have struck in the hearts of past Oxenhams, the omen appears to have run its course. Although several reliable accounts of the bird's appearance were recorded in the century following the 1638 holocaust, the last one took place as long ago as 1873, when the spectre materialised once more in the death chamber of one G.N. Oxenham, an elderly family patriarch.

Another bird of ill-omen marks the death of an English Bishopric, the See of Salisbury. If witnesses's accounts can be believed, huge white birds of a type unlike any native British species have regularly been seen hovering over the countryside before the last days of the incumbent bishop. One observer from the last century described them as being 'like albatrosses', but with dazzling white wings, whilst another witness from more recently said that they moved 'woodenly' through the sky, like gigantic overgrown gulls. The first recorded incident involving the white birds of Salisbury took place in 1414, when a flock of the creatures descended on the cathedral roof in time to mark the laying to rest of the local church leader.

Many times they have been sighted since, none more convincingly so than on 15 August 1911, the day on which the then bishop, Harold Wordsworth, died. Among the numerous witnesses was Miss Edith Oliver, an elderly spinster, who was returning home from choir practice. Upon seeing the birds, which she later attested to being a type she had never before encountered, she turned back to Salisbury Cathedral to warn her spiritual superior. In the event it was too late, for she reached her destination only to learn that the bishop had died suddenly of a heart attack.

There is nothing new about feathered omens, nor are they a peculiarly British phenomenon. According to the Roman *Chronicles of Plutarch*, ominous signs and portents preceded the assassination of Julius Caesar, among their number being the Stygian screech-owl which perched in the city's main square around the Ides of March. Later, at the emperor's funeral, a strange and unnatural bird flew into the hall of Pompeii carrying a sprig of laurel in its beak, only to be torn apart by a flock of predatory wonders who suddenly descended upon it from out of thin air. Today, two thousand years after the Roman Empire fell, Australian Aborigines believe that the death of a friend or close relative can be predicted by the sudden appearance of a bird of unusual species in their district or region.

In the United Kingdom it is the houses of the aristocracy which have tended to attract the most famous omens. Yet these preternatural creatures are by no means the exclusive preserve of the rich and powerful. Frank Podmore, a founder member of the Society for Psychical Research in the late nineteenth century, wrote of a doctor's daughter who had repeatedly seen a 'strange, tiny, graceful looking bird with a very slim head' every day for a week prior to a death in her family. During its regular visits the bird tapped upon the window of the house to announce its arrival, yet significantly it was never seen to eat and ignored water and breadcrumbs put outside. After the family's bereavement the bird was seen no more. The oddity noted by Podmore is far from unique. For years writers interested in curiosities have noted cases where flocks of birds have descended upon the roofs of houses in which a death is imminent or subsequently occurs unexpectedly. The eminent psychologist C.G. Jung encountered several of these oddities whilst researching his classic study of coincidences entitled *Synchronicity.* One involved the death of one of Jung's own psychiatric patients. After the man had gone to work his wife had become alarmed to see a large flock of seagulls descend upon the roof of her home. To the woman, the birds' arrival was portentous since a similar phenomenon had accompanied the death of both her mother and grandmother. Although she feared mainly for her own life, it turned out to be her husband's end that was foreshadowed. Later that same day she learned how he had collapsed at work and died of a cerebral haemorrhage.

C.G. Jung considered his patient's story evidential of coincidence's universal presence, the tendency of events to come together through synchronicity to form a pattern which was often bizarre. He firmly rejected a belief in the objective reality of omens themselves since he was unwilling to accept the existence of alien intelligences. To Jung all unexplained phenomena were accounted for by a more subtle understanding of the collective human mind's relation to the physical universe. As we shall see in a later chapter it is an intriguing theory, but on the evidence I have collected it would appear that omens are both real and dangerous. For these creatures, whatever force may direct them, do not always appear and disappear as simple reminders of what can or will happen. Occasionally they can themselves be the cause of death, not merely the bringer of ill-tidings. Where instances like these have taken place a new set of variables must be added to the equation ... with a result that is often incomprehensible.

One of the most alarmingly inexplicable aspects of spectral animal manifestations is their coincidence with outbreaks of unexplained physical attacks upon real members of the animal kingdom. Examples have appeared from across the world. In 1973, for example, panic set in across the American Midwest following a series of reports of cattle discovered slaughtered and mutilated. Stories came in from over a dozen states, involving more than a hundred separate incidents. Most striking amongst these was a number of cases where cows' ears, eyes, udders and bowels were removed, in many cases with clinical precision. Some carcasses were even found drained entirely of blood. Press accounts of these gruesome goings-on stirred the Bible-belt region into a state of near siege. Believing themselves to be under attack from they knew not what, farmers armed with rifles formed vigilante-style groups to defend their property and livestock, all to no avail. The attacks continued, and continued to defy explanation. The lack of tracks or footprints around the mutilated carcasses precluded the possibility of normal animal predators, yet a number of unidentified creatures were seen, confusing the issue further.

When some Red Indian tribes claimed that the killings were the work of a cat spirit from their own folklore the idea was roundly laughed at. Even so, although pumas have become extinct across Midwest states, big cats had been seen running wild across the countryside. One strange beast, looking like a 'black lion' was reported by two Indiana cowhands who watched it kill several of their herd. The lion was later hunted by police who found tracks suggesting a creature weighing more than five hundred pounds. Whatever the animal was, it was never seen again. Another mysterious black cat attacked and mauled farmer Ed Moorman; this time the state was Michigan, in the vicinity of Monument City. Several days later a neighbour of Moorman's found ten of his pigs dead – in each case their heart and liver only had been eaten.

In fact the 1973 cattle maiming outbreaks did not provide the first reports of big cats in the Midwest states this century. In August 1971, a cat-like animal which had the ability to appear and vanish at will slaughtered a variety of farm animals in Canton Township, Michigan. In September 1972 in Atlanta, Georgia, a black panther was seen to kill a goat and two cows before exploding into thin air. During spring of 1977 something unpleasant was visiting Richland, Ohio, where, in a series of nightly slaughters, several hundred sheep were torn apart by a huge dark creature which appeared able to walk through fences and barn doors with phantom-like ease. Never identified as a known species of feline, it was on one occasion chased by police into a wood where it disappeared.

1977, like 1973, turned in a plethora of phantom feline reports from across the USA. In Bay Springs, Mississippi, an entire herd of pigs died after having their ears eaten away by a strange creature described as half cat, half dog. A few weeks later, a farmer living forty miles away found his prize bull dead – its ears ripped out by the roots. Meanwhile similar reports emerged from across the states of Kentucky, Ohio, Michigan and Illinois. Characteristic of all these sightings was a curious lack of physical evidence to suggest the predator's presence. Only occasionally were paw prints found, and then enigmatically few. The injuries suffered by stock were terrible, although often of a type not associated with a large predator. Strangest of all were the numerous accounts of creatures vanishing into space like the black dogs of the English countryside.

Unlike the continental United States, big cats have never been a feature of the wildlife of Australia. Yet like their American counterparts, sheep farmers in the Antipodean continent have regularly been plagued by mysterious predators for more than thirty years.

In Emmaville, New South Wales, a strange creature resembling a black leopard was seen hunting the ranges during a twelve-month period beginning in the summer of 1956. Nearly 1350 sheep were slaughtered during this time, whilst repeated massive hunts with riflemen produced nothing. Much more recently, attacks by a black cat in South West Australia grew so commonplace that Mr James MacKinnon, Minister for Wildlife to the Australian parliament, admitted that only a 'phantom creature' could conceivably have been responsible for the carnage.

Astonishingly, even Britain has had its share of big cat sightings. Thousands of reports of black lions, tigers and pumas have emanated regularly from up and down the country over the past two centuries and continue to the present day. If anything, such sightings are more widespread in contemporary Britain than ever before. For instance, between 1962 and 1964 there were over three hundred sightings of alien felines in Surrey alone! The story of the Surrey pumas came to the attention of the national press in August 1964 when a 450-pound Friesian bullock was found badly mauled. The following week a calf was found having apparently been dragged across several fields. Prints near the carcass suggested the presence of a puma, three times larger than the largest fully grown adult puma ever caught. It was dubbed the Munstead Monster, after the nearby village, and sightings of this prodigious creature continued throughout the autumn of 1964. Respectable witnesses claiming to have seen the beast included clergymen, a doctor, gamekeepers and a number of policemen. In spite of massive armed searches, the creature was never caught and by the following spring sightings had dried up.

As elsewhere, Britain's phantom felines display bizarre predatory instincts and killing methods. Records show that in May 1910, for instance, up to fifty sheep were slaughtered each night in fields near the Cumbrian village of Ennerdale. In every case the bodies had been drained of blood through small incisions in the animals' jugular veins, yet no flesh was eaten. Much more recently, in 1976, Scottish farmer John Stewart of Ballageich Hill found a gaggle of his geese killed in a similar vampiric manner, the only marks on their carcasses being two puncture holes in their necks. Interestingly, Stewart's loss coincided with the appearance of a black lynx-like cat in the local area, though the two incidents were never positively proven to have been connected.

Some reports from the British Isles seem unaccountable outside the pages of horror fiction. Sixty sheep a night fell prey to a horror which stalked the farmland around Guildford for more than a month in 1910. Fifteen years later, in the long, dark winter of 1925, something huge and black terrorised the Edale region of Derbyshire, tearing sheep and cattle apart with preternatural strength. In 1964, in Bedford, carcasses of six horses were discovered horribly mutilated by a creature which some zoologists later described as having jaws the size of a small dinosaur; yet no tracks were found near the scene of the carnage. Twelve years later, in a strikingly similar incident, more than a dozen ponies were found dead in the New Forest, stripped of their hides. Afterwards, to the stupefied amazement of scientists, the ponies' bodies decomposed to skeletons within a few days. No explanation for the deaths of these animals or the remarkable rapidity of their bodily decomposition was forthcoming. Yet once again, a huge black cat 'like a tiger but bigger' was reported to have menaced a couple camping in the forest earlier the same week.

Reports of phantom feline activity show little sign of abating. In the early summer of 1981, several sightings were made of enormous felines in Wales. Dozens of sheep were savaged on three successive nights in June on farms around the village of Ysbyty Ystwyth. Then in August a 'big black cat' not only killed a henhouse full of chickens but also the guard dog left chained up to protect them. During the summer months of 1982 and 1983, a strange black creature 'bigger than a dog' killed more than five hundred sheep on the open Devonshire hillside farmlands of Exmoor. The 'Beast of Exmoor', as it became known – first locally, and then to the national newspapers – seemed capable of covering vast distances in order to commit its atrocities, to appear and disappear at will, and to be immune to the bullets of both farmers and police marksmen. It was never caught, and without warning its reign of terror ended as abruptly as it had started in the autumn of 1983.

In the past, reports of strange animals have had a tendency to be interpreted in terms of what already exists, or what the superstitious might believe to exist, even where those explanations are clearly implausible. Thus a creature which tore the throats of a hundred sheep in a single night in Ireland in 1874 was considered to be a wolf, despite the fact that wolves had died out as a species in Ireland more than a century before. By the same count a huge predatory quadruped which was variously described as a 'gigantic lion' and a 'wolf with a lion's head' by witnesses in the Languedoc region of France during the year of 1765 was labelled a werewolf by the authorities. Whatever the monstrosity actually was, contemporary records show that it ended the lives of more than forty people during its brief reign of terror.

Today those who attempt to explain the appearance of phenomenal creatures seem to convince themselves that a rational hypothesis is constantly being overlooked. This approach is rarely satisfactory. 'A pack of wild dogs' remains the official identity of the Beast of Exmoor, despite the many eyewitness descriptions of a large feline.

In Surrey, the many hundreds of reports of pumas in the mid-1960s were thought to be the result of hallucination, hysteria or mistaken identification, despite the reliability of witnesses and the frequent presence of physical evidence, such as droppings, tracks and the butchered half-eaten carcasses of farm stock. Even among those who do accept the evidence, many prefer the traditional explanation of big cat reports – that they are escapees from zoos or private collections – despite the absence of recorded losses from these sources. The truth is that no natural explanation comes close to fitting the facts. Mad dogs cannot have caused the variety of mutilations found on carcasses – indeed no known animal could. Nor could a single beast cover the distances between attacks that have taken place on the same night ... attacks which have often occurred simultaneously over a wide area. Whilst it is just about possible, though unlikely, that some big cats of the type sighted across Britain might have escaped unrecorded from private game collections, it is frankly inconceivable that they could live unnoticed in the British countryside for very long. In any case, not once have the massive armed searches in Surrey and Devon produced a single predator dead or alive. All in all, the fact remains that the sheer oddity of the reported attacks upon livestock, and the uncanny ability of these creatures to appear and disappear at will, leads strongly towards a conclusion that they derive their existence from a dimension outside our physical universe.

Not all manifestations from other worlds appear in the form of animal visions. Discarnate entities, both visible and invisible, have haunted men down the ages. Ghosts, goblins and other creatures of supernatural lore may or may not exist, depending upon your own viewpoint. Yet believe in them or not, enough scientific evidence has emerged during the past quarter-century to prove that invisible entities do exist in the most literal sense, whatever we may choose to call them. There are also plenty of examples of the physical harm they can do to humans.

With so many scientists still afraid to consider the possibility of discarnate forces, it is often the church which is left to do battle with the evil in our midst. One leading churchman who regularly confronts manifestations of mysterious energies is the Rev. George Tarleton, former minister of Chingford Congregational Church in London. A leading figure in the clerical establishment, Tarleton has often appeared on British television to denounce Ouija, the popular board game through which spirits can be contacted. In his denunciations, Tarleton points out that Ouija opens the door for other potentially dangerous non-human beings, and claims that in his parish physical injuries have been inflicted by Ouija spirits. One group of teenagers, for example, had asked for the invisible power they summoned to break the leg of one of their number as a test of its reality. The boy's ankle was snapped instantly. After another seance a youth became possessed and clawed his brother's face badly.

Another prominent London church leader, Canon John Pearce-Higgins, tells a similar story. A former Provost of Southwark Cathedral, Higgins knows of several cases where invisibles have physically attacked people during or after Ouija sessions, and has described several sudden suicides he believes were provoked by the incidents. One victim, a woman, fell under a bus as a result of her experiences, believes the minister. Yet another English cleric who has come face to face with the objective forces of evil is the Rev. James Song of Derbyshire. In 1977 Song exorcised a factory worker who had become the target of physical assaults by invisible entities. In these attacks, which usually lasted several minutes, the man named Peter was flung bodily across the room or strangled by unseen hands to the point of unconsciousness. Sometimes Song would witness Peter's head being twisted around to an impossible degree. Only after a series of exhausting exorcisms did these painful attacks cease.

Considered unbelievable by many, stories like those detailed above are by no means unusual. Countless numbers of violent manifestations have been recorded down the ages and from the four corners of the globe. The fact that such stories continue to be reported in our own scientific age supports the contention that invisible forces are not the product of superstition.

Among the most common of all invisible phenomena is the poltergeist. The German word 'poltergeist' literally means noisy spirit, and these outbreaks can occur spontaneously in homes without being invited by Ouija or some other occult means. That poltergeists exist is now almost totally accepted by academics, apart from the diehard sceptics who refuse to believe that anything occurs which cannot be explained. Nevertheless, what poltergeists *are* is very much in doubt. The phenomenon itself can vary tremendously: typically, tables and other furniture move mysteriously; household objects levitate or disappear altogether; strange noises are heard .·. rappings, scrapings, even disembodied voices. Usually the intelligence behind the phenomenon seems mischievous rather than malevolent, yet on occasions material objects are flung wildly across rooms, houses are damaged beyond repair, and the people who get in the way of the mayhem are injured. In the most disturbing poltergeist cases humans become the centre of a sadistic force which delights in inflicting pain and mutilation. Examples are numerous.

In 1919 a manifestation which appeared in the Portuguese town of Comeada, tore its victims' flesh with such violence that witnesses spoke of it having 'invisible fangs'. Eight years later a poltergeist outbreak in Poona, India, culminated in the entity attempting to strangle a small child with the bib she was wearing. In 1974 similarly hostile treatment was meted out to American teenager Anthony Rossi of East Hartford, Connecticut, who survived a poltergeist assault to find seven bleeding clawmarks slashed across his chest.

A particularly frightening case was reported to the Freiburg Institute of Psychology in November 1980. The institute's doctors were alerted to the plight of a young Spanish-born housewife living in Mulhouse, France. The woman, named Carla, had for two months been the subject of repeated attacks by a mysterious invisible entity present in her home. During these savage assaults, deep cuts had opened up involuntarily in her shoulders and thighs, and she had frequently suffered the sensation of being punched in the stomach. Inexplicable damage had also occurred to inanimate items in the house. A team of investigators from the institute moved into her home and conducted a study which proved conclusively that the reported phenomenon was genuine. Without question, the marks that appeared on Carla's skin were not self-inflicted and the investigators witnessed claw-like lacerations materialising on her agonised flesh. Nor did the invisible attacker feel inhibited by the presence of the parapsychologists; indeed, if anything, the maltreatment of Carla became more frequent and more vicious.

Other anomalous happenings convinced the investigating team that an energy unknown to science was present in the house. A recorder installed by the researchers to monitor temperature fluctuations produced a series of broken lines and impossible readings, whilst intricate infra-red cine-cameras suffered unexplained failures. On three separate occasions film even disappeared from inside cameras which had plainly not been touched. Finally, after months of evidence collation, the German team concluded that an evil presence definitely inhabited the house, but could not suggest a remedy. Carla's husband lost no time in finding his own. Hastily packing his belongings, he took his long-suffering wife to a new home in the Antilles. The invisible force, whatever it had been, did not follow them and the cottage in Mulhouse remains empty.

In 1965 a similarly evil-minded entity had plagued the life of Maria Jose Ferreira, a young child from São Paulo, Brazil. The infestation began its unpleasant behaviour by slapping the girl across the face and buttocks, then proceeded to pelt her with heavy stones which seemed to materialise from thin air. An exorcist was called in but things grew steadily worse. Sometimes Maria's clothes would ignite spontaneously and drop in flaming cinders from her body. On other occasions needles would be implanted into her flesh – sometimes appearing inside her leather shoes which remained unpierced. After one savage attack a total of fifty-five needles were extracted from her skin. Not surprisingly, the girl went mad and committed suicide at the age of thirteen.

Sinister tales of haunted houses, ghosts and other malignant forces have chilled the bones of cinema-goers ever since the advent of motion pictures, and recently the cash tills of the big movie companies have grown richer to the tune of hundreds of millions of dollars with such hits as *The Exorcist, The Entity,* and *Poltergeist.* In some cases these horror pictures are loosely based on true stories. In particular an intricate concoction of embellishment and myth was composed to market the successful *Amityville Horror* series.

Initially the *Amityville* fantasy gained attention after the Lutz family of New York complained of nightly visitations in their suburban home. Having had the house unsuccessfully exorcised by a Catholic priest, the Lutzes reported manifestations of green slime and swarms of flies. These tales captured the imagination of a continent and the rest, as they say, is showbusiness. A book on the subject sold three million copies and a succession of hit films followed. Only years later did it become apparent that the original stories were fabricated by a family anxious for an excuse to leave a home they disliked and a mortgage loan they could not afford. Movies like *The Amityville Horror* provide fuel for the sceptics who choose to deny the possibility of psychic phenomena. What the sceptics forget is that various manifestations described by the New York family were simply an amalgam of events which have been proven to have genuinely occurred in many other locations all over the world.

From newspaper reports published during the past decade it is clear that poltergeist-related anomalies include: human blood spurting from walls, floors and ceilings, the continuous pounding and shaking of houses, and the disappearance – and subsequent reappearance elsewhere – of solid objects. Add to these the frequently reported cases of spontaneous combustion described in Chapter One, and it becomes evident that the poltergeist has a reality outside of a scriptwriter's imagination.

Long before Hollywood discovered the box-office potential of the Devil, a genuinely diabolical entity was terrorising a pioneer family in their remote homestead in Robertson County, Tennessee. It was in the year 1817 that the Bell family began to notice strange noises in their frontier home. These began as a series of sharp raps, but were gradually replaced by guttural choking echoes and the screams of what seemed to be an old woman. The head of the household, John Bell, was a respected member of the local farming community and a God-fearing Christian. Believing the noisy intruder to be an emissary of the Devil, he invited a group of churchmen to witness the phenomenon and advise him upon a course of action. A contemporary tract records how the church committee found the Bells' house to be infested by evil, and that the air inside was corrupted by an obnoxious stench like that of a rotting corpse. Most disturbingly, the invisible being became violent for the first time – punching, slapping and biting one member of the church delegation while another was spat upon.

For the unfortunate Bells this was just the beginning of their misery. Over the next few months all were physically assaulted, John Bell, his wife and their nine children. Particularly violent attacks centred upon two teenage daughters who frequently found their hair being pulled out by the roots. Their screams of pain and fear were typically accompanied by loud raucous cries of delight from their unseen tormentor. As the story of the manifestation spread the Bell Witch, as it became known, was witnessed by more and more curious visitors, including a future president of the United States, Andrew Jackson. No one who saw it remained sceptical that the phenomenon was genuine, yet none could suggest a solution. Eventually, after four years of psychic intimidation, a despairing John Bell committed suicide. To the horror of his family, the entity then assumed an exact imitation of John Bell's voice and, uttering crude oaths and vile blasphemies, it continued to gloat over its victim's death for seven more dreadful nights. Once Bell's body was laid to rest in a local churchyard the manifestation abruptly ceased, never to return.

The story of the Tennessee poltergeist has become a part of American folklore. That the basic facts of the case happened must surely be beyond doubt, since the terror was attested to not only by the eleven members of the Bell household but by literally hundreds of other Tennessee people who were brave enough to cross the accursed threshold. Two hundred years on only the exact nature of the invisible entity remains open to question, not its reality.

It has been noted by some paranormal investigators that poltergeists often have a tendency to attach themselves to a specific individual rather than a particular place. This differentiates their presence from that of a haunting ghost. However, some mysterious attacks by invisible assailants appear to defy any logical pattern. For instance, in 1973, a Japanese woman was admitted to a Boston hospital suffering from deep lacerations to her tongue. At first she noticed, she said, a single sharp pain followed by a mouthful of blood. A doctor's examination ruled out the obvious scenario – that she had bitten herself – since the cuts appeared to have been made surgically, as if with a scalpel. She was passed on to a psychiatrist, who suggested that she might have inflicted the wounds upon herself possibly as a result of trauma. This diagnosis was also dropped when the same hospital admitted several other similar casualties later that week, each relating experiences which echoed those of the Japanese patient. In each case the injuries were suffered while the victim was walking in the same vicinity.

A similarly uncanny series of attacks occurred in London in 1922. Early in the morning on 16 April, a man was brought to Charing Cross Hospital with a deep stab wound to his neck. He claimed that no one had been close enough to have administered the thrust, and a witness to the incident, which had taken place at a turning off

Coventry Street in London's West End, corroborated the victim's strange testimony. Two hours later, another victim with a knife wound staggered into Charing Cross Hospital. He too spoke of an invisible attacker. Finally that evening, a third victim of the phantom knifeman was treated by Charing Cross doctors. Police subsequently found that each assault had occurred on precisely the same spot – the turning off Coventry Street. A full report of the bizarre crimes appeared the following week in the *Daily Express* newspaper.

More than fifty years apart the incidents in Boston and London's West End defy rational explanation, but they are by no means unique in the annals of mysterious violations.

In 1891 an American named Carl Gros was shot dead near Maspeth, Long Island. The bullets had passed right through his body without penetrating his clothing. A similar mystery surrounds the death of Isadore Fink, whose corpse was found in the back room of a laundry on East 132nd Street on the evening of 9 March 1921. Neither gun nor bullets were found in the room, which had been locked from the inside, yet Fink's chest exhibited two gunshot wounds. New York Police Commissioner Edward Mulrooney described the slaying as an 'insoluble mystery'. Likewise the murder of Englishwoman Lavinia Farrar in 1901 was never solved. Discovered lying in a pool of blood on the kitchen floor of her Cambridgeshire home, Farrar was found to have been stabbed repeatedly through the heart. Yet, incredibly, her dress remained intact. Could it be that she had had the strength to put on clothes after stabbing herself? It seems unlikely for she was seventy-two years old, blind and a cripple. In any case why should she have done so? Why indeed should any attacker? Any human assailant, that is.

If one cares to examine the pages of Charles Fort one will find listed outbreaks of invisible throat-cutters, stranglers, even in China the odd plague of pigtail choppers! The variety of this cabinet of curiosities is literally endless. Amusing though the panic spread by some of these bizarre activities can sometimes read, it is well to remember that the pain caused by the most horrifying violations is real enough. Frank Edwards, in his study entitled *Strangest of All*, details the tragic case of one Jimmy De Buin, a coloured South African farmworker who found himself the subject of a phantom slasher during the autumn of 1960. Investigated by a local police chief John Wessels, De Buin was seen to suffer deep lacerations to his legs and arms even though nothing was penetrating his shirt or trousers at the time. Throughout his ordeal De Buin screamed in agony, and eventually died from loss of blood.

Injuries caused by supernatural energies come in many forms, yet there can be no stranger or more disturbing example than the fate which overtook a peasant woman in Italy in 1761. The incident, which defies any conceivable explanation, took place as five women were returning after collecting firewood in a forest near their home in the village of Ventimiglia. As they were walking with their bundles, chattering happily, one of their number let out a stifled scream and pitched forward on to the ground. As the others turned towards her one can only imagine the horrified amazement on their faces. For there on the ground lay their companion not simply dead but torn apart, her body and clothes literally ripped to shreds. In an instant she had been rent asunder by some unimaginable force.

A full account of this extraordinary happening was reported to the French Academy of Sciences and an examination of her remains by Italian doctors appeared as part of a report the following year in the Annual Register. The astonished medical figures noted that wounds covering the woman's entire body – wounds which included a gaping hole in her side, deep incisions in her stomach, back, hips and pubic region – had been made from the inside. The body had been almost totally drained of blood. The doctors concluded their report by stating that, although no cause of death could be ascertained, it was clear that the force of the eruption had been from within. To put it simply she had exploded.

It is difficult to say whether the deadly enigma of Ventimiglia was connected with other invisible killings and mutilations detailed in this chapter. Clearly, like spontaneous human combustion, it was a manifestation of an incredible force beyond the reach of science to comprehend. As for phenomenal creatures, it has become perfectly obvious that they have nothing to do with mother nature. Birds of ill omen, black dogs and other portentous visitations may well be separate manifestations of a single unidentified force. Although we see them only seldom, they may exist permanently on an as yet unrecognised level of reality outside our mortal comprehension. Grim reapers from another dimension, they are the product of energies we are unwilling to recognise. Each leaves its own characteristic mark upon our world ... and sometimes those marks are hideous.

MALICE AFORETHOUGHT

Throughout recorded history there has remained a universal superstition among the races and civilisations of our planet. According to this belief select groups of individuals within a particular society are said to possess the unique power to harm others, either through the force of their will, or by using some secret magical art. Over the centuries hundreds of stories have been handed down, usually by word of mouth, offering supporting evidence for these beliefs, yet today in the closing decade of the twentieth century most enlightened people would dismiss the idea out of hand. They are 'old wives tales', we say, and nothing more. Our scepticism is perfectly understandable, for, like ghost stories, the vast majority of curse legends amounts to little more than a motley collection of uncorroborated hearsay from unreliable sources. Even so, after the dust-webs of time, ignorance and flagrant embellishment have been swept away, we are left with a convincing kernel of hard evidence which cannot be easily ignored. Moreover, as I have discovered during my research, curses and other psychic killings are still taking place each day in our own modern world of microtechnology and space-age avionics. Nor is the contemporary use of these invisible weapons relegated to the realms of the so-called backward countries. Voodoo's dark and unearthly rituals are as likely to be practised in the heart of a sprawling American metropolis as they are in the steaming jungles of Africa or the West Indies, while four hundred years after witches were burnt and hanged in their thousands for invoking the forces of evil, those same forces are to be found at work once more in the quiet peaceful villages of rural England.

Among the best known methods of psychic murder is the boning ritual of Australian Aboriginals. Early settlers to the subcontinent were amazed at the rapidity of death brought about by the secret methods of the Aboriginal sorcerers called *mulunguwa*. In fact this form of death magic had already been in existence for several thousand years and continues to be practised today. In the Aboriginal method, large bones, known as *kundela*, usually lizards' femurs, become a deadly pointer for those under the spell. Hardened in a charcoal fire, the bone is tapered at one end and finally wrapped around with human hair. Once prepared it is endowed with a concentration of sheer hatred and left in the sun for several days to increase in power. Having perfected his psychic spear the Aboriginal medicine man points the bone with short stabbing movements towards his intended victim. The affected tribesman then falls into a state of coma or sheer convulsions and ends his life in a writhing, twitching, vomiting heap. It is a singularly horrific way to die.

Dr S.M. Lambert, an associate of the International Health Division of the Rockefeller Foundation, noted several cases of sudden death following boning curses during his work at the Mona Mona Mission, North Queensland (1919–20). In a report published several years later, Dr Lambert concluded that the boning method of murder left no trace of a physical wound nor any medically acceptable cause of death. Yet in his experience it rarely failed. More recently evidence has emerged from other parts of the subcontinent to support Lambert's belief. In 1953 a sick Aborigine named Kinijika was transferred by air from his local Arnhem Land in the Northern Territories. Doctors at the modern hospital in Darwin found him to be dying though no wound was visible. An autopsy on Kinijika's body revealed that he had not been poisoned, nor was he suffering from any known disease. Only afterwards did the medical men learn that a curse had been placed upon their patient by his local tribal council. Even though the ceremony had been carried out in Kinijika's absence the death sentence was effective.

A similar story surrounds the fate of Lya Wakuma, a member of the Mailli tribe. In mid-April 1956 Wakuma fell ill after breaking a tribal taboo. Placed in Darwin Hospital Wakuma survived only a few days before dying in agony. Once more, doctors treating the man could find no clue to his demise, apart from the boning ritual. According to one who treated him, it was as if the man's life had slowly run out of his body 'like sand from an hour-glass'.

Antipodean anthropologists have long since recognised the reality of the boning curse without ever coming close to offering a satisfactory explanation for its success. Even more feared among native curses, however, and far better known to the civilised West, is voodoo – the magical death cult of the African and West Indian negroes.

The word voodoo itself is not derived from the French *vuadak* as is generally believed, but from a Ewe word *vudu* which simply means 'gods'. The Ewe tribes, who inhabit Togoland in Africa, believe that witchcraft is the highest power in the universe and that the voodoo gods control that power. In Haiti, where the inhabitants are descended from the slave trade, the voodoo rites of West Africa have become a perverted religion through which evil priests have kept a vice-like grip on the everyday populous. This hold is maintained through a mixture of physical violence and the threat of black magic. Haitian voodoo services involve repellent rites in which live cockerels are beheaded, doves, turkeys and other fowl throttled for the procurement of blood. This blood is then usually drunk from a magic chalice or smeared over the genitals of naked female dancers. For the terrible gods of voodoo – 'Loa' or eaters of men – sacrifices are offered, usually the testicles of an unfortunate pig. Sometimes dead bodies are removed from graves for the same purpose, and very occasionally a living person is sacrificed.

A belief in the evil gods lies at the root of the voodoo

curse. Petro Loa, the most powerful and terrible, is believed by Haitians to have been punished by the almighty for rebelling against the order of heaven, in a story curiously resembling the Biblical tale of Satan's fall. Petro Loa now walks the earth killing out of cruelty and spite, aiding and abetting those who wish to call upon Hell's legions. Since, in voodoo cultures, intercourse between the natural and supernatural worlds is considered easy, the idea that men can communicate with invisible spirits is readily acceptable. Few Haitians doubt the power of Petro Loa to possess or kill them, nor would they readily deny the power of the witch doctor to direct the evil one to possess their own souls.

The precise rituals used to evoke Loa are cloaked in secrecy, but the mechanisms used to direct the evil gods to their intended victims are well known. The doll or effigy is the most common. First a likeness is created and formally baptised and then a straw is placed into the doll's mouth so that life may be breathed into it. Once completed, the likeness is believed to have become the person. Hot needles, broken glass and splinters are then inserted into the effigy every day until the person dies. Another method regularly practised is the bowl of water curse. In this variety, a reflection of the victim is produced by magical means in a bowl of water. Through a series of incantations the enemy's face appears and is stabbed repeatedly. When the spell has become successful, the waters redden as if turned to blood.

Just how common these rituals are in the modern-day life of the West Indies is difficult to judge. Yet enough evidence exists to suggest that when curses are invoked by genuine voodoo priests results duly follow. Indeed it is often those filled with the most hate who are most likely to deliver the psychic dagger effectively.

Individual cases of voodoo killings are too numerous to mention. However, a particularly notable example of voodoo curse may be the fate of writer Robert Heini who, while exiled in the USA, published in the 1960s a book highly critical of the then Haitian regime led by the notorious dictator Papa Doc Duvalier. Angered by Heini's book the evil Papa Doc promptly ordered his own witch doctors to place a curse on the writer. In the months that followed an extraordinary chain of ill-fortune dogged Heini and although he was an educated man he gradually came to believe in the curse. Before the year was out Heini died of a cardio-vascular failure, despite having no history of a heart condition. At her husband's funeral Heini's widow, Nancy, professed her own personal belief that the curse had been responsible for the illness which claimed her husband's life.

If a voodoo curse really was the cause of Robert Heini's death in 1971, it certainly would not be the first time that a voodoo-related death has taken place inside North America – or the last. In the markets of contemporary downtown Harlem, black candles, bats' blood and grave-yard dust are amongst the least offensive items on sale. These macabre objects are not designed as jokes, mementoes or such like. They are manufactured exclusively for the serious business of effecting curses. The idea is to buy seven candles and burn them for seven minutes on seven consecutive days over a picture of the intended victim. When graveyard dust is spread across the portrait the curses become more deadly.

In 1978, speaking on a US television programme, police chief James B. Cassidy, commander of New York's 77th precinct, estimated that there were upwards of one hundred practising hourigans (witch doctors) in the Bedford-Stuyvesant section of Brooklyn alone. Cassidy, a black himself, was not taking the threat lightly, since he personally knew of several cases where deaths had apparently resulted from curses being laid. Moreover, black crime syndicates operating protection rackets in the ghettos were increasingly using voodoo to complement their more traditional Mafia-style intimidation.

Since Cassidy spoke out, New York criminologists have confirmed the growing spread of voodoo amongst the city's low life, and point to the details of several grisly murders to support their theory. In 1980 two Haitian refugees were found in the boot of a car parked in a downtown car lot, their ears cut off and their bodies covered in chicken's feet and feathers. In a separate case the following year, the head of a black man was found in a bag, the mouth stuffed with turkey bones. Both these killings bore the hallmarks of Petro Loa's disciples.

Medical authorities across America have also begun to express concern about the growing influence of voodoo in modern society. In 1980 Professor Kenneth Golden of Little Rock, Arkansas, began an extensive study of evidence of voodoo deaths for the *American Journal of Psychiatry*. By 1982 he was able to report more than a dozen cases of cardiac arrests which had no medical explanation apart from the known presence of maleficia. One man, treated by Golden himself, died under a curse laid by his own wife, a self-professed witch. Investigation showed that the woman's two previous husbands had also died in their middle years of sudden heart failures.

If voodoo is alive in the contemporary USA, then nowhere is it more so than in the deep South where large concentrations of blacks still live, a legacy of the slave plantation days. In the southern states deaths as a result of curses laid are not uncommon, yet some are far more striking than others. A particularly curious story came to light in August 1969, when a young black woman staggered into a Baltimore hospital claiming that she was about to die. The doctors at the city hospital who examined her were baffled, for although she seemed perfectly healthy the girl was falling into a slow but steady decline. A specialist was called in who diagnosed acute nervous anxiety and prescribed sedatives. Once the medicine was administered, the patient's heart rate steadied and her breathing returned to normal. Yet two days later, having made what appeared to be a near-total recovery, the girl suddenly died.

The post-mortem could detect no natural cause for the young woman's demise and for a while it appeared that the curious affair would never be solved. Then a nurse came forward with a strange story. It seemed that on the first night the girl was admitted, she had told the nurse something of her background. At her birth, in the Okefenokee Swamp area near Atlanta, Georgia, the girl's mother had apparently been warned by the midwife that her new-born baby was 'hexed' – a voodoo term for cursed. This hex was destined to affect not only the girl who, said the midwife, would not live beyond the age of twenty-two, but also two other girl children delivered the same day. They, she prophesised, would die on their sixteenth and eighteenth birthdays respectively.

Whether or not the mother believed this cruel tale was not clear, but the girl in the Baltimore hospital related that night how the two other girls had in fact died on the appointed dates: one in a car crash, the other shot in a freak gun accident. She now feared for her own life, since her twenty-third birthday was only two days hence. Upon hearing this odd tale, the Baltimore doctors quickly checked their medical records to confirm their patient's date of birth. It was her twenty-third birthday. Further investigation revealed the story was far from fantasy, for the other girls born twenty-three years previously *had* met their own deaths on their birthdays, and in the manner described.

The strange case of the Baltimore woman is by no means unique in the annals of modern medicine. Nor do such anomalies always involve voodoo.

In September 1965 three doctors from a Canadian hospital wrote to the *British Medical Journal* about their experience of a case of a white middle-aged mother in her forties who had suddenly and inexplicably died following a minor routine operation. To begin with the woman had regained consciousness normally, showing every sign of a satisfactory recovery. However, an hour later her condition abruptly relapsed, with rising blood pressure and a soaring pulse rate. Doctors battled to control the mounting crisis but her respiratory system collapsed and death followed within minutes.

As with the Baltimore doctors, the Canadian medical authorities learned only afterwards of the curse that had been placed upon their patient. In this instance it was the woman's daughter who explained how, twenty years before, her mother had been cursed by a gypsy fortune-teller, who had given her until her forty-third birthday to live. True to the prophesy, the day of the woman's death was the eve of her forty-third birthday.

In concluding their report to the *British Medical Journal*, the Canadian physicians professed their belief that the fear of the gypsy's curse had in itself been sufficient to kill off its intended victim. The racing heart rate and muscular spasms were most probably the result, they wrote, of an extreme state of self-induced shock. Quite literally, the woman had frightened herself to death.

Twenty-five years after the event the diagnosis of the Canadian doctors remains open to debate. However the ability of gypsies to effect curses has long been accepted and it is probable that the widespread fear of Romany magic is largely responsible for the hostility the travelling folk have engendered across many parts of the globe. In recent times, of course, gypsies themselves have actively promoted this superstition and encouraged belief in their psychic powers for commercial reasons. Nevertheless, there can be little doubt that many travelling people genuinely believe in the power of their incantations, and in particular the force of the dreaded 'evil eye'. Belief in 'the eye' is universal among Romanies and its contemporary use and misuse is perhaps most prevalent in the Middle East and southern Europe. In both Greece and Turkey, for example, the glance of concentrated hatred is so much feared that women are still officially employed by the state to cure those who have been overlooked in this manner. In Yugoslavia and other Baltic countries, gypsies will not travel without the protection of blue beads on their person as a defence against the eye, nor are they willing to be photographed since they believe that this part of their self may be taken and overlooked without their knowing. In Britain and across western Europe gypsy magic is invariably linked in the public consciousness with the realms of witchcraft and the occult. This is hardly surprising, since in the Middle Ages the spread of witchcraft and Diabolism was so great that an atmosphere of hysteria was generated across the continent. In the terrible purges that followed hundred of thousands were cruelly persecuted. Between the fifteenth and seventeenth centuries over a quarter of a million confessed to practising the art of black magic before being hanged, disembowelled or burnt at the stake. More often than not these witches were hideously tortured into signing their own death warrants and the orgy of official barbarism was doubtless out of all proportion to the actual crimes committed. Nevertheless, most experts agree that a real explosion of witchcraft was sweeping across Europe during this period, albeit on a smaller scale than was thought at the time.

Today the attitude of authorities to the practice of witchcraft is far more tolerant. Yet witches still exist and their numbers are again growing. In 1969, eighteen years after the Parliament of Great Britain repealed the ancient act outlawing witchcraft, English white witch Miss Sybil Leek was quoted as saying that she personally knew of some four hundred covens operating in England and Wales. In a long article which subsequently appeared in the *New York Times*, Leek described how interest in the occult had boomed during the sixties alongside an increased use of LSD and other hallucinogenic drugs.

Although many people felt at the time that the new covens would disperse like so many other fads of the swinging decade the opposite has proven true. Indeed, as we saw in the chapter 'Dark Shadows', so great has been the increased use of psychic evil in the United Kingdom that the British Parliament debated the subject in 1988. Incredible though it may seem, the most recent estimates conclude that the present numbers actively practising the witch's art in England and Wales are double those quoted by Sybil Leek, and the trend looks set to continue.

Has the increase in Diabolism led to a comparable increase in maleficia? It would be unwise to assume otherwise and, in any case the facts speak for themselves.

During the 1970s several mysterious deaths occurred in the Clapham Woods area of the South Downs, Sussex. A place noted for a medieval curse, the woods had more recently become the centre for nocturnal meetings of a black coven. Some said the curse had been reactivated as a result. One of the first victims was a police constable, Peter Goldsmith, whose body was found on 13 December 1972. A coroner's report revealed no signs of violence, nor any evidence of drugs or suicide. Yet no natural causes could be discovered either. Six months earlier the body of a young woman had been found close to the spot where Peter Goldsmith died. In her case, too, no cause of death was ascertainable. Three years later, the corpse of Mr Leon Foster, a walker, was found in Clapham Woods, in virtually identical circumstances. Once again there was no natural cause of death, yet neither was there a suspicion of murder or suicide. Next to die was the Rev. Harry Snelling, who fell prey to the curse on the 31 October 1978 – All Hallows Eve. Snelling had told his wife that he intended to take a short cut through the woods on his way home. He never made it. As in the earlier cases, an inquest failed to find a cause for the clergyman's death, natural or otherwise.

Since Reverend Snelling's death there have been many reports of strange events in the woods on the South Downs. There have also been more unsolved deaths. Can a centuries-old curse still be claiming lives, or were the spells cast much more recently? Either way few locals will venture into the area, and never after nightfall.

Among the phalanx of black artists some grow more famous than others. Britain's most notorious twentieth-century witch was Aleister Crowley, otherwise known as the Great Beast. During his lifetime Crowley, who claimed to have sold his soul to the Devil at the age of fourteen, was reviled by popular newspapers as 'the most evil man alive'. In fact he was a rather ludicrous figure whose pretended excesses were too incredible to be taken seriously, and whose powers of black magic were only seldom proven. But even some of Crowley's curses came true. One of his victims was a young general practitioner, William Brown Thompson, who had angered the ageing Crowley by refusing to prescribe him morphia. In a black rage, Crowley laid a curse upon his physician promising he would take the doctor with him the day he died. When Aleister Crowley descended to Hell on the first day of December 1947, Doctor Thompson died within twelve hours of a cerebral haemorrhage.

Another modern Satanist with the dark gift for prophesy was American Anton La Vey. La Vey, who was employed as a technical adviser on the film *Rosemary's Baby*, established a bizarre religious sect in the mid-1960s dedicated to the worship of the Antichrist. To many people the organisation appeared no more than a tasteless publicity vehicle for the headline-grabbing magician, but when a tragic accident involving one of Hollywood's sex symbols followed hard upon a La Vey death spell people began to take a different view. In 1966 Jayne Mansfield, an actress with little talent but a sensational figure, became interested in the cult Anton La Vey had created. Despite warnings from her studio, she joined the group which later became known as the Church of Satan. To begin with La Vey was delighted with the publicity Mansfield afforded him but things soon turned sour. After they had quarrelled violently Anton La Vey cursed his star disciple, reportedly drawing a red line across the throat of her portrait. A fortnight later, Jayne Mansfield was killed in an accident on the Los Angeles highway. When her body was cut from the wreckage she was found to have been decapitated.

Speaking to reporters the next day Anton La Vey openly claimed credit for her death.

*

In proclaiming publicly the success of his spell, the American magician was demonstrating the supreme advantage of maleficia as a weapon of hate and vengeance. Murder by curse leaves no evidence which can be physically linked to the wielder. Furthermore, the police are powerless to arrest those people responsible since maleficia is not recognised by the modern legal system. Even when a person claims responsibility, as Anton La Vey did, the authorities can do nothing. Of course most killers do not confess their crimes. Hardest of all to prove are those curses where victims expire from apparently natural causes, like Robert Heini who suffered a heart attack. In cases like these, the deaths may not even be considered suspicious, especially since in some instances the victims themselves remain unaware that they have been cursed in the first place. All in all it is not difficult to see why the curse has been called the perfect instrument for a perfect murder.

In China, there is an equally strange and silent method of killing which although not a form of curse is nevertheless a type of maleficia. The delayed death touch of 'Dim Mak' is a technique of assassination deeply rooted in the folklore of many eastern countries. Depending upon the force of the blow, it can bring about death in a matter of hours, days or even months. According to the belief internal injuries, comatose states and death can be deferred for an almost unlimited period of time simply by applying pressure from any one of several key points on a victim's body. Legend holds that Dim Mak is a forbidden technique known only to a handful of kung-fu initiates, or chosen ones, yet several modern martial arts experts from the USA as well as the eastern masters claim to have learned the skill. In fact, the mysterious death of actor Bruce Lee in 1973 was widely rumoured to have been the result of a lethal Dim Mak strike, though, needless to say this was never proven.

If the death touch does exist how exactly does it work?

Fundamental to the mystery may well be 'Ch'i', a concept of life force which eastern mystics believe flows through the human body. Oriental healing disciplines, of which acupuncture is the best known, are based upon the idea that a vital life energy pervades all of existence, and that all illness is caused by imbalances or inharmonies to that flow.

Healers are taught that seven hundred points exist on the human body on which manipulative pressure can be exerted or needles inserted. It is well known that some advanced martial artists believe they can control their own Ch'i rate. Could others have learned at which points deadly pressure could be applied to slowly starve an opponent's vital organs of the invisible life force that feeds them? One American physician who learned both the Oriental's fighting and healing arts is quite certain of the deadly efficiency of a Dim Mak blow. Dr John Painter, whose private clinic in America concentrates on the use of acupuncture, demonstrated the effects of the delayed death touch in a lecture delivered in Washington DC in November 1980. Using a volunteer male nurse, Dr Painter rapidly induced symptoms of rising temperature, wildly fluctuating pulse rate, profuse sweating and convulsions, all from a gentle tap on the forearm. Had Painter not then taken remedial action, as he did, the doctor assured the bemused audience that his guinea pig would have died. Yet Painter went on to claim that a full Dim Mak strike, carefully placed, could not be cured once delivered. Depending on the exact location of the blow, the victim would die in twelve hours or twelve months.

Fortunately for the rest of us, experts who have the knowledge to administer a lethal Dim Mak touch are few and the chance of an accident is apparently very slight. Yet an item in an English newspaper, the *Daily Express*, on 17 February 1976 might suggest otherwise. The newspaper feature told the story of how a brawl aboard a British Merchant Navy vessel, the *Empire Gull*, ended in the manslaughter of an elderly Chinese cook. The cook had been stabbed by a fellow compatriot, who subsequently told police that he had killed the man in revenge. In his statement to the law officers the Asian explained how he had suffered a blow which he believed would eventually kill him. 'He die first; I die later,' said the prisoner. And indeed he did die a few days later in his prison cell, awaiting trial. The reason behind his death proved beyond medical diagnosis.

Psychiatrists have a theory about curses. To the psychoanalyst, evidence that curses can work is nothing more nor less than proof that the human mind has the ability to control the workings of the physical body.

In that sense, and that sense alone, spells and curses are really a question of mind over matter. If a person believes that he will become ill then his mind convinces his body, which in turn begins to show real signs of that which is expected to take place. Thus, say the medical men, the Chinese cook probably died because he was convinced he would; the black woman who faded away on her twenty-third birthday came to believe in the hex placed upon her at birth; the Canadian mother scared herself to death because she believed passionately that her death was inevitable. Undoubtedly this neat psychological theory has much going for it. Psychosomatic illnesses have been proved to exist, and as a researcher who has studied the faith-healing powers of certain gifted individuals I have no doubt about the ability of the human mind to control bodily processes to a remarkable degree. Nor do I deny for one second that an individual can scare him or herself to death; in fact there is even a medical term for the condition – vagal inhibition. The trouble with the psychologists' pat theory, though, is that it does not go far enough to explain all the varieties of recorded curse deaths. For instance, one problem with the psychosomatically-induced suicide theory is that it assumes that the people whose health fails must themselves believe in the curse. This is fine in the examples of closed societies such as Haiti, Africa or India, where the reality of curses is accepted. But it does not go very far to explain cases where cursed individuals are firm disbelievers in the supernatural, and die nevertheless. Nor does it account for those cases where victims are unaware they have been made the subject of a curse in the first place. Vagal inhibition may well have caused the death by a process of auto-suggestion of, say, the young black woman who died in Baltimore because she had a background steeped in voodoo. Yet it would not so easily explain the death of the Canadian mother who was not herself a Romany. The most serious drawback of this death wish theory, however, is that not all curses are effected through illness. For those lives brought to an end by accident or other forms of violent death no logical explanation can be forthcoming.

Some of the most striking examples of curses are those which have been directed against a group of individuals rather than just a single person. Some tales of family curses go back into legend. The fables of the ancient Greeks are full of maleficia, and their most celebrated families suffered worst of all. A notable example was the curse placed upon the house of Atreus by the god Hermes. According to the tale, Hermes was angry because Atreus had killed his son in combat. In revenge he placed a spell upon the entire family of his son's murderer, a spell which eventually was to account for Atreus's son, his grandson and his wife.

Of course, the tale of Atreus and Hermes may have little or no foundation in truth. Like all legends the Greek heroes were most likely the creation of story-tellers' minds and even if the fable had a broad basis in fact, the details were probably embellished. A more recent example of a family curse at work, and therefore a more interesting one, is provided by the events surrounding the death of Scottish prophet Kenneth Ohdur in the early seventeenth century. Ohdur, known as the Brahan Seer, was born with the extraordinary gift of predicting the far future with an uncanny accuracy. His most spectacular prophesies included the coming of the steam railways to Scotland and the discovery and exploitation of the 'black gold' in the sea – a clear reference to the modern oil fields of the North Sea. Like Nostradamus before him the Brahan Seer used his powers of second sight for his own fortune; in this case under the patronage of a Highland aristocrat, the Earl of Seaforth. For years all went well for the Seer until, in 1667, he angered his master's wife by casting an unfavourable prophecy, and was promptly condemned to execution. Ohdur died in agony, boiled alive in tar, but not before he had cursed the Seaforth clan in ominous and quite explicit detail. Speaking to those assembled at his place of execution, the Brahan Seer told of a future Seaforth chieftain, the last of his line, who would be struck deaf. This Seaforth would, proclaimed Ohdur, have four sons all of whom he would follow to the grave. Of his two daughters, one would kill her own sister through a cruel twist of fate. These deaths were to signal forever the demise of the house of Seaforth, yet even this was not to be the end of the curse. As he was being lowered into the tar, Ohdur spoke of a Laird of Tulloch who would be present at the funerals of the accursed Seaforths, and who would himself kill four wives in succession.

Decades passed before the Brahan Seer's words began to be fulfilled. Then, in the early 1700s, a boy child of the Seaforth clan was taken ill with a severe bout of measles, an affliction which rendered him deaf. Despite this handicap the boy grew to manhood to become a baron and Member of Parliament. He married and sired six children: four sons and two daughters. Having fulfilled the necessary criteria for the maleficia to continue, the curse began to work in earnest. First the baron's eldest son William died aged six. The second, George, ended his life in infancy. The baron's third son Francis fared better and reached his early manhood, only to be killed serving in the Navy. The fourth Seaforth heir, Ross, survived the longest and followed his father into politics, becoming elected to Westminster at the age of twenty-four. He died suddenly later the same year of a heart attack. Mortified with grief, Baron Seaforth MP expired soon afterwards, dying some said of a broken heart. Present at his funeral was a lifelong friend Duncan Davidson, Laird of Tulloch, a man who had known his own share of tragedy. Davidson had been married four times and each of his young brides had died in childbirth. In a sense he had killed them, since he had been responsible for their condition.

So concerned was Davidson at the working out of the curse that he spoke to Seaforth's two surviving daughters to warn them once more of the words of the Seer's curse: that one of them would die by the hand of the other. Whether they heeded his advice we shall not know. In any case it was in vain, for five years afterwards the final part of the cruel prophecy came true. The tragedy occurred as the eldest of the two girls, Mary MacKenzie, was driving her sister Caroline towards the place of their birth – Brahan Castle. For some reason the horses bolted and the carriage overturned. Lady Caroline was trapped underneath and died several days later of her injuries, her demise registering the end of the curse and the fall of the House of Seaforth.

The many details correctly predicted by Kenneth Ohdur prior to his death curse provide us with the clearest evidence of maleficia at work. The fate of the Seaforth clan remains a permanent testament to the efficacy of the sorcerer's art long after its victims became dust.

Not all curses take so long to become effective, however. A particularly odd example of a curse affecting an entire community appears to be the evil which descended upon the Lincolnshire seal-hunting village of Fosdyke during a year-long period in 1973–4. Unusually, the curse, which accounted for the deaths of some fifteen people, would seem to have become activated by a form of collective hatred directed towards the inhabitants of Fosdyke rather than one specific individual source. The trigger for the curse was a television film made about the small community and broadcast on British television in April

1973. In the film, a documentary about seal hunting, interviews with local men were interspersed with some particularly unpleasant shots of seals being battered to death. One Fosdyke villager, Len Lineham, described in graphic detail how, along with other local fishermen, he had caught and clubbed over three hundred baby seals the previous year.

The British are a nation of animal lovers and predictably a storm of protest followed the screening of the programme. Whilst thousands wrote to the television company to complain, dozens more wrote poison-pen letters to individual members of the Fosdyke fishing community. Among these were several death threats and curses. Such was the sustained level of hatred engendered by the documentary that the Lincolnshire villagers began to feel as if they had become the subject collectively of a national curse. For sixty-year-old Len Lineham the pressure soon became unbearable. Nine days after the film was shown he shot himself in the head. If the villagers of Fosdyke hoped that the curse would be lifted by Lineham's death they were mistaken. His suicide was to be the beginning of a macabre series of events in the locality. Three weeks after Lineham took his life, his grandson was killed in a road accident and a day later Lineham's niece choked to death. Other deaths in the community followed within months. Two more men were killed in road crashes and a further seven in as many weeks from supposedly natural causes. Most mysterious of all was the drowning of thirty-year-old Colin Runnals, a Fosdyke man whose body was found floating face down in a shallow dyke. Runnals was known to be an excellent swimmer.

As an atmosphere of hysteria began to haunt the Fenland village, religious help was sought to lift the spell. Canon Henry Cooper, then chaplain to the Archbishop of Canterbury, visited Fosdyke, to reassure them that the powers of evil could not finally prevail against the greater power of God. Nevertheless, further deaths continued to dog the hapless seal fishermen until the curse ran its full course, a year and one day after the TV programme was shown.

The ill fortune experienced collectively by the inhabitants of Fosdyke lends credence to the theories of some para-psychologists who believe that hatred itself can be a destructive force. Yet can it be possible that material, inanimate objects might also be imbued with the same hate energy? Objects which themselves become the focus of death and misery over a period of centuries? Many believe so, and there is some evidence to suggest that they may be right. For instance, among the annals of world-wide curse legends, there are countless examples of misfortune befalling grave-robbers and other tomb-defilers. Often these examples involve treasures or sacred relics which have been reputedly bewitched by a subtle form of psychic protection. In such cases ill luck befalls all those who inherit the relic.

The clearest example of this scenario is the chequered career of the gemstone known today as the Hope Diamond, a piece of jewellery destined to bring doom to those who are foolish enough to buy it. The origin of both the curse and the gem itself are lost in the mists of anti-quity. The diamond probably came from northern India and one legend holds that it was stolen from the third eye of a Hindu idol. According to this version, the thief, a Frenchman, escaped the clutches of the Hindu priests who guarded the temple only to be torn to shreds by a pack of rabid dogs lurking outside. True story or not, the details would fit neatly into the pattern of ill luck the Hope Diamond brought to subsequent owners. It was, for instance, acquired by no less a personage than Louis XVI of France, who gave it to his wife Marie Antoinette. Their fate needs no recounting here. Several decades later, after a long disappearance, the stone turned up in London where it became the property of a succession of wealthy people all of whom died whilst in possession of it. Mr Hope himself, a London banker, purchased the diamond in 1830, just in time to see a scandal ruin his reputation.

His business career was finished and he ended his life in a mad house. Further nineteenth-century owners suffered at the hands of the curse. The list includes the French millionaire, Jacques Colet, who died by his own hand; a Polish aristocrat, Prince Ivan Von Kanivorsky, who was murdered; and a Turkish sultan, Abdul Hamid who lost his throne. Unluckiest of all was one Simon Montharides, an Englishman who died along with his wife and small child in a freak riding accident.

In the early part of the present century the Hope Diamond passed into the hands of a wealthy American family, the McLeans, for whom it continued to be an unlucky acquisition. Mrs Evalyn Walsh McLean, who paid $40,000 for the gem in 1922, saw her entire family decimated in the years that followed. Her son died in an accident; her husband went insane, her daughter killed herself. When Mrs Evalyn Walsh McLean herself died some years after this triple tragedy, ownership of the gem passed to her granddaughter, also called Evalyn. The heiress had little time to benefit from the family fortune. In an incident which was never satisfactorily explained, the younger Evalyn was found dead in the room of a Dallas hotel. She was twenty-five.

The history of the Hope gemstone may well demonstrate that diamonds are not necessarily a girl's best friend! More seriously, it also provides as strong a case for the existence of maleficia as one could wish to find.

Those who profess a disbelief in curses and other mysterious forces find examples like the Hope Diamond difficult to explain. Certainly it is hard to apply the psychologists' theory of self-induced death by fear to such examples, since the owners choose to acquire the object of their own free will and usually at considerable expense. If Mrs Evalyn Walsh McLean had believed in the curse, would she have paid $40,000 for it, I wonder?

Archaeologists, that group of investigators whose profession it is to disturb ancient buildings, ruins and burial grounds, would appear to be the ones most likely to fall foul of a curse. If the story of the most famous modern archaeological find is anything to go by, the facts speak for themselves. The discovery of the tomb of Tutankhamen, in 1922, was without doubt the find of the century. For the first time in history a royal tomb of ancient Egypt was seen in all its magnificent splendour complete and intact. Yet the world-wide sensation over the riches was soon to be replaced by stories recording the deaths of the men who found it. Thus was born the legend of the curse of Tutankhamen.

The expedition which uncovered the tomb of the boy emperor began in the autumn of 1922, but the men who headed the team – Lord Carnarvon and Howard Carter – had been on the trail of the Pharaoh for more than fifteen years. Carnarvon was an amateur archaeologist who financed the 1922 expedition from his own pocket. Carter, on the other hand, was a dedicated and highly regarded professional in the field of Egyptology. Together they had searched for years to find Tutankhamen's tomb yet together they were to regret their final success. Neither man could claim to have been ignorant of the curse. In August 1922 Carnarvon received a warning from the famous mystic and clairvoyant Count Louis Hamon. Hamon described how he had received a cryptic message through his spirit guide. The message, written in a trance state through automatic writing read: 'Lord Carnarvon not to enter tomb. Disobey at peril. If ignored would suffer sickness. Death follows.'

The English peer, whilst not being a man given to superstitious beliefs, was nevertheless sufficiently concerned to contact his associate in the venture. When asked for advice, Carter told him that such talk was not for sane men. So, dismissing all thoughts of the curse, Carnarvon went ahead with his plans. The story of Count Hamon's mediumistic warning soon reached the pages of the British press, however, and by the time the archaeologists set sail for their destination, the tales of impending doom had captured public imagination around the globe.

For several weeks nothing was discovered in the Valley of the Kings, and it appeared increasingly likely that this mission would once again end in failure. However, on 4 November 1922, a team of native workers led by Carter found some steps leading down into the sand. Later, with the steps uncovered, the tomb was found. Above its entrance was an inscription in hieroglyphics which, when deciphered by experts in Cairo Museum read:

'Death will come to those who disturb the sleep of the
    Pharaohs.
They shall sicken, they shall thirst.'

Carter ignored the warning and cabled the exciting news to his partner, who had returned briefly to his Hampshire home to conduct some pressing business. Carter's Egyptian work crew were afraid of the curse and refused to go on and it took some time to hire enough men willing to continue the excavation, and then only at greatly inflated wages. But on the morning of 16 February 1923, the excavation was finally completed and the tomb opened. Howard Carter and Lord Carnarvon were the first to enter, followed by distinguished archaeologists from around the world, all drawn magnetically towards the unique event. As it turned out they were not to be disappointed. The boy king's last resting place consisted of four rooms – two antechambers, the burial chamber itself, and a treasure room piled high with fabulous riches. The lid of the Pharaoh's sarcophagus was lifted to reveal an inner compartment of solid gold. The archaeologists were staggered. Clearly this was the most remarkable find of all time, its historical value exceeding every expectation. For Carnarvon and Carter it was the greatest moment of their lives, the consummation of their long search.

As news of the sensational discovery was telegraphed around the world, mention of the tomb's inscription took second place and the legend of the curse faded into the background. Not for long, however. On 6 April 1923, only eight weeks after his moment of triumph, the fifth Earl of Carnarvon died. His passing from the mortal plane was attributed to an infected mosquito bite which had, in turn, brought on a severe attack of pneumonia. Was this the curse at work? asked the newspapers. It looked distinctly possible for, coincidentally, the golden death mask of Tutankhamen had a blemish on its cheek in exactly the same spot that the English aristocrat suffered his fatal insect sting. Moreover, the Earl's death was accompanied by some very strange events, not only in Egypt but in England also. To begin with, a phenomenal vision, a so-called 'wild man' was seen several times running around Carnarvon's Hampshire estate during the first week of the month of April. Odder still, the hour of Carnarvon's death in a Cairo hotel coincided with an unexpected power failure plunging the entire city into an eerie darkness.

Meanwhile, at precisely the same time in England, the Earl's pet dog let out a piteous yell and died.

The demise of Lord Carnarvon was an auspicious beginning for the boy king's curse, since it accounted for one of the two men most responsible for the tomb's defilement. Next to die was not Carter, however, but one of the Earl's closest friends, George Gould, who was unable to make the funeral but travelled to Cairo the following month to pay his respects at Carnarvon's grave. While in Egypt, Gould also visited another burial site – the tomb of Tutankhamen. Within six hours he had collapsed into a coma and a day later, to the bafflement of doctors, he was dead. No reason could be found for his illness. This second mystery delighted the popular press of the day, and, as other members of the excavation team began to die off one by one, the newspaper men gleefully kept count. Within six years, twelve of the original twenty-two people present at the opening of the tomb had themselves been laid to rest. These included: Lord Carnarvon's wife, also a victim of a poisoned insect bite; the Earl's half-brother, who committed suicide; Professor Newberry who opened the royal sarcophagus and subsequently died of heart failure; and Professor Derry who conducted an autopsy on the mummified remains and who first concluded that the boy pharaoh had probably been murdered. When Arthur Weighall, who wrote a book on the subject of the curse, himself fell victim in 1930, only two men were left alive of the group that had witnessed the opening of the tomb. One of these was Howard Carter who died nine years later. The other, an Englishman named Richard Adamson, lived to a respectable old age, although his life was not without tragedy, as we shall see.

Following Howard Carter's death in 1939 interest in the curse story waned and the consensus of rationality was wheeled out once more to explain the mysterious deaths of the Egyptologists in terms of the orthodox. It was, the sceptics agreed, a choice bit of fun while it lasted, but when all was said and done the whole thing was just a coincidence. Archaeologists who had not been present at the tomb's opening stated categorically that there was no proof that a curse existed. 'A contemptuous invention' were the words used by one notable Egyptian expert in the 1950s. His name was Mohammed Ibrahim. Ibrahim, as director of the Cairo Museum for Antiquities, had personal responsibility for the Tutankhamen treasures. He had always decried talk of a curse, yet in 1966, after he was instructed by his government to arrange for an exhibition of the relics in Paris, he apparently received strong sensations of foreboding. The museum director even told a friend how he had been warned, in a dream, to stop the treasures leaving the country.

In the event Mohammed Ibrahim did his duty and defied the threat. The Paris show went ahead as planned, yet two weeks after it opened in the Louvre, the museum director was killed in an automobile accident outside the Egyptian capital. Once more, said believers, the curse had claimed vengeance.

Ibrahim's successor was Dr Gamal Mehrez, also a famous authority on Egyptian history. Since interest in the curse had been revived, Mehrez went out of his way to emphasise his personal unbelief. At the age of fifty, he was, he claimed, living proof of the nonexistence of the curse, since he had himself been working with the antiquities all his adult life. In 1972 Dr Mehrez was, like his predecessor, charged with the task of transferring the Tutankhamen treasures, this time to London for an exhibition at the British Museum. He complied, despite an extraordinary anonymous note he received warning him of his own death if he went ahead. On the evening that preparations were finalised for the transport of the tomb relics, Gamal Mehrez was found dead in his office. An autopsy showed that he had suffered a massive circulatory collapse.

The removal of the antiquities went ahead. An RAF transport aircraft was loaned for the purpose of conveying the treasures in sealed, carefully padded crates. One of the men on that historic flight, Sergeant Brian Rounsfell, then thirty-five, later described how the crew joked about the curse and played cards on the crate containing the royal coffin. As it turned out the crew's levity may have been unwise, for within five years every member of that crew suffered death, or serious accidents. Rounsfell himself survived the period at the cost to his health of two heart attacks. Speaking years later, the RAF man had no doubt that the curse was to blame for his ill fortune.

The 1972 London exhibition was an enormous success with huge publicity fuelled partly by renewed speculation regarding the curse. Of the original excavators only one remained alive, the aforementioned Richard Adamson, then seventy years old. Despite his surprising longevity, Adamson's life had contained a series of personal tragedies at least two of which seemed to be eerily connected with his vociferous opposition to belief in the curse. Some years earlier, the Englishman's wife had died less than twenty-four hours after her husband had spoken out on radio to denounce the legend. Then, on another occasion, Adamson wrote an article voicing the same sceptical viewpoint. On the day it was published, his son broke his back in a plane crash. In 1972, Richard Adamson was due to appear on British Independent Television to explode the myth of the curse once and for all. Before he could reach the studio, however, his taxi collided with an articulated lorry in the city rush hour. Adamson survived, but suffered serious head injuries. Recovering in hospital, he finally accepted, in a statement to the London *Evening Standard*, that the legend may just be true.

'Until this week,' he said, 'I have refused to believe that my family's misfortunes could have had anything to do with the curse. Now I am not so sure.'

Archaeologists are, on the whole, an unromantic bunch. Mention the curse of Tutankhamen to an archaeologist today and you will most probably be met with a tirade of derision. Such was the reaction of the celebrated few who stepped inside the Pharaoh's funerary chamber on that fateful day in February 1923. These learned professors, flushed with excitement at the find of the century, had no intention of allowing some superstitious mumbo-jumbo to get in their way. But get in their way it did, and fatally. It is interesting now to note that in the case of the Egyptian curse, the power of the death spell was indifferent to the disbelief of its victims. There is little room here for cosy psychological explanations. The truth is we have no idea how curses work. To science, it seems irrational that latent psychic power can remain dormant in ancient inanimate objects to bring about disease, accidents and death to those living today, yet enough facts have emerged to support the hypothesis against any amount of logical scepticism. Moreover, methods of cursing hundreds, even thousands, of years old are still practised today and are seen to be effective.

Of the fact that curses exist we can be certain. Why they exist or how they work must remain, at least for the present, incomprehensible.

OUT OF THE BLUE

On 5 May 1982 a funeral taking place in the small American town of Blairsville, Georgia, was interrupted by an extraordinary twist of fate. In contrast to the dismal occasion, the sun was shining brightly as the local preacher, the Rev. Raymond Hewitt said a few final words over the lowering coffin. Doubtless the thoughts of those present were focused upon the slow death from cancer of the deceased, yet it was a different kind of death – sudden and inexplicable – which was about to strike without warning from the clear sky above. Moments before the ceremony could be completed the priest's voice was drowned by a deafening peal of thunder; at the same time a tremendous flash blinded the mourners. When they recovered, it was to find one of their number dead – struck headlong by lightning into the open grave. Some witnesses said afterwards that the words Rev. Hewitt uttered immediately before the strike were, 'We never know what may happen next'. If true, then rarely can a sermon have proved so prophetic.

The ecclesiastical nature of the Blairsville incident provides an appropriate starting point for this chapter, for the gods have long been thought to hurl thunderbolts earthward to administer divine retribution. In Greek and Roman legends lightning was the dart of the heavens. To the Greeks it was the weapon of Zeus; to the Romans, Jupiter. Neither ancient culture allowed victims of lightning strikes to be buried, and the Greeks of the Hellenistic period fenced off areas that had been struck by lightning because they were considered dangerous. For the Israelites of the Old Testament, death by lightning bolt was a sign of the wrath of Jahweh, while the early Christians believed that acts of perjury, profanation and the desecration of holy places would attract the same heaven-sent punishment.

Most people would agree that lightning is an awesome phenomenon and it is probably unsurprising that so many early societies assumed its enormous destructive power to be the work of the gods. For modern man lightning has long since been explained in terms of the scientifically comprehensible. It is, say the meteorologists, merely a spectacular discharge of atmospheric electricity brought about by a natural separation of positive and negative charges. As the charging process increases a 'static field strength' rises to a point where the air itself breaks down electrically, bringing with it the familiar flash. Today, few would argue with the scientific explanation, and only a handful of religious fundamentalists would still claim that the thunderbolt is evidence of God's wrath. However, this is not quite the end of the story. The fact is that lightning strikes occasionally follow a highly selective pattern, quite inexplicable in terms of conventional meteorology.

Moreover, some fatal bolts, like the aforementioned Blairsville example, appear from a clear sky – bolts from the blue in the most literal sense and wholly incompatible with the current explanation of lightning's creation. It is these curious anomalies as well as the odd and quite unnatural side effects that lightning occasionally visits upon its victims which have led many parascientists to the disturbing conclusion that lightning is occasionally directed by a subtle form of intelligence. The kind of intelligence in which we have long ceased to believe ...

It is a common belief that lightning never strikes twice in the same place. This is manifestly untrue. Indeed, some individuals or groups seem to attract lightning with such regularity that they can only be described as moving targets. Consider the following cruel twist of fate, an historical oddity catalogued by several past collectors of anomalous data. In 1899, a man named Luigi Calvi was struck down in the garden of his home in Taranto, Italy. Thirty years later, almost to the very day, the son of the first man was to die in exactly the same way while standing at almost exactly the same spot as his father. Finally the grandson of the original victim was himself struck down by lightning while playing with his own infant son in the garden of the same family home. In this last incident the child was unhurt but the parent paralysed. Vendettas may be fashionable in Italy, but they are not usually conducted by the elements!

This is by no means the most extraordinary example of the vindictive nature of the lightning bolt. It is not always the locality which seems to hold the key to the coincidence; occasionally a person will become the focus. One unfortunate individual who would readily agree is an American, Mr Roy Sullivan, who earns an unenviable place in the *Guinness Book of Records* as the world's most prolific survivor of lightning strikes. Up until now Sullivan has been hit no fewer than five times: in 1942, 1969, 1970, 1972 and 1973. Incredibly the American has not once been seriously hurt, although various parts of his anatomy have dropped off, including his eyebrows and fingernails! A less amusing example of a human conductor is exemplified in the career of one Major William Alan Summerford, a professional soldier in the British army and veteran of the Somme. Having survived the horrors of the trenches unscathed, this luckless officer was struck down by lightning on three successive occasions in the four years following the end of World War I. The last of these assaults led to the major's rapid physical deterioration and subsequent death. Even then Summerford was not spared, his gravestone being shattered by another bolt of lightning a few months after his burial in 1922.

Sometimes whole communities can become the focus of a sustained assault from above. In a two-year period between 1983–4 ten villages in west Donegal, Ireland, registered over one hundred hits on buildings and inhabitants. A wave of hysteria swept through the small rural communities and locals asked priests to seek Papal intercession to save them from God's wrath. Only when the plague of freak bolts ceased did the villagers' terror subside.

Ignoring the cases of specific individuals who attract lightning to a degree which cannot be rationally explained, the overall statistical distribution of lightning fatalities follows a quite bizarre pattern. For instance, it is a fact that women are more likely to be hit by lightning and die of their injuries than men. There would appear to be no logical reason for this. Indeed, given that tall things attract lightning and that the average male is taller than the average female, the reverse might be expected to be the case. Yet the gender gap is enormous, for when one examines the annual global averages three women die for every one man killed by lightning.

It has long been noticed by pathologists that the bodies of those killed by lightning decompose more rapidly than usual. The reason is unclear. However, a stranger property of the lightning bolt is the way in which pictures are sometimes imprinted on to the bodies of victims through some unidentified photographic process. Such impressions appear in the form of light burns on the skin and recorded examples from our own century have included pictures of birds, trees, horseshoes and other multifarious man-made objects. In one example from the late 1880s a rancher from Nebraska, USA, was found to have a detailed outline of the surrounding countryside imprinted on his naked back. In another incident (from 1906) a woman from Unionport, New Jersey was found with burns resembling a pheasant, snakes and Chinese letters. Recent examples of skin pictures appearing upon the corpses of lightning victims include the Midwest of America in 1973, a year in which an unusually high number of individuals died as a result of strikes. Injuries commonly suffered by survivors include a peculiarly intense form of concussion accompanied by a profuse bleeding from mouth, nose and ears. At the same time mysterious red marks appear on the necks and ears of those unlucky enough to be affected. For many, these patches of skin, like strawberry birth marks, have remained as a permanent reminder of their ordeal. Doctors were at a loss to explain the injuries.

Being struck by lightning does not invariably bring about death despite the fact that the lightning charge is estimated to exceed sixty million volts of static electricity and to be five times hotter than the surface of the sun. Occasionally men and women have been known to suffer no ill effects whatsoever, even when their clothing has been blown off in flames, whilst others have survived despite having their skulls cracked open and the soles of their feet burned as the tremendous power surges through them. Perhaps the strangest cases of all are those which involve the therapeutic effects occasionally reported following a lightning strike.

In the nineteenth-century work *The Anomalies and Curiosities of Medicine* by American physicians Gould and Pyne is an account of the recovery from partial paralysis, occasioned by a lightning strike, of a farmer from Careret County. Other instances mentioned by Gould and Pyne include the recovery of an emaciated negress from Georgia, and a blind ex-collier from Ettingsmall, England, who regained his sight after being blasted to the ground during a thunderstorm. Further evidence of the beneficial qualities of the thunderbolt appeared in the form of a story printed in *Fate* magazine in February 1953, which told the remarkable tale of Mr H. Cantrell of Nashville, Tennessee, who was cured of terminal brain cancer after being struck by a lightning bolt outside his house on Thanksgiving Day. The *Fate* report included signed testimonies from doctors and witnesses confirming the miraculous cure.

Traditionally thunderbolts of vengeance are supposed to strike from a clear sky, like the one in Blairsville. Clear sky bolts are impossible scientifically, yet they continue to be reported. According to the publication *Monthly Weather Review* No. 28, there was a well-witnessed occurrence of a bolt from the blue in the long hot summer of 1900, when two Englishmen were struck dead whilst fielding during a cricket match in Somerset. In his book *Lo*, the veteran compiler of oddities, Charles Fort, quotes an example from the French journal *Ciel et Terre*, in which nineteen French soldiers were blasted by a thunderbolt from a clear sky whilst route marching near Bruges in 1893. For several of these men the incident proved fatal. Fort goes on to mention a further curiosity involving two climbers who died on successive days whilst climbing twin mountains in the Alps. In both these incidents, according to witnesses, the mountaineers fell to their deaths after being struck by lightning bolts emanating from above the cloud line. A much more recent counterpart to these stories was witnessed in 1986 by gun experts at the Millpool Rifle Range on Britain's bleak Bodmin Moor. RAF cadet Douglas Davidson, of Helston, Cornwall, was struck down by a single freak bolt according to the *Observer* newspaper, following a light fall of rain from an apparently cloudless sky. Coincidentally, the weather had been freakish across much of Britain that weekend. Still meteorologists could find no satisfactory explanation for Davidson's death.

Bolts from the blue are not the only type of lightning phenomenon which modern science has failed to account for. Ball lightning is a rare and little understood phenomenon in which glowing balls of light materialise and slowly float through the air. Up until recently many scientists were sceptical that ball lightning existed at all. Nevertheless, studies have confirmed that a majority of eyewitness accounts was likely to be genuine and now most meteorologists grudgingly accept that globular luminous masses can be created through some unknown process. What makes ball lightning so strange is that nothing else in nature behaves in quite the same way. Its unique properties include the ability to move against air currents, defy gravity, and pass through solid objects such as walls and doors with ghost-like ease. Sometimes these glowing balls move along wire fences or other conductors; on other occasions they mysteriously materialise inside closed spaces like chimneys or ovens. On rare occasions they have even appeared inside aircraft cockpits.

Much controversy surrounds the size of lightning balls. Most scientists think that the glowing spheres cannot grow larger than twenty centimetres in diameter, yet there have been several reports of balls one hundred times as large. These unnatural monsters appear to behave in a far less benign way than the average lightning ball, which rarely causes damage. For instance, the ancient Hittite King Mursilis II recorded in his Annals that a huge fireball had struck down his arch-enemy Ephesus, the King of Apashash. Three thousand years later, the Archaeological Commission of St Petersburg, Russia, recorded an account of a similar phenomenon falling from the clearest of skies upon the fishing town of Robasero, burning fishermen and townspeople. During the last century, the *Bulletin of the Astronomical Society of France* carried an account of a seventeen-year-old girl from Brittany who was incinerated by a large glowing ball in the kitchen of her parents' farmhouse. A similar fate befell a Devonshire man who stood in the path of a fireball which ploughed up earth for over one hundred yards in December 1895, and a man from Grimsby was blasted by ball lightning in the winter of 1923.

Fireballs can certainly kill more than one victim in a single strike. On Sunday 21 October 1638, a thunderstorm raged along the English valley of Widecombe. During the service of evensong, lightning struck the north-east pinnacle of St Pancras Church, and a huge fireball tore through the assembled congregation, killing four worshippers at prayer, and injuring a further sixty-two. The incident has become part of the local folklore and scorch marks on the wooden beams of the chapel mark the day when a lightning ball brought terror to the simple country community. An incident similar to the one described above took place in France on 11 July 1819, when a fireball created by three successive bolts of lightning manifested itself inside the main church of the town of Châteauneuf, southern France. On this occasion, nine people were killed including the pastor, and a further eighty-two seriously burned.

Examples of fatal encounters with ball lightning prove difficult for scientists to explain. Balls of light often end their life with an explosion, yet usually little heat is given off and bystanders remain unharmed, provided there is an absence of inflammable material in the immediate vicinity. The slaughter at the churches of Widecombe and Châteauneuf does not fit into any available pattern, but as so many witnessed the phenomenon in each case, the evidence cannot be easily derided. Even more troubling for meteorological experts to explain is the growing evidence that fireballs can occasionally act with what appears to be a form of intelligence. According to paranormal investigator Vincent H. Gaddis writing in his book *Mysterious Fires and Lights*: '... They display an independent will and curiosity, circling objects and human beings, entering and exploring houses ... They exhibit either innate intelligence or control by intelligence ... after brief visits they must return to their invisible natural habitat and their temporary vehicles explode or fade away.' Gaddis may well be right to say that lightning balls have an independent will. What he failed to mention was that their will is often homicidal. Examples are not difficult to find. One of the most murderously destructive attacks by a fireball was the incident which took place in the Soviet town of Voronezh, where in the summer of 1952 a glowing ball of fire slowly descended upon a factory producing heavy armaments. The resulting explosion devastated the factory and the surrounding area and, although there were no official figures for dead and injured, it is safe to assume that casualties must have been considerable. Curiously, in the aftermath of the disaster, survivors reported seeing a myriad of small shining globes floating above the rubble. These globes, claim witnesses, actually seemed to be deliberately following those left alive setting their clothes and hair on fire.

Many other accounts tell a similar deadly story. In 1953 a

fireball came to rest beside a thirty-foot-high water tank in Tucumcari, New Mexico, causing it to collapse; a number of houses were demolished and four people killed. In July 1958 several fireballs fell from an overcast sky on to the remote Lappland community of Parajaevarra, fatally burning one man and seriously injuring several others. More recently, on 7 July 1977, two large luminous globes descended upon the audience at an outdoor cinema in Fujian Province, China, killing two children and causing a panic stampede in which more than two hundred were injured.

Two well-witnessed accounts from Third World sources suggest that the force behind the lightning ball may be even stranger than we have so far believed. On 7 August 1970, at eleven thirty a.m., a large spinning fireball hit the small Ethiopian village of Saladore. The glowing ball, about the size of an elephant, proceeded to roll over the village, crushing walls and houses in its path. People and livestock touched by the fiery persecution were badly burned and more than twenty died. After a terrible few minutes the fireball rose once more into the sky and at an altitude of about three hundred feet exploded with a huge flash, leaving misery and destruction in its wake. What troubled Ethiopian officials most about the Saladore incident was the way that eyewitnesses described the fireball's behaviour as wilful and deliberate. It was as if the malicious phenomenon had systematically destroyed the lives of its victims like some messenger of a terrible deity. A similar story emerged in 1980 from Kuala Lumpur, Malaysia. In this incident a row of houses in the Port Kuang district had been gutted by fire following the appearance of a huge glowing ball of red light. Three survivors described how their houses had been attacked by the fireball, approximately ten feet across. Seven residents died in the resulting inferno, and some in the street outside were, they said, chased by the fireball which ignited their clothes. The bemused Malaysian police department blamed these tales on hysteria, and asserted their firm belief that the cause of the fatal blaze must have been arson. No one was charged, however, and the witnesses resolutely stuck to their original story despite aggressive cross-examination.

Perhaps the most convincing proof that lightning balls can display both intelligence and aggression is a reported attack on a party of climbers which took place high up in the Soviet Union's Caucasian mountain range.

On the night of 17 August 1979, the five-man team were awoken by the sudden appearance of a glowing object in their tent. One of their number, Victor Kavunenko, described the ordeal which followed: 'I woke up with the feeling that a stranger had made his way into our tent. Thrusting my head out of the sleeping bag, I froze. A bright yellow blob was floating one metre above the floor.' The 'blob' proceeded to burn each man in turn, 'methodically observing a pattern known only to itself' according to the Russian climber. As it entered the sleeping bags of the men there were screams of agony – Kavunenko himself blacked out after contact with the object, which had the heat of a welding torch. When he regained consciousness the light sphere was still present and the pattern of attack repeated again and again. By the time it disappeared one man, Oleg Korovin, was dead and the rest seriously hurt. Flown to hospital by helicopter, the survivors' injuries were found to be far worse than normal burns; pieces of muscle had been seared right down to the bone. Soviet doctors had never seen anything like it.

No one yet knows how or why ball lightning appears. Antimatter, electromagnetic energy and nuclear fission have all been put forward as a possible energy source, at least among those scientists prepared to accept its reality. As we have already seen with other phenomena, some sceptical physicists maintain that the unnatural cannot and therefore does not exist. Just about the only thing that all experts will agree upon is that lightning is a terrestrial phenomenon which derives its energy from within the earth's atmosphere.

But not all fireballs begin their life in this way. Meteors – large pieces of space gravel – enter the earth's atmosphere at a fantastic speed and in prodigious numbers. A century ago scientists and astronomers alike insisted that meteors were a physical impossibility. Today the US Space Agency NASA reckons that something like two hundred million enter the earth's atmosphere daily. All but a tiny proportion of these are incinerated in the upper regions of the stratosphere, for such is the protective shield of the earth that only a very few fall to the ground. Some of the larger space debris may appear as bright lights in the night sky – shooting stars – and of those that do fall to earth it is rare to find one which weighs more than a few ounces. However, the rare exceptions have disturbing implications for the future of mankind.

At seven twenty a.m. (local time) on 30 June 1908, something massive hit the remote valley of Tungaska, northern Siberia. It had the destructive power of a thermonuclear bomb. The blazing heat of the explosion laid waste an area the size of Leningrad, obliterating forests, herds of reindeer and the sparse population of Russian peasants. To the handful of observers who witnessed it from up to a hundred miles away, the vision appeared like an enormous fireball, filling the entire northern sky. A few seconds after a blinding flash the still, cold air of the tundra region was filled with a low thunderous roar. Then for some hours afterwards the sky turned as dark as night.

Due to the vastness of the Asian continent, this extraordinary cosmic event went almost unnoticed in the outside world, and it was not until nearly twenty years later that it received official recognition in the Soviet Union. In 1930 Professor Leonid Kulik of the Soviet Academy of Science reached the scene of the blast with a team of investigators. In the Tungaska river basin, Kulik found a landscape devastated. Trees in a radius of twenty miles from the blast's epicentre were either flattened or ripped from the ground by their roots. Over two thousand square miles showed after-effects of the explosion. The destruction was on a scale unprecedented in recorded history, and Kulik's men expected to find a giant crater in the middle of it all. To their astonishment, the team of Russian scientists found that the forest at the centre of the affected district remained relatively unharmed. Whatever had happened the explosion had taken place above the earth's surface – in the air.

What really happened at Tungaska? Since the Hiroshima holocaust, the pattern of damage caused by a nuclear air burst has become recognised as being uncomfortably similar to that which scorched the Tungaska region in 1908. In the years following the Second World War, various theories emerged to account for the gigantic explosion. The most startling of these conjectures was that an alien spacecraft may have been destroyed by a malfunction of its nuclear reactor. A second equally fanciful scenario contends that the explosion was the result of a black hole colliding with the earth. Other somewhat more conventional theories suggest that a giant meteor, miles across, may have broken up high in the earth's atmosphere, or that a comet may have changed course to cross paths with our own planet. To this day the truth remains a total mystery. All that we can be sure of, and be eternally thankful for, is that the explosion occurred in perhaps the least destructive area possible in terms of human life on our planet. Apart from the few hundred herdsmen, subsistence farmers and nomads, the loss of human life was minimal. Had the disaster taken place over a city the size of New York or London the death toll would have been counted in millions. On 30 June 1908 the world was lucky. Next time may be different.

Though on a less dramatic scale than the Soviet cataclysm, it is quite possible that several disasters have extraterrestrial (or at least unearthly) origins. On the night of 8 October 1871, the American Midwest fell victim to a series of dreadful blazes. States which suffered widespread fire damage included Iowa, Minnesota and the Dakotas. Large areas of Chicago were enveloped in a veritable firestorm whilst a conflagration in Peshtigo, Wisconsin consumed every single structure and took over nine hundred lives. In all, the trail of fiery devastation left two thousand dead and tens of thousands homeless.

How could so many fires start simultaneously? One survivor of the Peshtigo outbreak spoke afterwards of 'countless fiery tongues' raining down from the skies. Others talked of 'red hot bolts' and 'electric flames'. The tornado of fire which destroyed the entire community apparently lifted burning buildings into the air where they exploded into cinders. Similar stories emerged from each of the twenty-four towns which ignited that night.

The events of 8 October 1871 may go some way to put into perspective the various biblical and historical accounts of 'rains of fire' from the Middle East and Europe. Our own century has, thankfully, been almost entirely free of these heaven-sent terrors, although occasional reports suggest that anomalous phenomena of this type may strike at any time. On the clear, apparently normal, evening of 15 June 1960 thermometers in the small Texas community of Lake Whitney recorded a temperature rise of 70 degrees Fahrenheit in ten minutes. The intense heat activated sprinkler systems and terrified locals went outside to see the sky above glowing bright orange. The following morning farmers awoke to find their crops scorched black. The Lake Whitney incident, the effect of which was highly localised, has never been repeated in the Lone Star state and remains inexplicable to geoclimatic experts.

Some say the world will end in fire, some say in ice. Giant hailstones have often proved fatal to those caught beneath a particularly violent shower. Accounts of hailstones the size of golf balls are considered scientifically possible in some tropical countries, yet falls of hail even larger still have baffled meteorologists from around the world.

The *Bombay Telegraph* reported on 21 May 1850 that

between the hours of four and five o'clock in the previous afternoon, hail the size of mangos fell on a village near Scattara. Several houses fell under the onslaught and many cattle were killed. Much more recently, on Monday 31 September 1985 a similar hailstorm killed twenty-two and injured nine hundred in the Brazilian state of Minas Gerais, whilst in a massive Chinese hailstorm of 1986, an estimated one thousand people died and thirty-two thousand were made homeless. In the last case some hailstones were recorded weighing several kilos. Not all bombardments of this variety emanate from extreme climates.

The US monthly *Weather Review* documents an occasion in the early 1900s when thousands of sheep in Texas were the victims of an icestorm. In 1950 a farmer in Exmoor, England, woke one morning to find his fields littered with ice lumps the size of soup plates, one of which was embedded in the neck of one of his flock. Even more extraordinary than the giant hailstorms mentioned above are the occasional falls of single ice blocks. For decades meteorologists have dismissed such reports but in April 1973 a particularly prodigious item fell conveniently a few feet in front of weather expert Dr R.S. Griffiths of Manchester University as he was walking home one evening. The block disintegrated on impact, but the quick-thinking scientist picked up the largest piece and put it in his deep freeze at home. It soon became part of vital evidence to support the belief of parascientists that unnatural ice falls do take place, since chemical tests proved that the ice Griffiths found could not have fallen from an aircraft. Even more interestingly its structure was quite different to that of conventional hailstones. What tests failed to identify was the probable cause of the ice formation.

That a single mass of ice could crystalise in the upper atmosphere seems improbable, yet modern examples of ice falls are too numerous to dismiss as fantasy. In Britain alone more than a dozen large ice blocks have dropped from the skies during the past decade, in several cases causing serious structural damage to property. It is inconceivable that any atmospheric process could form and sustain heavy objects in the sky long enough to grow into such a mass; nevertheless that is exactly what would appear to be happening.

Occasionally, ice falls take place which defy rationality completely. On 14 August 1849 the London *Times* reported in detail the fall of a single large ice mass, weighing over half a ton, upon grassland near Ord, Ross-shire in Scotland. Luckily, no one was close enough to be hurt, although many witnessed the object's descent which followed a single massive peal of thunder from an unnaturally darkened sky.

Less fortunate was a German carpenter who died whilst mending the roof of a house near Dusseldorf on 10 January 1951. Killed instantly, he was found skewered through the chest by an ice spear six inches in diameter and with a length of no less than ten feet.

The contemporary explanation for the phenomenon of single ice bombs is that they are the result of ice building up on the underside of aircraft wings. This explanation is clearly inadequate since, as we have seen, many examples of heavy ice falls predate the invention of powered flight. Indeed the aircraft explanation backfired somewhat in 1930 when five human corpses fell out of the clouds on to the Rhon Mountains in Germany, each individually encased in ice! Yet the strangest of all forms of aerial phenomena have yet to be mentioned. These are the falls of solid matter, beside which the forms of coloured ice, salt crystals, hailstones of calcium carbonate and rains of nitric acid seem almost commonplace.

Oddest among all falls of material are the falls of organic matter, living or dead. Curious examples include rains of live frogs and fish, fresh flowers and rotting animal flesh. Such reports have come in from all corners of the globe and regularly pop up today in the human interest columns of the popular press. Fantastic they may be; fantasy they are not.

The list of physical matter which has inexplicably found its way from above is endless. Live eels in Wessex; grilled catfish in South America; dead canaries in Louisiana. In 1718 gelatinous matter fell upon Lethy Island, India, accompanied by a glowing fireball. In 1880 milk fell in thousands of gallons upon Morocco. In California strips of human flesh floated to the ground in 1869; flakes of dried mutton descended in Kentucky seven years later.

The procession of bizarre sky-born curiosities has continued during the present century. On the afternoon of 2 July 1901 toads fell in such quantities upon Minneapolis, Minnesota that roads and sidewalks across four blocks were covered in the living green mass to a depth of three inches. Just after dawn on the morning of 25 October 1947 thousands of fresh-water fish landed on roofs of buildings in Marksville, Louisiana. Sometimes even large animals have been known to fall. In 1911 a two-foot-long crocodile dropped into a garden in Evansville, Indiana; in 1960 an even larger specimen of the same species fell to earth at Long Beach, California.

Compared with previous centuries the modern world seems particularly rich in strange falls, though this may simply be because people are reporting them more frequently. In North America during the 1980s alone falls of organic matter have included eels, crabs, snakes and, on one notable occasion, a monkey! During the same period the United Kingdom has seen localised rains of winkles, jellyfish, eggs and a wide variety of vegetables. No less extraordinary are falls of inanimate objects. World wide these include molten lead, red-hot pieces of cast iron, heavy chains, nails, crockery, crucifixes, limestone boulders, hot ash, sulphur and various unidentified slimy substances. That the reliability of such reports is held in question by orthodox science is quite understandable for stories such as these defy all scientific principles. Any speculation upon the origin of creature falls is pointless, and talk of freak winds and the like merely serves to emphasise the hopelessness of such a direction of rational inquiry.

Fortunately, falls of man-made and organic matter rarely result in injury or death for humans. However, rains of blood or fiery crosses double as omens for coming misfortune, wars, plagues and pestilence. Homer tells of bloody showers that fell upon the Greek heroes of Troy before they were destined to fall in battle. Reference to similar events can be found among Roman legends and chronicles. Invariably they were followed by some general misfortune and their appearance caused widespread panic among the populace. St Gregory of Tours the sixth-century French historian recorded in AD 582 that a prolonged rain of blood preceded a plague, whilst a similar preternatural phenomenon was recorded across Europe prior to the Black Death pandemic of the mid-fourteenth century. In March 1181 blood red rain fell widely upon central regions of France and Germany on the three days and nights prior to an outbreak of war between the two states; a similar three-day-long shower of blood on the Italian town of Brescia was followed by the death of Pope Adrian II on the fourth day.

A list of unnatural rainfalls and other weird aerial phenomena was compiled by the nineteenth-century French astronomer and writer Camille Flammarion. In his book *The Atmosphere*, Flammarion mentioned over forty examples of showers of blood before 1800 and a further twenty-four since. In almost all these cases, the red rain preceded some specific death or general disaster.

Lightning bolts from a clear sky ... fireballs ... ice bombardments ... rains of blood and frogs ... these are not your common meteorological hazards. Nor are they, in fairness, particularly dangerous when compared to more traditional sky-born agents of death – hurricanes, torna-does, whirlwinds, floods, swarms of locusts etc. which between them are responsible for millions of fatalities every year. Yet here in this curious selection of oddities we are once again faced with the irrational, things which logic tells us should be impossible. They exist nevertheless.

In accepting this evidence, we are faced with the truth that we live in a universe whose laws are alien to us, whose forces are not only beyond human control, but are also beyond human comprehension. It is a truth that official bodies would prefer us not to recognise.

<u>INTO THIN AIR</u>

In 1978 a world-renowned atomic physicist Professor John Halstead of Birkbeck College, London, produced some remarkable evidence for the potential reality of the telekinetic movement of solid matter. Halstead placed pieces of metal in a hermetically sealed glass container and attempted to influence them psychokinetically so that they would bend, twist or fracture. For his tests he invited children with a history of psychic powers to concentrate upon the objects. Some of the metal pieces did bend, whilst others, when examined under an electron microscope, were found to have had their molecular structure altered. Most sensational of all, and quite unexpected, were occasional examples of objects disappearing altogether. Sometimes these disappearances were only temporary; other times they were permanent. In his conclusions published the following year, Professor Halstead considered it likely that there is around us a parallel space or subuniverse into which under certain conditions terrestrial matter can dissolve. He considered teleportation to be a faculty of the human mind whose discovery was only just around the corner and he further conjectured that by the middle of the next century it may have become the most common form of travel. Not surprisingly, Halstead's conclusions were derided by many fellow scientists. Yet since his research was published in 1979, similar experiments have been carried out in Berkeley and Stanford Universities in the United States with comparable results.

Startling though Halstead's projections for tomorrow's

modes of travel might seem, human teleportation is really nothing new. Between the years 1620 and 1631 a young Spanish nun made over five hundred teleportations from her convent in Agreda to Central America, where she set about converting the Jumano Indians to Christianity. At first Sister Mary's superiors were infuriated by her tales of flights across the ocean, yet her story was conclusively confirmed by officials of the Catholic Church who were themselves working at the time with the Mexican Indians. James A. Carrico's *Authorised Life of the Venerable Mary of Agreda* sets out in clear detail the evidence of her missionary visits: 'That Mary really visited America many times is attested by the logs of the Spanish Conquistadors, the French explorers, the identical accounts of tribes of Indians a thousand miles apart ...'

Not all such stories have a happy ending. In 1655 the Inquisition put on trial a man who, to his own considerable surprise, was suddenly teleported from the Portuguese colony of Goa in India back to his own native country. Found guilty of witchcraft he was burnt at the stake.

Extraordinary though these teleportations may seem the subject of this chapter is a far more bizarre and much more disquieting phenomenon than matter transference from one terrestrial location to another. The possibility of the complete and permanent vanishment of human beings into thin air is something that most of us would prefer not to consider. Yet the uncomfortable fact remains that there is a long and growing list of instances where solid flesh-and-blood human beings have vanished, not metaphorically – but quite literally – into space. We cannot talk of the deaths of such people, yet we can date precisely their last moments on earth. What happens to them after their disappearance is anyone's guess. The nature of the force which claims them is beyond our comprehension. All we can know for certain is that such vanishments strike suddenly, silently and without warning.

The list of those among the missing is endless, covering all classes of people and all manner of circumstances. On

12 December 1829 a New York State Supreme Court Judge named John Lansing walked out of his hotel to post some urgent mail in a box thirty yards away. He never returned. On the afternoon of 28 March 1905, Charles Austin, an unemployed labourer from Yonkers, went into his back yard to fetch some coal. When he failed to come back in his wife found the yard deserted, though the walls were too high to be scaled. Mrs Austin never saw her husband again. On 12 December 1910 a society girl called Dorothy Arnold went missing after stepping inside a fitting booth in a fashionable Fifth Avenue store. When she failed to come out, assistants found the cubicle empty. Dorothy Arnold remains a missing person to this day. In January 1975 Mr and Mrs Jackson Wright stopped in the Lincoln Tunnel whilst travelling to America's biggest city. Mr Wright got out to wipe snow from his windscreen, a task taking only a few seconds. When he got back inside his car his wife was gone.

Four unsolved disappearances from a single American state. Yet despite its high crime rate, people are no more or less likely to vanish in New York than anywhere else – at least not unnaturally.

Might there not be a perfectly rational explanation for these enigmas? Perhaps ... but then what of the many similar examples? How might we explain, for instance, the fate of James Regan, a passenger aboard the liner *Prince Heinrich* who vanished on the night of 28 January 1914 from inside a locked cabin whilst en route from Marseilles to Naples? What became of Louise le Prince, the brilliant French inventor who disappeared from a sleeping compartment of a train in September 1890? Did a similar fate befall Carnegie Whiteland, heir to a fortune, whose plane was lost over a densely populated area after taking off on a twenty-two-mile hop from Long Island on the clear bright morning of 17 April 1938? No trace was ever found of the aircraft or its young pilot, a fact which, as the press remarked at the time, was impossible. No less impossible was the total oblivion which marked the last journey of the Mississippi riverboat steamer *Iron Maiden*, lost along with every one of its fifty-two passengers and crew in June 1872. A search of the river waters found no sign of wreckage; it was as though the boat had never existed. Only the mystery of its whereabouts remained.

The phenomenon of strange disappearances goes back to the beginning of recorded history and some examples have entered into the realms of folklore. In the English West Country county of Somerset a particularly celebrated mystery surrounds the vanishment of Owen Parfitt two centuries ago. Parfitt, an old man at the time of his disappearance, had been a wild and colourful character in his early years. He had adventured in the New World and skippered a slave trader before he was thirty. Later, according to his own boasts, he had carved a bloody reputation for villainy on the high seas and sent many an innocent soul to a watery grave. All this may or may not be true. We do know, however, that Owen Parfitt was by 1769 a crippled and arthritic old sea-dog who was spending his retirement years at his niece's comfortable cottage near Shepton Mallet, Somerset. It was from there that he was to vanish.

Parfitt was last seen by his niece Susanna Snook, who had left him sitting on a chair on the veranda while she ran a short errand. When she arrived back at the cottage, having been away less than half an hour, she found the old sailor gone. This somewhat surprised her since she knew her uncle to be feeble and immobile; yet it soon became clear that he was not inside the house, nor was there any sign of the old man in the surrounding countryside. Susanna Snook assumed that he must have been carried off by a third party, yet when she spoke to labourers at work in the next field they informed her that no cart had passed that way all morning – nor had they seen her relative. Only then did it begin to occur to the young woman that something truly inexplicable had happened.

In the days following Owen Parfitt's disappearance the

area was thoroughly searched by local officers of the law who treated the case as one of criminal abduction, even though nobody could imagine why anyone should wish to kidnap the irascible old man. Meanwhile, superstitious locals whispered darkly that 'Old Nick' had spirited away Parfitt's body in payment for his life of sinful misdeeds. As the weeks passed with no sign of the cripple this supernatural theory gained ground and the disappearance of the ex-mariner gradually entered into West Country folklore. Today, more than two hundred years after the Shepton Mallet happening, it is most unlikely that the truth will ever be known.

The fate of the eighteenth-century cripple bears stark similarities to many disappearances which have taken place more recently. In particular it mirrors closely the circumstances surrounding the vanishment of a Cambridgeshire man who went missing from his home on the night of 5 June 1975. Donald Dent, a forty-year-old stallion keeper, was last seen by his wife, Valerie, sitting in his front room watching television. Having spent several days off work with a throat infection, Dent was taking it easy and allowed his wife to cook him a supper of ham, eggs and sausages while he sat back and put his feet up. Valerie Dent then left her husband to enjoy his meal while she went upstairs to talk to her teenage son who also was unwell with mild influenza. A mere fifteen minutes later, at a quarter past nine, Mrs Dent left her son's bedroom and returned downstairs to make the family a hot drink. Pausing to ask her husband whether he would prefer tea or coffee, she was surprised to find the front room deserted. The ham and eggs she had prepared were half eaten and lay on the tray beside his empty chair; the television was still on. Yet Donald Dent himself was nowhere to be seen, nor would he ever appear before human eyes again.

To begin with Mrs Dent thought that her husband must have gone outside for some fresh air. Then, when after a short while he did not return, she got into her car and made a small tour of the local lanes. There was no sign of her husband. On returning, Valerie set about phoning all the people she could think of that her husband could conceivably have visited. Finally, when this line of enquiry also proved negative, she reluctantly called the police. The official investigation launched by the Newmarket Constabulary in June 1975 included a thorough search of the surrounding farmland. It uncovered no clue as to Dent's whereabouts nor was anything ever found to suggest that he had deliberately chosen to leave. To this day none of Dent's family or friends have heard from him, nor have any been able to offer a logical explanation for what took place that night. As Mrs Valerie Dent was later to say to a reporter, 'The whole thing is an unbelievable nightmare, it all seems so impossible'.

A still more recent disappearance to baffle those who knew him was that of the Rev. Philip Smith, a minister of the United Reform Church, from St Helens, Liverpool. On the afternoon of 27 February 1984 the clergyman was driving home after lunching with friends; he never arrived. His car was found with a flat front tyre parked on the side of a busy dual carriageway. From its open car boot it would appear certain that Smith had been attempting to change the faulty wheel. What force removed him suddenly from the spot is less clear.

Those people who prefer natural explanations to supernatural enigmas will probably take comfort from the fact that the vanishments of Parfitt, Dent and Smith were unwitnessed. Is it not possible therefore that the men could have removed themselves physically or at least have been removed by other people from the vicinity in which they were last seen?

Unlikely as this seems it clearly cannot be ruled out. However, there have been many examples recorded where human beings have actually been seen to vanish before the eyes of others. In some cases the same incident has been witnessed by several individuals – and the stories they tell are strange tales indeed.

One incident which occurred in the full view of several

other people was the case of Tennessee farmer David Laing who vanished from this earth in September 1880 whilst walking across a forty-acre field on his Sumner County homestead. Details of this preternatural happening, which has now become something of a classic in the annals of the unexplained, can be found in almost any book on the subject of mysteries. Minor details may vary, but the significant ones remain consistent in the published accounts. According to most versions the events of the morning of Tuesday 15 September 1880 were as follows: Laing was expecting a visit from his brother-in-law, August Peck, a local judiciary in the nearby town of Gallatin. Seeing his relative's horse and buggy approaching, Laing set off across the pasture to meet him. Meanwhile, Laing's wife and two of their children watched and waved from the porch of their farmhouse. It was at that moment, as Judge Peck's carriage drew closer to his brother, and in the full sight of all his relatives, that the physical form of the farmer vanished, instantaneously melting into thin air. When his horrified family reached the spot where he had been they found only empty space.

The incredible story of David Laing's vanishment spread like wildfire across Sumner County and for months the morbid and the curious came to view the scene of the extraordinary phenomenon. The local sheriff, who might otherwise have dismissed the story out of hand, was persuaded by the learned August Peck to treat it as a serious investigation. Consequently, the bemused lawman did the only practical thing he could think of – he directed a party of volunteers to drill and dig down into the pasture at the precise spot where Laing was last seen. Their quest proved fruitless. Even so the efforts of these men did result in one bizarre sequel to the Laing story. For whilst they were working several believed that they heard the faint voice of the vanished farmer calling out for help. Curiously, the sounds did not seem to come from beneath the ground but from above their heads. Later, almost a year after the initial disappearance of their father, Laing's two youngest children also claimed to have heard his voice distinctly on two consecutive evenings. The aural phenomenon, real or imagined, did not recur after the anniversary of Laing's disappearance. Yet even though the phantom voice was not heard by humans, it may well have remained audible to animals, for accounts relate how in the years following no livestock ventured close to the original spot where Laing disappeared and the grass surrounding the area grew rank for a diameter of some thirty yards.

Three decades later a fate similar to that of the Tennessee farmer was suffered by a young Welsh boy, Oliver Thomas, who vanished outside his home near Rhayader on Christmas Eve 1909. Whilst a party was in progress inside, the thirteen-year-old Oliver was sent to fetch some water from the family's well. When he did not return, a search was carried out by lantern light. The boy's footsteps could be traced in the snow to a point seventy feet from the house, where they abruptly ended. No other footsteps were apparent. The next morning, Christmas Day, a search party was formed from the congregation which had arrived to sing festive carols at Rhayader Chapel. They scoured the countryside to no avail. However, once again this was not quite the end of the story. For although Christmas Eve 1909 was the last time the parents of Oliver Thomas saw their son, it was by no means the last time they heard him. For several weeks following the boy's disappearance, Oliver's mother and father both claimed to have heard their son's voice at the location where his footsteps had halted. Like David Laing, the boy seemed to be calling out in distress. Similarly the ghostly pleas seemed to be coming from above.

What unnatural fate could have befallen these two people? Might they perhaps have remained alive, trapped within some invisible force field? Or did they unwittingly step through a transparent portal into a different, but not entirely separate dimension? Faced with a set of possibilities so unpalatable to the rational mind, it may seem

197

pointless to attempt to construct theories to explain these incidents. Nevertheless some have tried to do just that. Earlier this century author and investigator Harold Wilkins made a study of all aspects of psychic phenomena including the disappearance of material objects. In particular he was intrigued by the instances where people were transported or teleported across vast distances, as well as those cases of permanent disappearance such as the ones outlined above. Wilkins knew of the scientific belief that matter could not be created or destroyed and agreed with it. Yet like the eastern mystics he also contended that mind and matter were inextricably intertwined: that matter was mind stuff in itself, 'mind-modified'. In this way Wilkins postulated an opinion that the bodies and minds of people who disappear have not been destroyed at all but are simply transformed by some unknown process, imprisoned in a kind of supernatural suspended animation. Backing up his theory, Harold Wilkins cited a mystery from 1906 where three English children vanished from outside their home only to be found four days later in exactly the same place. In this case, the Vaughan children, a boy of ten and his two sisters aged eight and seven, went missing while playing in a field adjacent to their parents' farmhouse in Gloucester, England. The alarm was raised and for three days an extensive search was carried out by the local constabulary with the assistance of helpers from the village. By the third day of the hunt more than two hundred people were involved, yet despite this abundance of manpower no clue was uncovered as to the children's whereabouts. As day four of their search dawned, the police were planning to widen their search area when they suddenly discovered all three Vaughan children safe and well, sleeping peacefully in a ditch less than fifty yards from their home. The searchers were stupefied as they had combed the area thoroughly and crossed the ditch several times at the point where the children were found. It was wholly unreasonable, therefore, to assume they had simply missed them during the previous seventy-two hours.

Equally unlikely, however, was the possibility that the three youngsters had re-entered the search area from outside. For their part, the Vaughan children could offer no explanation for their absence, nor had they any recollection of the missing time period. The whole experience was a blank, just as if it had been erased from their collective memories.

Referring to the missing time period apparent in the Gloucester enigma, Harold Wilkins considered the 1906 incident evidential of his own 'suspended animation' theory. Making a detailed study of this and other similar occurrences from the United Kingdom, Wilkins then went on to construct a second hypothesis: that strange disappearances only take place, or were at least much more likely to take place, in areas where the evidence of unknown energies was present. Places in this category, said Wilkins, included those countryside areas where witchcraft had been practised in the past or where a configuration of ley lines came together. Neolithic burial mounds and places used in the distant past as centres for ritual sacrifice were also, he felt, conducive to vanishing phenomena and a whole range of other preternatural manifestations. Drawing together a patchwork of reported experiences he had accumulated during his years of research, Wilkins published his findings in a book entitled *Mysteries Solved and Unsolved*. One reviewer called it 'an exercise in wild guess work which dealt with largely unproven and unprovable stories'. In fact it was an earnest and intelligent attempt to make sense of indisputable and verifiable facts. Yet *Mysteries Solved and Unsolved* is, in its final analysis, unsatisfactory, for whilst Wilkins suggests areas where strange vanishings might occur, he is never able to tell us how or why they actually happen. And this, as I have long since discovered, is the key question.

Not all mysterious disappearances require supernatural explanations, however. Some stories of vanishing people are no more or less than that – just stories. One celebrated incident which turned out to be a fiction pure and simple was the Hanging Rock affair of 1901, where three girls from a private school supposedly went missing in the Australian Outback. Although most people assume otherwise, neither Peter Weir's excellent film nor the atmospheric novel on which it was based hold a single grain of truth.

The mystery never took place and the individuals portrayed never existed. At the same time people do go missing in reality for a whole range of distinctly unmysterious reasons. A particularly common type of disappearance which owes little or nothing to supernatural causes is the one in which a person deliberately leaves home in order to make a fresh start. Pressures of life are great and many people become so frustrated, unhappy or bored with their everyday existence that they feel the need to escape completely from their own identity and begin a new life under a different name. Many individuals are neurotic or suffering from a more serious mental illness when they do this, but many more make the decision consciously and rationally. Either way their sudden exit from the presence of their friends and families may seem uncanny to those left behind – but in fact the event was predictable.

A separate version of this self-exiled vanishment is the fugitive from the law. Of all those modern instances of this type the most memorable disappearance must surely be that of John Stonehouse, a Labour MP and former Cabinet Minister, who faked his own death in 1974 so that he might run off with his mistress. Having previously perpetrated a fraud in London, Stonehouse went missing after going swimming whilst on holiday in the West Indies. He had hoped that his death would be accepted by the authorities, yet the whole affair was bungled and within weeks the embezzler was brought back to England to face a prison sentence. Stonehouse was not the only British Member of Parliament to disappear this century. Victor Grayson, also a politician on the Left, vanished in August 1920 after boarding a night train to Liverpool. Like his later counterpart, Grayson had enjoyed a measure of political success and had won respect as a fiery orator and dedicated campaigner against injustice. Unlike Stonehouse, however, his own vanishment was to prove permanent and was never explained. Having stepped aboard the northern-bound train at London's Euston Station Grayson was never seen again. It was considered unlikely that he could have fallen or thrown himself from the carriage since a search of the line produced no corpse, and none of his colleagues could suggest a reason why the Labour man might have chosen deliberately to end his career in such a fashion. To this day the curious fate of Victor Grayson remains an enigma, and is just one more case of an individual who vanished into thin air.

Examples of disappearances which were later proved to have been planned by those at the centre of the mystery provide helpful ammunition for those disbelieving rationalists who prefer to think that natural explanations lie behind all such cases. However, if the vast majority of vanishments can be explained in this way, a stubborn few defy all the known laws of science. One such example was the subject of a report carried by the Scottish *Daily Express* newspaper dated 27 December 1971.

The feature comprised an interview with two brothers, the Cleghorns, who described how, as they had been walking along a Glasgow main street five years earlier, they had seen their younger brother disappear before their eyes. The incident had, they told, happened on New Year's Eve 1966, when the three kinsmen were on their way out for a drink. According to their tale, their brother Alex, then nineteen, was walking between them when instantaneously he vanished like a ghost into the crisp night air. Due to the fantastical nature of this story the *Express* report went on to point out that the city's police department compared it to other similar cases this century. The report also mentioned how the two surviving Glaswegian brothers had gone back every New Year's Eve to the same spot, hoping that their lost kinsman might return by some miracle. To that date he never had.

The Scotsmen's testimonies, impossible though they sound to most people, are in fact only one of many similar tales told by vanishment witnesses over the years. One equally well-authenticated case comes from the last century. The victim was James Worson, a cobbler by trade and a hard-drinking bruiser by reputation. A boastful, arrogant fellow, Worson had, it seemed, a penchant for vain and foolish wagers, and on 2 September 1873 he bet a man that he could run all the way to Coventry, a distance of some fifteen miles. The wager was accepted, and according to the story the half-drunk cobbler set out the next morning accompanied by two friends, Hamerson Burns and Barham Wise. Shouting encouragement and abuse by turns, the two cronies followed a few paces behind in a horse-drawn cart watching delightedly as Worson's legs grew steadily weaker. Long before the halfway stage was reached it became clear that the braggart had bitten off more that he could chew; out of breath and sweating profusely, he was on the verge of exhaustion. Yet before he had a chance to give up, something inexplicable occurred. Still in the middle of the road and in the full view of his comrades, James Worson stumbled, pitched forward and with a single sharp cry of pain or fear, disappeared into the cobblestones beneath him. Burns and Wise, dumbstruck with astonishment, jumped down from their cart and rushed to the spot. There they found not a single trace that their friend had ever existed, nor a sign of what might possibly account for his sudden demise. No hole was visible that could have admitted his physical form, nor was there even a crack which could have conceivably closed above him. Neither they nor any other living person was to see Worson again.

Stories like the two above leave little room for the rationalist viewpoint. If one accepts that they happened at all then the reasons behind them must be unnatural. One man who made a detailed study of the Worson case and other witnessed dematerialisations was an American journalist called Ambrose Bierce.

A serious-minded individual who accepted the value of human testimony above all other things, Bierce had no time for the rationalists whose sole argument was that if a thing was impossible then it could not happen. He knew that impossible disappearances were happening because men were regularly reporting them. Fascinated by the phenomenon, and using all available material and accounts of witnesses, the American compiled a complete dossier on the subject over a period of several years. The evidence gathered, plus his own thought-provoking conclusions, was eventually published in a lengthy magazine article entitled simply 'Mysterious Disappearances'. In the article Bierce put forward an interesting theory as to the possible reasons behind vanishing people. In certain places, so he argued, a psychic whirlpool or vortex might become created in the ether – the mind stuff which occultists believe to lie behind the physical universe. In this void, which he conjectured may be like a dark room, no light, sound, heat or thought could ever enter or emanate from once closed. Like the cells in Swiss cheese the etheric whirlpools might exist within our visible world yet remain separate from it, and only those unfortunate enough to be trapped inside one would know positively of their whereabouts.

To those who seek an explanation for vanishment Ambrose Bierce's psychic whirlpool idea is attractive since it accounts for the way vanishing people sometimes seem to melt or dissolve into apparently solid forms, such as the cobbled road into which James Worson fell headlong. Not only that, but the void in which men are held, perhaps for eternity, may conceivably occupy the same geographical location, explaining the voices noticed after the disappearances of both David Laing and Oliver Thomas. Most intriguing of all, however, is the fact that Ambrose Bierce's conclusions, published over seventy years ago, parallel almost exactly the opinions of some modern scientists with regard to one of the universe's astronomical mysteries: the black hole. Whilst the exact nature of black holes is little understood, it is taken as proven that they are the product of collapsed stars, or star systems, whose gravitational mass has caused an area to be created from which nothing, not even light, heat or radio waves can escape. Could it be that such geometric quirks exist not only in deep space but also on the surface of our own planet as a small supernatural counterpart to the huge natural aberration in physical laws?

One piece of testimony that points towards the possibility of mini black holes was the reported experience of two elderly Victorians, staying in a Bristol hotel in 1873. Their story was reported in *The Times* in December of that year, a few months after the same paper carried a piece about the vanishment of James Worson in the West Midlands.

The Times story related how the couple, a Mr and Mrs Cumpston, had witnessed a black chasm slowly open up in the floor of their hotel suite. Apparently Mr Cumpston almost fell into the yawning pit as, panic-stricken, he and his wife fled the room. The report went on to describe how the couple were found an hour later by police, huddled in the waiting room of the local railway station suffering from severe shock. Did the elderly Cumpstons simply have a bad dream or had they encountered a horror more frightening than any human nightmare could produce? Ambrose Bierce would probably have favoured the latter alternative, and had he have lived he may well have included the strange story of the Cumpstons in his planned sequel to 'Mysterious Disappearances'. Instead the American journalist himself vanished without trace whilst covering the Mexican Revolution. His fate was never discovered.

Whatever natural or unnatural end may have befallen Bierce, his whirlpool theory has lived on to be taken up and adapted by a new generation of researchers. Amongst these are a group who feel that the phenomenon first identified by the American could hold the key to the mysterious losses of ships and planes evident in areas such as the Bermuda Triangle. The Bermuda Triangle, or Devil's Triangle as it is sometimes called, has long been notorious among the seagoing fraternity but the mystery surrounding it only achieved widespread notoriety when occult author Charles Berlitz published his book in the early 1970s. An interesting, if sensationalised, account of odd happenings, Berlitz's *The Bermuda Triangle* sold more than five million copies and was translated into twenty languages. Its success was followed by an avalanche of paperbacks, periodicals, magazine articles and television documentaries on the same subject. As the cottage industry grew, so others claimed that the whole thing was a hoax designed to fool gullible believers and earn millions of dollars for the Triangle experts. In part this was true. Nevertheless, despite some justified criticism from the sceptics, few debunkers felt able to deny that strange events were regularly taking place in the waters between Florida, Bermuda and the Sargasso Sea. For one thing far too many disappearances of boats and aircraft have occurred in fine weather; odder still was the fact that in typical Triangle vanishings no wreckage was found, no lifeboats, life jackets, not even an oil slick to mark the spot where the vessel or plane was lost. Whilst the various agencies of the establishment – marine scientists, government oceanographers, coastguards and naval spokesmen – all strenuously denied the existence of a mystery, the appalling losses continued unabated. During 1976, as Charles Berlitz's book went into its umpteenth reprint, an average of one plane per fortnight disappeared in the Bermuda area and every week at least one boat went missing.

One of the greatest mysteries to have occurred in the Triangle surrounds the fate of Flight 19, a group of naval training aircraft which vanished during a routine exercise just after World War II had ended.

At two o'clock in the afternoon of 5 December 1945, five Avenger Torpedo bombers took off from Fort Lauderdale

Naval Station, Florida. Each plane, carrying a crew of three, had been given the usual pre-flight checks and refuelled before leaving for what was meant to be a strictly unhazardous mission. As the ground crew watched the formation fly off and away over the blue Atlantic Ocean, none could have guessed that their colleagues would never return. To begin with, Flight 19 proceeded normally along its scheduled route, parallel with the Florida coastline. For an hour everything seemed okay, yet at three forty-five p.m. the operator at Fort Lauderdale tower began to receive a series of astonishing messages from the training mission's flight leader, Lieutenant Charles Taylor. In a voice which betrayed both fear and amazement, the group's commander indicated that his instruments were going crazy. Indeed not only his but all the planes' controls were malfunctioning simultaneously.

'What is your position?' asked the radio operator.

Taylor could not say. 'Everything,' he yelled, 'seems wrong. We are lost. Even the sea isn't right.'

Alarmed by this incomprehensible turn of events the radio operators at Fort Lauderdale continued to ask their officer to verify his position, yet Taylor's voice became more disturbed and confused, his messages making even less sense than before. The last words he uttered sounded like a warning: 'Don't come after us, for God's sake ...' Then silence. Yet come after him they did. Following the loss of radio contact, a Mariner flying boat was sent out towards the area where the base command estimated Flight 19's probable position to be. The navy knew that whatever else might have happened, the Avengers would soon be running out of fuel and would have to ditch in the sea. However, the rescuers were themselves about to become the Triangle's next victims. As the flying boat reached the stretch of ocean designated as the search area, it disappeared from radar screens, vanishing into oblivion along with its crew of thirteen.

For the US Navy the loss of six planes in the space of as many hours represented an unprecedented peacetime disaster. An inquiry's report into the events of 5 December ran to some four hundred pages. This official document took the line that Flight 19 had fallen into the sea following an unlucky coincidence of a number of chance factors: sudden bad weather, electrical interference and pilot error. It also concluded that the flight leader Lieutenant Charles Taylor must have panicked, thus compounding the situation and destroying the nerve of his young and relatively inexperienced men. As for the loss of the Mariner flying boat, it was assumed that a mid-air explosion had claimed it, though no evidence was ever produced to support this hypothesis.

For a time the natural explanation behind the Flight 19 mystery was accepted by almost everyone. When aircraft continued to go missing in the area with a regularity that belied such rational solutions, the picture began to appear more ominous. In most of these air losses, the vanishings occurred so suddenly that the planes' pilots were unable to give a mayday signal or even hint that they might be in trouble. When messages had been picked up, they served only to deepen the mystery still further. One typical example was the final signal received from the British Lancastrian Airliner *Star Dust* which ceased to exist a dozen miles from its airport of destination on the night of 12 August 1947. Approaching the Bermuda runway, the pilot of the British passenger craft broke radio silence to utter the cryptic word 'Stendec' three times. A few moments later the *Star Dust* disappeared from the control tower's radar screens. No trace of bodies or wreckage was ever found; nor could the word Stendec be deciphered. In an incident which Civil Aviation officials later described as 'impossible', a large aircraft had simply vanished along with a full complement of passengers. Another doomed aeroplane whose fate echoes that of the *Star Dust* was the similarly named American Airlines DC-3 *Star Ariel*. It disappeared on 28 December 1948 whilst on the last leg of its journey from Bermuda to Miami. The *Star Ariel*'s pilot, Captain Robert Linquist, gave a confident warning of his plane's approach to Miami tower before his jet was plucked into invisibility.

'I can see the lights of the city,' said Linquist. 'We are approaching the field ... all's well.'

All was not well. Nothing more was ever seen of Linquist or his aircraft. The *Star Ariel* never landed, nor, incredibly, was any wreckage of the DC-3 discovered in the shallow waters of the Florida Everglades. It was, in the words of a fellow American Airlines pilot, as if a 'huge electronic camouflage net had come down and swept them away'.

Just as the usual dangers of air travel do not seem to have been responsible for many of the plane disasters in the Devil's Triangle, the circumstances surrounding shipping losses in the area would also appear to rule out most of the traditional maritime hazards. By far the most common cause of a ship sinking is deemed to be adverse weather conditions, but relatively few of the mysterious Triangle happenings occur during hurricanes or severe storms. In fact, many of the oddest cases involve ships and small boats which have vanished during spells of fine weather, often within a few miles of the coast. The majority of these incidents involve small boats, but in some instances very large vessels have disappeared while still within sight of land, leaving no trace whatsoever to explain their sudden departure from the visible world. Among the strangest of all shipping losses was the vanishment of the USS *Cyclops*, a nineteen-thousand-ton cargo vessel which disappeared on a fine, clear day in February 1917 en route to Barbados.

The loss of the *Cyclops* was an incident so bizarre that the US Navy never even bothered to concoct an official explanation. The only fact sheet ever issued by the service stated, in words of unusual candour that it was 'one of the most baffling mysteries in the annals of the Navy. Many theories have been advanced for its disappearance but none which is remotely satisfactory ...'

Particularly inexplicable to naval experts was the fact

that no distress signal of any kind had been sent from the USS *Cyclops*. This is typical of sea vessels lost in the waters of the Bermuda Triangle. As is usually the case with missing planes, disappearing ships seldom get the chance to make their impending danger known to the outside world. One notable exception to this rule seemed to have been the Japanese freighter *Raifuku Maru*, which was lost whilst sailing between the Bahamas and Cuba in 1924. Having issued the standard mayday signal the Japanese craft's radio operator went on to deliver a short and chilling warning: 'Now!' he cried. 'Now come danger like daggers!' Nothing more was picked up. For Triangle researchers, the exact translation and meaning behind those last desperate words has since become the source of much controversy. What is not contested is that the danger spoken of was real and deadly.

Few people encounter mysterious forces inside the Triangle and live to tell the tale. However, some travellers have reported odd experiences and their evidence may give an insight into the true nature of the phenomenon. Characteristically these stories involve the malfunction of radio and guidance equipment on ships and aircraft. In July 1955 the skipper of an American cargo ship, the *Atlantic City*, described how the automatic steering device on his vessel had taken on a mind of its own whilst crossing the Gulf of Mexico. Nineteen years later, in March 1974, the crew of the USS *Vogelgang* experienced a series of electrical and mechanical failure whose coincidence appeared to be without precedent. The source of these events was never established and the captain later described the episode 'as though an invisible force field was tearing her apart'. Aircraft have also encountered unnatural interference in the area. Among those pilots who have reported instrument malfunctions was a Commander Jack Billson, whose navy PBM handled erratically during a flight to the Bahamas in March 1945. As he began to lose height, Billson also noticed that his magnetic compass was going round in circles. The trouble ceased after a few minutes and Billson reached his destination safely. In November 1943 Lieutenant Robert Ulmer had experienced a similar inexplicable anomaly on his instrument panel during a mission over the same latitude. First Ulmer's compass had gone haywire, and then his radio died. If this was not enough, the fighter plane then began to shake violently and lose altitude. Luckily, Robert Ulmer managed to regain control before he hit the sea, and made it back to base. Another pilot who may count himself fortunate to have survived the mysterious forces was Gerald Hawkes, a retired Air Force officer whose twin-engine craft suffered a control failure exactly like those described above. During a flight from Bermuda to Idlewild in 1952 Hawkes lost radio contact before dropping several thousand feet. He said later that it was like 'being in an invisible lift shaft'.

Aviation experts have ruled out thermal draughts and other natural causes as being responsible for these peculiar experiences. An even more weird effect sometimes reported by Triangle fliers is the 'glowing plane' enigma. In these cases, pilots have described how their aircraft have slowly become enveloped by a yellowish phosphorescent haze. Such a story was related by American Chuck Wakely who encountered it whilst flying solo from Nassau to Miami in November 1964. First the plane's wing-tips began to glow, then the luminescence crept slowly along the wings and over the fuselage. Eventually, according to Wakely, it enveloped the whole plane, at which point the aircraft radio ceased to function. Unlike his predecessors the American pilot suffered no loss of control, and within half an hour the glowing yellow mist had evaporated. Ten years later, in 1974, Jack Stubbe, another American aviator, told how a fuzzy yellow glowing steam had covered his light aircraft whilst flying off the coast of Florida. Simultaneously his radio stopped working and his navigation instruments began to spin wildly. Yet once again this episode lasted only a few minutes before everything returned to normal.

Some observers prefer to believe that these glowing

plane stories must be the product of an aerial version of St Elmo's Fire, the strange but harmless atmospheric phenomenon which occasionally appears to surround the masts of ships. This possibility cannot be altogether discounted, yet in no way does it explain the other factors frequently reported by pilots, such as instrument failure and loss of radio contact etc. Nor would it account for the ever-growing list of aircraft that never reach their destinations at all. A second theory, which has gained much ground with dedicated Triangle watchers, holds that reported instrument malfunctions are the result of electromagnetic fluctuations emanating from within the earth's surface. This magnetism theory is attractive to many, since it not only explains the spinning compasses and gyros, but could also, if massively powerful, have been responsible for the literal disintegration of the planes. One investigator who strongly supports this hypothesis is the British writer Ivan Sanderson.

Sanderson noticed that the Bermuda waters were not the only area where an unusually high number of disappearances have been reported. Indeed, far from having a unique reputation the Bermuda Triangle was only one of a whole series of waterways in which strange happenings were commonplace. After a period of exhaustive research, Sanderson concluded that there were twelve regions, of roughly similar size, where magnetic aberrations regularly occurred. These areas, shaped more like lozenges than triangles, formed a symmetrical pattern around the globe, lying along roughly the same latitude – thirty-six degrees north of the Equator. Sanderson named them the twelve 'vile vortices', regions in which localised electromagnetic pulses could coincide to produce a vortex of unimaginable proportions. During such a concurrence of forces those sailors or aviators who travelled close to the fringes of the invisible maelstrom would notice their instruments begin to produce eccentric readings. The unfortunate ones who entered the epicentre of the magnetic whirlpool would never be seen again.

One of the vile vortices identified by Ivan Sanderson is the so-called Devil's Sea, an area of the Pacific south of Japan. In these waters all manner of vessels have been lost on a regular basis for over a century. Nevertheless it was not until 1955 that the Japanese authorities took the mystery seriously. In the early months of that year, after nine fishing vessels went missing in a series of inexplicable disappearances, the Japanese government declared the area to be a danger zone and tried to restrict shipping access. At the same time an official investigation was ordered. In conjunction with this inquiry, a team of scientists set sail aboard the research vessel *Kaigo Maru V*. Their mission was to monitor weather conditions, take seismographic readings and report any other abnormalities they might encounter in the region of the Devil's Sea. One week after it left port the *Kaigo Maru V* ceased radio contact with the mainland; it was never seen again.

In the thirty-five years since the loss of the research vessel Japan's vile vortex has continued to claim victims. One of the most uncanny incidents involved the loss of the British oil tanker the *Derbyshire* which vanished on 9 September 1980 along with its crew of forty-four. The official inquiry into the disappearance of the vessel – at 170,000 tons the biggest British ship ever lost – concluded that the *Derbyshire* had probably been overwhelmed by the forces of nature. But many nautical experts remained unconvinced, for the doomed tanker had been extensively refitted prior to its final voyage and held an AI certificate of seaworthiness issued by Lloyd's Shipping Registry. Even if severe weather had overcome the vessel – which must be counted as unlikely – then it still failed to explain why no mayday signal was sent, why no oil slick was detected, and why no bodies or wreckage were ever recovered by the Japanese patrol boats which searched fruitlessly for five days.

Several years later, when confidential Whitehall documents relating to the disaster were leaked to a British newspaper in January 1989, they suggested that the force which overpowered the *Derbyshire* was so sudden that none of its crew had even had time to don life-jackets. As one journalist wrote, 'There was a normal radio message – then oblivion.'

Clearly the vile vortices are areas one should avoid at all costs. Yet even if we discount those areas of maximum danger identified by Ivan Sanderson, the rest of the world's oceans provide a rich source of mystery for the investigator of unexplained disappearances. The list of ships that have set sail for never-to-be-reached ports of destination would fill a volume in itself. In a sense this is unsurprising, since the sea is powerful enough to destroy and deep enough to hide any vessel mankind could construct. However this is not the whole story, for there have been many extraordinary cases where only the crew vanishes, and not the vessel itself. In such circumstances awkward questions must inevitably be posed. What fear can lead men to abandon their only hope of survival – their ship – in mid-ocean? Or was the choice not their own?

The most famous crewless vessel was the legendary *Mary Celeste*, an American brig-schooner found drifting in the mid-Atlantic in December 1872, well provisioned and quite seaworthy. Built in Nova Scotia and launched originally under the title of the *Amazon*, the ship suffered a chequered history which earned it the unenviable reputation of a hoodoo vessel. Its ownership changed hands several times until, in 1868, it became the property of a consortium headed by the financier J.H. Winchester. Under Winchester's direction the two-masted brigantine named *Amazon* was extensively modified into a brig-schooner and her name changed to the *Mary Celeste*. After four years of relatively successful and trouble-free navigation, the captaincy of the *Mary Celeste* passed to one Benjamin Briggs. At thirty-eight years of age and with a family tradition of seafaring behind him, Captain Briggs must have seemed an ideal choice. Not only was he an experienced skipper with excellent references but he was also noted as a man of high moral character, a teetotaller and devout Christian. With the ship's jinxed history Winchester's consortium believed they needed someone who scorned superstition and Benjamin Briggs was just such a man. The first cargo the *Mary Celeste* was engaged to transport under her new skipper was commercial alcohol, seventeen hundred barrels of which had to be taken from New York to Genoa. For the trip two new mates were hired, plus a cook and four German seamen. On the journey there would also be two passengers, Briggs's wife and two-year-old daughter. In the days when transatlantic voyages were hard, those aboard probably watched New York harbour disappear into the distance with some reluctance. Yet when they left the American city on the morning of 5 November 1872 they could scarcely have imagined that they were sailing towards one of the greatest mysteries of modern times.

The ship was not seen again by human eyes for more than a month. Then on 4 December Captain David Moorhouse, skipper of the three-hundred-ton brigantine *Dei Gratia* noticed a sail about five miles from his starboard bow. At first disinterested, Moorhouse became curious when, having regarded it through his telescope, he saw that the vessel's foretop sail and mainsail were missing. Furthermore, there were no signs of life visible on the deck; even the helm was unmanned. The *Dei Gratia*'s skipper ordered a change of course. As they approached the ghost ship, the crew of the US brigantine repeatedly attempted to hail her. When no response was received a boat was lowered and the *Dei Gratia*'s second mate led a boarding party. As the men climbed over the deck railings they were greeted only by an eerie silence. It took them less than a minute to realise that there was no living soul aboard. Reporting back to their captain, the investigators could offer no logical explanation for the situation. Although it was clear that the *Mary Celeste* had run into rough weather (hence the condition of the rigging), the ship was far from unsailable and in no danger of sinking.

One lifeboat was missing, which suggested that the crew had abandoned ship voluntarily, yet nothing gave a clue as to the reason. A survey of the ship below decks only served to deepen the enigma, since there was a plentiful supply of food and drinking water. Indeed everything seemed neatly in place. Most intriguing of all was the fact that the ship's logbook revealed no hint of approaching difficulties, nor any account of a developing situation which might have conceivably led to the present circumstances.

Baffled as he no doubt was, Captain Moorhouse lost no time in seizing upon the discovery to claim the *Mary Celeste* for himself. Setting his men to repair the damaged craft with all haste, he split his crew in half and sailed both ships to the nearest port of Gibraltar, where he formally claimed salvage rights. The news of the *Mary Celeste*'s latest misfortune soon became common knowledge and revived the story of the ship's hoodoo. An Admiralty court subsequently investigated the curious episode; unable to reach any feasible explanation it returned an open verdict. Of the unfortunate Briggs, his family and crew, nothing more was ever heard. The only satisfied party involved in the affair was Moorhouse, who received his due reward.

So what really happened? In the hundred-plus years since Briggs and his men disappeared, many ingenious theories have been put forward to explain their vanishment. Insanity has become a favourite explanation, centred usually upon the person of Captain Briggs himself. History has shown how unnatural urges have occasionally led men to slaughter their comrades or family and such behaviour is more likely to occur in those whose religious beliefs border – like those of Briggs – on the fanatical. Perhaps Briggs murdered his fellows in a spiritual frenzy, threw them overboard and himself afterwards. Others seeking to explain the mystery have suggested that the crew of the *Mary Celeste* got drunk on the fumes of the alcohol spirit in the hold, and fell overboard one by one. On reflection neither of these natural causes seems likely since both lack supporting evidence. When the men of the *Dei Gratia* inspected the cabins and lower decks of the *Mary Celeste* they found no sign of a struggle as might have been anticipated had Briggs gone mad. Nor were any of the barrels stored in the ship's hold found to be leaking their contents. Thus the alcohol fume theory can be ruled out. The truth is that no explanation fits well with the circumstances of the disappearances and the perplexing ambiguities surrounding the hoodoo ship remain unlikely ever to be solved.

Celebrated though the *Mary Celeste* incident has become it can hardly be described as unique in the annals of sea mysteries. Rather than consider the 1872 vanishings as a special example, readers would be advised to think of it as just one in a whole line of vessels whose crews have inexplicably gone missing. In the year 1849 a Dutch schooner, the *Hermania*, was discovered drifting off the Cornish coast. Her rigging was in disarray and her crew missing, yet the *Hermania* remained seaworthy with her lifeboats firmly in their place. A commission of enquiry suggested that a freak wave might have swept the crew overboard, but few sailors thought it likely. In any case, the seas off Cornwall had been unusually calm for some weeks beforehand. In contrast to the *Hermania*, the *James B. Chester* was in fine condition when discovered adrift and deserted in the North Atlantic during February 1855. Once more, however, all the lifeboats remained intact.

Our own century has also seen ghost-vessels. In October 1917, for instance, the yacht *Zebrina* left Falmouth Harbour, Cornwall, for the small port of Brieux, France. No storms were reported and the voyage should have taken less than forty-eight hours. However, after four days the *Zebrina* was found deserted, in excellent condition, and giving no clue as to the fate of her missing crew of five. Like the *Mary Celeste* no explanation has been satisfactorily put forward to account for the tragedy. Two years later, in 1919, the *Lucienne*, a schooner out of St Malo was found washed up on the Goodwin Sands of Kent. A half-eaten meal lay on the table, a true Conan Doyle touch, yet those who sat down to the repast remained permanently absent. In July 1941 another ship lost its crew, this time a Portuguese lugger, the *Islandia*. A Red Cross charter vessel, the *Islandia* was commanded by a Captain Amandio Mathias, a former naval officer and one of the most experienced skippers in the European merchant service. Like the *Mary Celeste*, the Red Cross vessel was found drifting aimlessly upon the open sea, this time near the Gulf of Lions. When a boarding party from the French cutter *Belle Isle* investigated her they found her to be perfectly seaworthy. There was no sign that she had weathered a severe storm, nor was there any reason to suppose that some form of violence had occurred on board. Nevertheless, the ship had apparently been abandoned. An even more recent example of a ghost ship was the *Joyita*, a twin-screw pleasure cruiser which met with disaster in 1955. Having left the port of Aria in Western Samoa on 5 October, the *Joyita* was not seen for more than a month. Then on 10 November a fishing vessel found her abandoned a few miles off Fakaofo in the Tokelau Islands. Nothing more was ever seen of the twenty-five missing passengers and crew.

Ironically, the sea story which provides us with perhaps the strangest disappearances of all did not occur aboard a ship but on an island. The Eilean Moor Lighthouse was built on the rocky expanse of Flannan to guide mariners safely around the Hebrides and the western coast of Scotland. Manned by two seamen, a third was always on hand to act as a reserve should the others fall ill. It was believed that with this fail-safe precaution, the 140,000 candlepower warning beacon need never go out. But on 15 December 1900, sailors navigating the icy waters of the North Sea watched in amazement as the Flannan Isle Lighthouse suddenly ceased to function.

The first to report the mystery to the Scottish authorities was the captain of a steamer, the SS *Archer*, which had been sailing close to the Hebrides on the night of the fifteenth. Immediately a relief vessel, *Hesperus*, was sent to investigate, manned by, among others, one Joseph Moore who was also a lighthouse keeper on Flannan. Moore was a friend of the three men whom he had left on Eilean Moor, Thomas Marshall, Donald McArthur and James Ducat, and knew them all to be experienced and able keepers. They had been in good health two weeks previously when he had last seen them before going on leave, and it seemed incredible to Moore that all three could have gone down with an illness so serious that it made their duties impossible. However, sickness was not to blame; for something far stranger had happened. As the *Hesperus* approached the bleak island of Flannan, its crew saw that no preparations had been made for their arrival on the jetty, nor did repeated blasts from the ship's foghorn provoke any response from the lighthousemen. First ashore was Joseph Moore himself, striding purposefully towards the whitewashed walls of the lighthouse. Inside he found no sign of life. The place was cold and empty, yet otherwise normal. Everything was neat and in its proper place; even the wicks of the lanterns had been cleaned and trimmed, with their bowls filled with oil ready to be lit at sunset. Checking the logbook for a clue to the mystery, Joseph Moore noted with some astonishment that on the night of the fourteenth a storm had apparently raged in the seas surrounding the island. This entry was inexplicable, for in fact that night had been in the middle of a period of comparatively calm weather. The following entry on the record sheet was the last. It said simply: 'Storm ended, sea calm, God is over all.' The date was 15 December ... the night on which the great light was extinguished.

Reporting this curious situation to the skipper of the *Hesperus*, Moore suggested that a full search should be made of the island. His advice was duly followed but at the end of their investigations the crew of the relief vessel had found nothing and on the following day the *Hesperus* returned to Scotland bereft of survivors, bodies or explanations. As news of the mystery spread the story made headlines on the mainland. Meanwhile, on Flannan itself Joseph Moore was left alone charged with the grim task of manning the lighthouse single-handed. During the next few weeks as he paced the harsh rocky terrain of the tiny island, Moore must have had plenty of time to ponder upon the fate of his former comrades. Did they venture too close to the sea, perhaps to be swept away by a huge wave? It was unlikely, he believed, for the men knew only too well the dangers of the Atlantic Ocean. Had one become insane, killed the others and thrown their bodies from the jetty before following them to a watery grave? This Moore could not countenance. He knew the men personally to be of sound mind and body and had waved them goodbye only a fortnight before the tragedy. And what of the storm mentioned in the log on the night of the fourteenth? How could such an impossible occurrence be accounted for? These and other macabre speculations must have preoccupied the mind of Joseph Moore during the lonely days of late December 1900 and January 1901. Much later, after he had been relieved of his solitary spell of duty, Moore told of how during those sombre weeks he had become aware of an unnaturally depressing atmosphere which pervaded the entire island. Moreover, he believed that whilst searching in vain for clues to the enigma of his friends' disappearance, he had distinctly heard their voices calling to him on the wind. Whether or not this was his imagination or the cries of the gulls circling overhead we shall never know. However, Joseph Moore never again returned to the bleak island of Flannan.

In one important respect the mystery of Flannan Island differs from those mentioned in the earlier part of this chapter. The difference is that the enigma of the lighthousemen involved more than one person vanishing on land. Though they remain a thankfully rare phenomenon, multiple vanishings have been recorded from all parts of the globe. Indeed, if we include occurrences where several people disappear from the same vicinity within a short period of time, recorded instances increase alarmingly. In one week in 1926, for example, six people vanished from the

Essex coastal town of Southend. The disappearances, all apparently unrelated incidents, involved three adults and three children. None was ever seen again. Six years before a similar string of inexplicable vanishments had taken place in Belfast, Ireland. In these happenings eight girls were lost from a city street in the space of a single week. The American continent has also suffered its share of multiple disappearances. In July 1892 so many people mysteriously went missing from the Canadian city of Montreal that an atmosphere of near hysteria seemed to have been abroad on the streets. Meanwhile, in the USA, the New York *Sun* of 14 August 1902 reported the witnessed dematerialisations in one day of no fewer than five men in the town of Buffalo.

Bizarre stories such as these are commonplace if one bothers to research the world press for an extended period. Of course, few of us have the time or inclination to do so, and for this reason it comes as a shock to many who had previously believed that such events just couldn't happen. But there is an even more incredible and far more frightening phenomenon yet to be considered – the mass disappearance syndrome.

Fortunately mass disappearances, in which hundreds or even thousands of people vanish without warning or explanation, hardly ever happen. For that we must be grateful. Yet happen they do and their existence presents perhaps the most disturbing mystery included in the pages of this book.

Some of the most striking examples of these large-scale vanishments seem to have occurred in Asia. There are, for instance, several Russian examples from medieval times, but since they cannot be corroborated they must be considered suspect. A more recent example from China, however, appears ominously reliable.

In December 1937 China had been at war with Japan for more than six months. With the invaders pushing northwards to advance upon Nanking, a forward guard of approximately three thousand Chinese troops was deployed to defend a vital bridge south of the city. Taking up entrenched positions, the troops waited for the expected Japanese onslaught. It never came. What did occur was much more alarming. On the morning following his tactical deployment the Chinese commanding officer, General Li Fu Siea, was awoken by a frantic subordinate who told him that radio contact had been lost with the division guarding the bridge. Fearing that his men had been overrun, Commander Du Siea gave orders for an immediate reconnaissance to be made of the forward lines. He was prepared for the worst, yet the tale his officers returned to tell was so strange that he could scarcely believe it. For what they found south of the bridge was simply lines of empty trenches, devoid not only of life, but of death also. No corpses or other signs of a recent battle remained to suggest an explanation for the men's whereabouts. Li Fu Siea was baffled, for he knew that if the soldiers had deserted en masse they must have recrossed the Yangtze Bridge – but they had not done so. Southwards lay the enemy and certain destruction. So what had become of them? The puzzle was never solved. Two days after the division vanished, hoards of Japanese swarmed across the bridge into the city. The assault that followed culminated in the Rape of Nanking, a massacre unequalled in the bloody history of Asian warfare, and the loss of the three thousand men defending the bridge was forgotten in the general carnage. However, many years later, following the peace at the end of World War II, an official investigation by the Chinese government could uncover no evidence to suggest a logical explanation for those strange happenings in the days before Nanking fell. A later inquiry set up by the Communist regime of Chairman Mao Tse Tung established categorically that none of the Chinese defenders who held the bridge in 1937 was ever seen or heard of again.

Although it might seem amazing, the Chinese story was not without precedent in the annals of twentieth-century warfare. A similar fate seems to have befallen a company of

British soldiers during the Gallipoli campaign of World War I. This multiple vanishment, in which a total of 145 men were lost, was witnessed by a platoon of twenty-two volunteers of the Number Three Section, 1st Division Field Company NZEF. The full details of the remarkable happening were not available until 1965, when a veteran of the battle first published his eyewitness account.

Frederich Reichart's story, which reads like some fantastic fabrication, was nevertheless accompanied by an affidavit signed by other elderly survivors of the campaign who also bore witness to the phenomenon. Fifteen Anzac veterans remained alive and were prepared to attest to the accuracy of the account.

Briefly what the men of the 1st Division supposedly saw was as follows: on the morning of 21 August 1915, a company of men from the First-Fifth Norfolk Regiment advanced upon Hill 60, a Turkish stronghold. All that morning the lower slopes of the hill were shrouded in a curious mist, a mist which apart from being unprecedented in that region appeared to defy natural laws since it remained unaffected by a stiff breeze blowing from the south-west at the time. Into this mist the men of the First-Fifth advanced, never to emerge. According to Reichart's testimony he and his fellow Anzacs watched in amazement from their positions near Suvla Bay as the English Tommies disappeared one by one into the swirling fog. Seconds later the unnatural haze lifted to reveal ... nothing. The empty slope of Hill 60 appeared before their eyes devoid of men or bodies. Reichart finished his account, published fifty years later, by pointing out that upon the cessation of hostilities in 1918 the victorious British Military Authorities sought the return of prisoners captured in the battle. Turkey handed over her POWs but replied that although many British soldiers were captured that day, no contact was made with the First-Fifth Norfolk Regiment. Indeed, no captured British prisoners ever claimed afterwards to have seen or heard of any of the men who disappeared on 21 August 1915.

Further corroborating evidence for Reichart's claims appeared when a declassified edition of the final report of the Dardanelles campaign was made public in 1967, some fifty years after the classified document was written. Although heavily censored by the Ministry of Defence there remained some details which lent credence to the vanishment story. In the final report, the loss without apparent cause of a large body of men is conceded and the descriptions of the weather in Suvla Bay on the morning in question seem similar to Reichart's interpretations. The slopes of Hill 60 were, said the official report, 'wrapped in a strange and unnatural mist'. Could 145 Englishmen really have vanished into that unnatural mist as those who witnessed the event claim? One argument which is still put forward to explain the Suvla Bay incident contends that the company was simply wiped out by the machine guns of the Turkish defenders. This explanation is unconvincing, since it does not account for the lack of corpses on the battlefield and ignores the testimony of fifteen witnesses.

Nevertheless, the possibility remains that the ordinary hazards of battle were responsible for these men's disappearances, as well as those of the Chinese warriors. A similar explanation cannot be put forward for every example of large scale vanishment. For one thing, not all have taken place during situations of conflict. Among the most intriguing examples of a mass disappearance to have occurred this century is the thin air migration of an entire Eskimo village from their traditional homelands on the shores of Lake Anjikuni in 1930. To this day the Canadian authorities have never been able to solve the riddle or make contact with members of that tribe or their descendants. The mystery emerged in November 1930 when a fur trapper named Joe Labelle snowshoed into the Eskimo village to find the familiar shanty-style huts devoid of population. Only two weeks before, when Labelle had been last there, the village had been a noisy settlement teeming with life. Now instead of the usual friendly welcome an unearthly silence greeted him. Unable to find a single soul, the trapper looked desperately for clues to explain the situation; he searched in vain. Tied to their normal mooring places were the Eskimo kayaks. In their homes were the villagers' essential items, their rugs and their rifles. On the cold camp fires stood pots of congealed stew made from the caribou meat which formed the tribe's staple diet. All was just as it should have been except for the people. It was as if the entire community of over two thousand had suddenly left in the middle of an otherwise normal day. There was one other detail notable by its absence. Labelle saw, to his utter astonishment, that no tracks led away from the encampment.

Feeling, as he later described, 'a strange sick feeling of dread' in his stomach the grizzled trapper made his way to the nearest district telegraph office and alerted the Royal Canadian Mounted Police. The Mounties had never heard anything like it. Immediately an expedition was despatched to investigate the village and a search was begun across the borders of Lake Anjikuni. The second measure failed to locate the lost tribe whilst the first served only to deepen the mystery further. Arriving in the deserted encampment the Canadian Mounties found two chilling pieces of evidence, both of which strongly suggested that an unnatural event had occurred. Firstly it was discovered that the Eskimos had not taken their sleigh dogs with them as Joe Labelle had originally assumed. The frozen carcasses of the huskies were found buried deep inside a snowdrift on the camp's perimeter. They had starved to death. Secondly, even more incredible, was the discovery that the graves of the tribe's ancestors had been opened up and their bodies removed. Both of these details baffled the authorities. Clearly the Eskimos could not travel without using either one or other of their means of transport, their sleighs or their kayaks. Nor would they leave their faithful canine servants to a slow and painful death. Yet gone they were and the dogs had been abandoned. The second enigma – the opened graves – was in many ways odder still for tomb disturbance was unknown among the customs of the Eskimo tribes. Besides, the ground was frozen as hard as iron and was virtually undiggable by hand.

As one high-ranking officer in the Mounties said at the time: 'The whole affair is physically improbable'. Improbable certainly, yet the vanishing Eskimo settlement of 1930 is only one spectacular example of a world-wide phenomenon which is as yet hardly recognised. Moreover, it is a phenomenon which may well be growing more widespread as time goes by. According to the latest statistics, the London Metropolitan Police receive roughly twenty-five thousand missing persons reports annually, a figure mirrored by other big cities around the world. Though the vast majority of these are juveniles who return home subsequently, there remains a small but disturbing kernel of vanishing people who never return, and for which no explanation appears to suffice. These are the lost ones, the forgotten ones, unrecognised by society apart from the small group of friends and family who are personally aware of the mystery and know the disappearance to be inexplicable. How many of these may have stepped, unknowingly, into a different dimension, a limbo state from which there is no escape? A state where a man neither lives nor dies, but simply exists?

Whatever their fate may be the roll-call of the lost continues to lengthen. At the time of writing, a Malaysian newspaper has recorded the disappearance of one Abdul Mutalib, an eighteen-year-old soldier who vanished in front of other recruits at a rifle range training centre at Port Dickson near Kuala Lumpur. The centre launched a search without success. From Germany there has come a story of a British football supporter who walked out of a bar in Cologne and disappeared into thin air. In the very same week from Basildon in Essex there came a report of a woman who vanished from her kitchen suddenly and inexplicably, leaving a pan of potatoes boiling on her cooker. No one saw her leave the house and police have admitted that they have no clues as to her whereabouts. In the words of one constable it was as if the woman had 'vanished off the face of the earth'.

DOOMWATCHERS

For Mrs Lesley Brennan, a housewife from Grimsby, Lincolnshire, 1 June 1974 began like any other normal Saturday. Having returned from her morning shopping, she made herself a light lunch and settled down in front of the television to watch her favourite sport of wrestling. Instead of the normal programme, however, the screen contained pictures of fiery devastation, while the news reporter's voice described in graphic detail how a large chemical plant at nearby Flixborough had exploded that morning killing dozens of workers. Since Flixborough was only twenty miles away from her home town it was natural that Mrs Brennan should mention the disaster to two friends who visited her – Janice and Peter East. Neither had seen the newsflash and were understandably dismayed.

That evening all three watched the early evening broadcast which contained once again the scenes of flaming horror. In all, twenty-four people were dead, and over a hundred buildings in the area had been damaged. All this Mrs Brennan and her friends expected to hear. Yet to their astonishment the news reader now said that the Flixborough nypro disaster had occurred that afternoon – several hours after Janice and Peter East were told of the tragedy by Mrs Brennan. A phone call to the television company confirmed that the series of explosions at the plant had begun at ten minutes to five and no special midday bulletin had been screened.

The full story of Mrs Brennan's strange premonition appeared in the *Grimsby Evening Telegraph* the following week. The nature of her foresight – through the medium of television – may be unusual but the gift of prevision itself would appear to be the most common expression of man's psychic powers. For whilst scientists insist that the future cannot be foretold, evidence of decades of parascientific research has long since proved otherwise. Among those who have seen the future are a small group who have been forced to look upon death itself – perhaps their own, perhaps someone's they have never met. These glimpses of the end are usually brief, always unexpected, and often terrifying. Whether they arrive in the form of a dream or waking vision they are seldom welcomed.

In this chapter we examine the role precognition plays within the wider context of unnatural deaths – and the people fate chooses to be the unwilling spectators of the dark drama ... the Doomwatchers.

Since precognition is such a common manifestation of man's psychic powers, it is probably not surprising that amongst those who have seen the future are many who have become famous for other reasons. The American writer Mark Twain is just one amongst many literary figures who have been blessed – or cursed – with the gift of prevision.

In an article he wrote late in his life, the American author recalled a dream that he had experienced many years earlier whilst he was still in his mid-twenties. At the time, Twain's younger brother Henry was employed aboard the Mississippi riverboat, the *Pennsylvania*. One night, whilst they were both staying at their sister's house, Twain dreamt that his brother had died and that his body lay downstairs in the front room with a bouquet of white flowers on his chest. Twain's dream must have been particularly vivid for when he awoke he was so upset that he immediately checked to see if it was true. Of course the room was empty.

The details remained so markedly stuck in the novelist's mind that the next morning he confided his fear to his sister, who scoffed at him and told him it must be the product of his legendary imagination. But she was wrong. Two weeks later the Twain nightmare became tragic reality, as the *Pennsylvania* blew up, killing more than a hundred and fifty passengers and crew. Among the fatalities was Henry. Two days after the sinking, the young man's body was returned to the sister's home in a metal casket. Upon arriving for the funeral, Mark Twain was astonished to find his brother's coffin topped with a bouquet of white roses surrounding a solitary red bloom.

If Twain's premonition bears the hallmarks of the master story-teller's art, it is merely typical of many dreams-come-true that have been claimed by others who lack his gift for fictional narrative. For example, in his biography of United States President Abraham Lincoln, historian Walter Hill Lamon described a conversation he had with the statesman in March 1865, a few weeks before the end of the Civil War. According to Lamon, Lincoln was preoccupied with a peculiar dream which had been troubling him for several nights. In this nightly dream tableau Lincoln would be awoken by sounds of wailing voices and ghostly cries. Always he would get up and follow the voices until he reached their source, the East Room, where upon opening the door he would see a catafalque draped with the colours of the Union.

The President was certain that this represented a forewarning of his own imminent death, and so it proved to be. Within two months the leader had been assassinated, shot in the back of the head by John Wilkes Booth.

Owing to the subject's stature in history, Abe Lincoln's premonition has become a cause célèbre among paranormal investigators. It is certainly a notable example, but there are far more astonishing cases of dreams-come-true.

One particularly odd example surrounds the case of seventeenth-century French actor Champmesle who experienced a recurring nightmare in which he saw his dead mother beckoning to him. Interpreting the vision as foretelling his own impending doom, and believing absolutely in its accuracy, the ageing thespian set about organising his own funeral. Undeterred by the hopeful report of his physician, the actor booked a local church, arranged for flowers, a hearse and mourners. On the appointed day of his burial, Champmesle turned up alive and seemingly well, joining his bemused friends and relatives throughout his own funeral mass. At the end of the service he thanked the priest, bade farewell to all those who had attended, and promptly dropped dead of a heart attack.

Stories of deaths predicted are plentiful enough yet they are only of value to a researcher if they can be corroborated by witnesses. One notable case which is beyond suspicion concerned the murder of Field Marshal Sir Henry Wilson in London on 22 June 1922. Ten days before Wilson was gunned down by Irish Nationalists, a wealthy socialite and friend, Lady Londonderry, dreamt that she saw the officer shot dead by two men. Although her ladyship told several other acquaintances about the dream, she declined to warn the Field Marshal himself because she knew that he would say it was nonsense. Afterwards she regretted her reticence, yet from the point of view of parascientists the fact that she told other people before the event occurred was enough to prove the reality of the phenomenon.

British political assassinations are rare, but another example, the death of Prime Minister Spencer Percival in 1812, was also witnessed previously by Cornishman John Williams in a night-time prevision. Williams, an innkeeper from Redruth, had the same dream three nights running and spoke of it freely to friends and customers. He saw an important man shot dead, he said, though he did not know who it was. Only after Percival was gunned down by a madman in the lobby of the Palace of Westminster on 2 May 1812 did Williams realise that he had foreseen the death of the Prime Minister himself, and when he saw a picture of Percival in the newspapers he quickly recognised it as being the face of the victim in his nightmare.

The premonition dreamt by the Redruth innkeeper was

unusual because it did not involve anyone he knew. Precognitions of death generally focus either on the receivers themselves or someone very close, usually a member of the family. A third variety involves premonitions where the receiver is given prior knowledge of a person or persons whom they know only vaguely. An example of this variety was reported to the British Society for Psychical Research in 1975.

On 9 April of that year Mrs Eileen Lickness, a social worker from Hull, dreamt that she saw the death of a man she had not seen in real life for sixteen years. Troubled, she told her husband of her impression the following morning. Mr Lickness allayed her fears and promised to check through the public records for their former acquaintance's address. In the event it proved unnecessary for, by a considerable chance, Mrs Lickness herself saw the very man in question that next morning whilst she was shopping. He was alive and well, and although they had a short conversation, she said nothing of the premonition.

Seeing the subject of her dreams turn up so coincidentally after all those years did little to dispel the social worker's anxiety, and later that day her worst fears were realised. In the early evening her husband phoned her to say that he had tracked down her old friend's address and had turned up just in time to see a body being put into the back of an ambulance. It seemed that their friend from the past had collapsed with a heart attack minutes before. As it turned out the man had died only an hour after Eileen Lickness had met him in the shopping precinct.

Incredible though it may seem, the story told by Mr and Mrs Lickness is absolutely true. Her husband was not the only person whom Eileen Lickness told about the premonition and the couple from Hull, together with several other friends, later signed statements attesting to the genuineness of the phenomenon. For their part the British Society for Psychical Research considered it to be one of the more remarkable instances of precognition to have emerged in recent years.

Although we may be astonished by stories of dream premonitions and perhaps choose not to believe them, the idea of dreams foretelling the future is hardly new. The ancient civilisations of Greece and Egypt analysed dreams long before the theories of Sigmund Freud.

The oldest recorded prophetic dreams are those in the Old Testament in which Joseph interpreted the Pharaoh's vision of the seven cows. Centuries later, in 650 BC, King Assurbanipal of Assyria filled his libraries with tablets recording the substance and interpretation of his own dreams. Even the early Christians believed that dreams could hold the key to future events and Catholic scholar St Thomas Aquinas wrote in his thirteenth-century work *Summa Theologica* that divination by dreams was a valuable practice.

Of dreams themselves little is known. Although some people continue to believe that they do not dream during sleep, science insists that we all do. When in 1952, an American paediatrician conducted a study into REMs (Rapid Eye Movements) in babies, it was soon concluded that the activity indicated dreaming, and that the process was observable in all adults without exception. Since every man, woman and child on earth has between five and seven REMs during a normal night's sleep, and therefore the same number of dreams, it follows that the total number of dreams formed in the collective sleeping mind runs into billions each year. Obviously dreaming is an important activity in the human brain, yet psychologists are still unable to agree on a likely reason for its existence. Freud, the father of modern psychiatry, described dreams as the 'Guardians of Sleep', though he never arrived at a more precise explanation. If dreams themselves are difficult to quantify, predictive dreams throw the experts headlong into confusion. Unfortunately, statistics relating to genuine cases of predictive dreams have never been surveyed closely enough to form an objective conclusion as to the proportion of the population that might experience them.

However, the few statistics that do exist tend to support the theory that such dreams are widespread. In response to a questionnaire published in *The Times* in the mid-1970s, over half the correspondents outlined personal experiences of precognitive dreams. Meanwhile, in the USA, Dr David Ryback, a lecturer in psychology at Georgia University, polled four hundred students to discover that no less than thirty per cent regularly experienced dreams which came true.

Probably the most in-depth study to have been undertaken by a person from outside the parameters of conventional science was the survey launched by English writer J.B. Priestley, in preparation for his book *Man and Time*. Priestley, a celebrated novelist and playwright, was intrigued by the anomalies in time apparent in his own life and became determined to study time-related phenomena in order to arrive at a more satisfactory concept of what time itself was. He was especially interested in precognition, the existence of which would shatter the rationalist viewpoint of linear time and an unchanging, unknowable future.

In order to increase his already prodigious volume of data, Priestley appealed in 1963 on British television for anyone who had had a predictive dream to write to him with the details. To his astonishment, he received over a thousand replies.

Many of the letters he received were discarded as useless because the witness seemed unreliable, or because the stories themselves appeared to be suspiciously fictional. Yet there remained a significant minority – over two hundred – which had been corroborated by witnesses other than the prediction-receivers themselves. Of the ones Priestley considered worth studying, the majority of predictions appeared in the form of dreams; but there were some notable exceptions. In *Man and Time* the writer gave these a special precedence.

One example concerned the sensation of dread felt by a young London woman whilst walking past a hospital during the height of the Blitz in 1940. The woman was unable to find a reason why the sight of the building upset her so much yet on several occasions the emotions it aroused moved her to tears as she passed it on her way to work. Eventually she used a different route to avoid the illogical reaction.

It was twenty years before the reason for the distress became apparent. In 1960 her best friend died in the hospital after a long and painful illness and the girl, by then a middle-aged woman, found herself staring once more at the same exterior walls, the exact same feeling swelling inside her breast as she had felt so inexplicably two decades earlier. In this instance it was a case of death being felt rather than seen before.

Few of the precognitive sensations took so long to materialise. Another letter Priestley published in his book concerned a fellow writer who gradually realised through some sixth sense that her teenage son was soon going to die. The woman novelist, whom Priestley chose not to identify, first realised that her son was doomed during a church service in which she had begun to cry uncontrollably. Comforted by her husband the woman recovered before the service ended, yet two days later the same eerie feeling returned and once more she broke down. Up until that time her son, then nineteen, had been in the best of health, but within a fortnight he became seriously ill and before the end of the year he was dead.

To J.B. Priestley examples of prevision were to be considered as quirks – aberrations in 'personal time'. Time itself, he believed, could not be considered outwardly in separate modes of past, present and future, but as a construct that existed within people's minds. That the general view of time remained the same was not remarkable, since there existed such a thing as a collective intelligence or subconscious – the concept first formulated by psychologist C.G. Jung. Nevertheless, to Priestley the fact remained that current notions of time were false in a sense that a future already exists; as the occasional, and not infrequent, cases of precognition proved.

In reaching his conclusions, J.B. Priestley acknowledged the enormous debt he owed to another Englishman: John William Dunne. J.W. Dunne first made his name as an aircraft designer, the man who built the first British war plane. But it is as a writer and time theorist that he is best remembered today.

Since 1889 Dunne had been interested in predictive dreams and kept a personal record of his own. These 'night-time revelations of the future', as he called them, were largely unremarkable though elements of his dreams regularly came true. Then, late in 1916, Dunne had a night vision of unprecedented clarity in which he saw an explosion in an armaments factory. Two months later, in January 1917, a gigantic blast occurred in a London bomb factory killing seventy workers and injuring more than a thousand. The aircraft designer linked the two events, and from that moment on his fascination with precognition and the future became an obsession. Giving over his life to the task he set about studying all reports of time/future anomalies and carefully constructed theories which might account for them.

In 1927 J.W. Dunne published his ideas in a book entitled *An Experiment with Time* which can fairly claim to be the first genuine attempt to treat the subject of prediction on a serious level. Dunne's concepts, which he called 'serial time', were complicated and controversial, though not entirely implausible. Basically, he considered a man's mind as being conscious only of what it is doing and thinking at that precise moment; past and future then become irrelevant. At the same time, according to Dunne's conjectures, a man's mind might be conscious of what he is doing – aware of itself – at any given moment. Not only that but it must be aware of being aware and so on and so on ... ad infinitum. Thus, to Dunne, the human mind became a mental hall of mirrors.

If one accepts this thesis, it was not hard, claimed the writer, to go a step further and accept also that our perceptions of time itself are misleading. This, in turn, naturally opens up the possibilities for precognition to exist, since the time we experience (and believe in) during our waking life would be quite different to that experienced during sleep.

Dunne's ideas challenged the accepted view of the universe and, not surprisingly, they received little serious attention from the scientific mainstream. Those who condescended to oppose him in print pointed out that amidst all the precognitive examples chosen by Dunne most were taken from the author's own diary of dreams. They were uncorroborated evidence and therefore worthless.

Nevertheless, *An Experiment with Time* created considerable interest among the general public, and Dunne was flooded with letters from readers who claimed similar clairvoyant experiences to his own. The book sold well, went into several reprints and encouraged the author to continue his research. In the next fifteen years J.W. Dunne wrote several other books, each redefining and reinterpreting his theory that human beings experienced time on different levels.

Dunne died in 1949 yet interest in his work has continued to the present day. In 1971, a Cambridge University research team led by Dr Carl Sargent carried out a series of experiments based upon Dunne's techniques of dream recording. Unlike the English theorist, however, the Cambridge group worked in laboratories, inducing sleep in their subjects through a form of sensory deprivation. Upon waking, the sleepers would be asked to write down details of their dream memories. These transcripts were then matched with preselected cards upon which drawings had been made. The results showed that over forty per cent of the subjects' dreams bore a direct relation to the images on the cards – which, of course, none had seen previously.

An even more interesting set of experiments was undertaken between 1976 and 1977, in America, by the two physicists Russel Targ and Harold Puthoff, both resident lecturers at the Stanford Research Institute. In these Dunne-inspired tests, a subject would be induced into a sleeping state, be awoken at an appointed time, asked to write down or draw details of what they had seen whilst dreaming, and then be driven to a predetermined destination unknown to them. The basis of Targ and Puthoff's experiments was to see whether laboratory dreamers could describe in advance visual details of places the research assistants were to drive them to following their periods of sleep. To the researchers' disappointment, the results of the tests were patchy, apart from one individual subject, a woman who was known to possess psychic gifts. Her visual interpretations were invariably close to her chosen location.

Targ and Puthoff were anxious to avoid the possibility that extrasensory perception (ESP) might be causing the woman to score so highly. Therefore they changed the experiment slightly: this time even they themselves would remain unaware of the woman's destination, which would be chosen at random later. Nevertheless, under the new conditions their star guinea pig remained able to predict her future destination accurately, proving beyond reasonable doubt that precognition was somehow involved.

In summing up their findings the Stanford researchers considered that the correspondence between real destinations and previously dreamed ones was so clear that no doubt could remain in the case of their female psychic. Over a period of several months she continued to match a consistent ratio of distant viewing impressions with the real thing. Evened out, that ratio remained at a steady seven out of ten – seventy per cent correlation of dreams with actual physical locations.

Despite the reputations of the men who carried out these tests, fellow scientists refused to countenance the presence of precognition in the findings of Targ and Puthoff, and today J.W. Dunne's theories are no closer to achieving even the slightest measure of academic respectability. Why are today's scientists so steadfastly opposed to the possibility of precognition? Arguments against stories of predictions are many and varied, yet most can be knocked down quite easily. For instance, some critics point to the fact that certain personality types love the irrational and the miraculous; such people (it is argued) would enjoy the thought of being picked out by fate, and so persuade themselves that they are psychic. For these wishful thinkers, dreams and hunches are touched up so that they comply with the facts learned with hindsight. 'Hindsight prophets' no doubt exist, and J.B. Priestley for one recognised many among the thousand-plus letters he received when researching *Man and Time*. Yet self-deluders cannot account for the literally thousands of corroborated examples that have been recorded.

Another objection made by sceptics is that many predictions do not come true. This is a valid argument, since people, especially professional soothsayers, tend to forget their misses whilst remembering their spectacular hits. Yet the clarity and persistence of some previsions cannot be possibly accounted for in this way. Nor can a genuinely predictive dream be confused with an ordinary dream or nightmare, as any person who has experienced one will testify.

Since the vast majority of presentiments of death involve the demise of the receiver, some doctors have conjectured that sensations of foreboding could be the body's way of warning the brain that trouble is ahead. Certainly there are innumerable cases recorded by physicians down the years of people somehow sensing an undiagnosed terminal illness. Even the ancient physicians Hippocrates and Romanus spoke with dread of the cruel effects of death presentiments on their patients. In their massive tome entitled *Anomalies and Curiosities of Medicine* nineteenth-century doctors Gould and Pyne mention several examples they had encountered of predictions unaccountably becoming fatally true, and concluded that presentiment of death was a dangerous symptom which should not be treated lightly. Much more recently, doctors have begun to give serious consideration to the possibilities opened up by the human body's early-warning system.

During the 1980s a Soviet medical scientist, Vasli Nikolagevich Kastakin began to analyse data relating to dream precognition. As a student, Kastakin knew a friend who had nightmares of a huge snake crushing his body. A few months later, the young man was diagnosed as having a spinal tumour which subsequently paralysed him. Another case Kastakin noted concerned a woman whose dreams of being smothered preceded a confirmation that she had tuberculosis. Since he began studying the subject in detail, the Russian has found some other notable cases, including a stroke victim who previously dreamed of having his head covered in blood-stained bandages, and a man who saw himself in a wheelchair months before he was told he had multiple sclerosis. Only time and many more years of patient research will conclusively prove whether or not the human body can predict a malfunction in advance, but already it's looking an even-money bet.

Just as a message from body to brain may account for some previsions involving the receiver's own condition, so deep anxiety felt for a close friend or relative may serve to explain many of the precognitive instances where a person foresees the death of someone near to them. If, for example, a wife knows her husband to be ill, her suppressed feelings may well outpicture themselves in a dream – perhaps symbolically. At the same time, it is possible that extreme emotional disturbance following the death of a loved one may lead a person to unconsciously falsify their belief that they had a precognitive feeling prior to the death itself. Similarly, anxiety could also be the cause of some apparently inexplicable premonitions which have been felt immediately before a particularly stressful moment.

In some cases one must seriously doubt the genuineness of the phenomenon. For example, soldiers often foresee their deaths on the night before a battle, a fact that is not surprising since in wars many men die. Such sensations cannot reasonably be said to prove precognition. In the same way competitors in high risk sports appear to attract a noticeably marked incidence of doom-laden premonitions.

So when is a premonition not a premonition?

On 4 January 1967, Donald Campbell, the British motorboat racer, attempted to break the world water-speed record on Coniston Water in the English Lake District. Two hours before his attempt was due to begin, Campbell received a mental impression that someone in his family was going to die – though not specifically himself – and relayed his premonition to friends and helpers who were present. That afternoon those same people watched in horror as Campbell's speedboat *Bluebird* somersaulted to destruction on the placid surface of the lake. The racer's body was never recovered.

Another sporting story involves the boxing match between the world welter-weight champion Sugar Ray Robinson and Jimmy Doyle, which took place in 1947. On the night before the fight Robinson had dreamt that he had seen his opponent lying dead in the ring. The next day he told his manager and the fight promotor that he did not wish to go ahead with the contest. Threatened with breach of contract the unwilling champion was forced to enter the ring and meet Doyle as arranged. The horror of the previous night came true: Robinson floored the contender in the seventh round ... and the luckless Doyle never regained consciousness.

Could the premonitions felt by Sir Donald Campbell and Sugar Ray Robinson have been evidence of real future-seeing, or were they simply macabre hunches brought about by the natural stresses their dangerous sport involved? The truth in these cases will never be known.

As we have seen, many experiences of premonition involved the deaths of the recipients themselves or the deaths of people for whom the recipients have strong personal feelings. For another type of doomwatcher the rationalists, sceptics and medical psychologists can find very little explanation. These are the people who witness moments of disaster and mass destruction; like Mrs Brennan they are unwilling observers to events beyond their understanding and control.

These horrified onlookers often not only see but actually share the pain, anguish and grief of the victims in these strange visionary events. They may see, hear and sense the physical presence of the scene itself. It is as though all of a sudden and for no apparent reason they are quite literally there – actually part of the tragedy. Disaster premonitions, whether they occur in a dream or waking state are brief, spontaneous, happening seemingly without warning, and without discernable cause. They often appear to people who have absolutely no connection with the real event itself. Why or how they happen is a complete mystery. They are unpredictable, uncontrolled and terrifying phenomena which do not conform to accepted theories of what is and is not possible.

A typical case of a disaster prediction was the experience of an Eastern Airlines stewardess who was working on a New York to Miami shuttle service in 1972. One day in November, during her leave period, the young woman had a sudden visual impression of a Boeing 747 Jumbo jet crashing into water at night. Throughout the vision, which lasted only a few seconds, she could clearly hear the screams of the injured and drowning passengers. Afterwards, she was extremely upset, knowing with a sick feeling of dread that her next flight might be her last. Indeed the stewardess's anxiety was only muted by the knowledge that she herself did not fly a Boeing 747 like the one she had visualised crashing. However, on 29 December 1972 the standard aircraft used for the Miami to New York flight was unavailable, and a 747 was requisitioned as a last-minute replacement. On hearing of the scheduled change the doomwatcher asked to be transferred. Thus, when the plane crashed into the Florida Everglades killing seventy-nine people, the one person who had foreseen the tragedy was not among their number.

Fear of flying is a commonplace anxiety and it is not difficult to imagine how this everyday phobia might account for the prevalence of air disasters among those premonitions recorded by regular air travellers. Even so, some air crashes are foreseen by people who do not fly themselves.

In Britain in July 1972, Mrs Monica Clarke of Letchworth, Hertfordshire, 'saw' an airliner nose-diving into a field. It crashed 'without noise' she claimed to her bemused friends and family. Mrs Clarke had never knowingly possessed psychic powers, nor had she ever flown personally or feared to do so.

Given the distress that the premonition caused her, Mrs Clarke's family suggested that she saw a doctor. Three days later, on 18 July a BEA Trident jet ploughed into countryside near London's Heathrow Airport killing 118 people. Curiously, the Trident, which had suffered a complete engine failure, was described by eyewitnesses to have fallen silently to earth.

Occasionally recipients of disaster premonitions take steps to avoid their destiny. In 1973 a large group of women from three villages in Somerset organised a skiing holiday in Switzerland. Through their local Women's Institute they chartered a Vanguard jet and arranged the block booking. For many, it was to be a holiday of a lifetime. But fate had other ideas. On its outward journey the plane crash-landed into a mountainside near Basle and so great was the impact that all those on board perished. Yet in a strange sense there was one survivor: Mrs Marion Warren, a farmer's wife from the Somerset village of Churchill Green, who had received a vivid warning three weeks before the departure date. In her sleep, she had seen the aircraft skim low over trees before ploughing into a white hillside. As the smoke cleared she could see the crushed and mangled bodies of her friends and neighbours lying in the snow. Purely as a result of the nightmare Mrs Warren sold her ticket for half the face value and refused to consider going on the holiday, despite her husband's protests. Sadly, she feared being disbelieved and chose not to tell anyone else the reason for her change of plan. Only afterwards when the dream had become grim reality did her full story appear in the London *Evening Standard*.

The fear of ridicule is common among doomwatchers. Just as many people who see ghosts or UFOs decide to keep silent in case they will be thought of as mad, so many witnesses to unnatural premonitions prefer to keep their experiences to themselves, or else tell only those they completely trust.

One notable exception to this rule was an American doomwatcher, David Booth of Cincinnati, who dreamt in 1979 for seven consecutive nights that a DC10 airliner had crashed at an American airport. Booth took his premonition so seriously that he pestered the various US airlines until at last he got someone to listen. He was interviewed by Paul Williams, an official of the Federal Aviation Association. Initially wary, Williams was impressed by the clarity of detail contained in Booth's mental impressions. He also became convinced of the man's integrity. However, since neither Williams nor his superiors could think of any practical way to avert the future disaster – short of grounding all American based DC10s – they simply did nothing and prayed that it would not come true.

The tormented David Booth went away unsatisfied and continued to experience his nightmare. Three days after his conversation with Williams his vision was tragically fulfilled when a Pan Am jet crashed in flames at Chicago airport. In all there were 270 fatalities making it the worst death toll in US aviation history. Seeing pictures of the plane, American Airlines flight 191, David Booth knew for certain that it was the same one he had seen in his vision. Horrified though he was, his ordeal was over for his dream never returned.

*

Some parapsychologists have conjectured that disasters attract (or project?) premonitory influences in proportion to their size. The greater the scale of the tragedy, the higher becomes the likelihood of previsions. Some of the major disasters of the twentieth century have provided much evidence to support this theory.

For instance, before the 1975 Moorgate tube disaster, which was the London Underground's worst accident for sixty years, there were numerous accounts of Londoners dreaming of being trapped in a long, dark tunnel filled with choking smoke. So many were reported that the British Society for Psychical Research made an individual study of each case. Afterwards the investigators published their conviction that the previsions could not be explained away in terms of coincidence.

An even more striking example surrounds the sinking in 1912 of the *Titanic*. Literally hundreds of people claimed afterwards to have foreseen the catastrophe, and so widespread were these accounts from sources around the world that an entire book was able to be written devoted solely to that one terrible incident.

A similarly unparalleled human disaster took place in Wales in 1966. At exactly nine fifteen a.m. on the morning of 21 October a huge heap of coal slag located outside the village of Aberfan slid down upon Pantglass Junior School. A total of 144 people lost their lives under the advance of that terrible avalanche, including 128 children. The British public's sorrow was heightened by the knowledge that the disaster could have been avoided. Like the *Titanic* fiasco many years before, human folly was to blame for the misery of Aberfan. Yet whilst most of the population looked for scapegoats in authority, one man, Dr J.C. Barker, was interested in a different aspect of the affair.

Barker, a psychiatrist from Shrewsbury, was aware that large-scale disasters had frequently been the subjects of previsions in the past and set out to discover if this was also the case with Aberfan. Through a contact in Fleet Street, Peter Fairley, who was then science correspondent for the London *Evening Standard*, Barker appealed for people who had experienced a premonition to contact him. Over one hundred letters were received of which thirty-five were adjudged to be reliable. These Aberfan premonitions, which included dreams, trances and waking visions, were varied in their particular visual representation. One woman dreamt that she saw hundreds of black horses charging down a hillside pulling hearses, whilst several other correspondents spoke of a suffocating sensation and a black mist appearing before their eyes. Some previsions were alarming in their directness.

Mrs Grace Eagleston, a housewife from Kent, had dreamt the week before the actual event that 'hundreds of children' were to die in a mining village, crushed by a mountain of coal. Another doomwatcher, Mrs Hennessy of Barnstaple, heard a voice telling her how the tragedy would kill dozens and saw a vision of children struggling frantically to escape from the choking dust. Most of the examples revealed to Barker were from people who lived nowhere near Aberfan and had probably never heard of the obscure Welsh valley community. By far the most poignant premonition focused upon ten-year-old Eryl Mai Jones, a victim of the disaster, who on the night before told her parents how she had seen a 'big black thing' coming down on her school. The next day she was dead along with more than a hundred of her school friends.

Dr Barker believed that premonitions – if analysed carefully – could one day warn of impending disasters in a useful, practical way, provided this undeveloped faculty of the human mind could be harnessed and trained. Along with Peter Fairley, he set up the British Premonitions Bureau in January 1967. In the end the bureau met with little success, for, while premonitions continued to be collected, no discernible way was ever found to adapt the knowledge to avert the future. Unfortunately, few people who saw disasters recognised the time or place where the events were to take place. In 1969 the researchers eventually admitted defeat and the bureau ceased to exist.

So can previsions never be made useful? Perhaps they already are ...

Whilst scientific attempts to quantify and use premonitions have failed, there may well be unofficial, or perhaps we should say unconscious, ways of avoiding disasters already at work. In the early 1960s an American parapsychologist, William Cox, conducted a series of statistical surveys on the numbers of rail passengers using trains which had subsequently crashed. Cox was trying to ascertain whether doomed trains carried the same ration of passengers as did ones that had reached their destination safely. If the proportion was lower on the day of the accident than was usual for that particular run, then Cox felt it might indicate that people had a tendency to avoid the fateful day.

To many it seemed an extremely long shot, but the results of the American parapsychologist's surveys were startling. Data from over one hundred accidents spread over a six-year period confirmed Cox's suspicion that fewer passengers travelled on doomed trains than those who travelled on other days, and that the statistical differences were far higher than could reasonably be explained in terms of mere chance. Using a computer Cox estimated that the odds against the set of figures occurring coincidentally were well over a million to one. He concluded, therefore, that whether they realised it or not, people do predict disasters and take evasive action, albeit on a subconscious level.

One day it may be proved that we all experience unconscious predictive sensations, only some of which surface into our conscious minds. However, there is a special group of people who are already quite aware of the reality of their premonitions and use the power seemingly at will. These are the professional doomwatchers, the soothsayers, prophets and seers who have made a living throughout history predicting the rise and fall of princes, rulers, kingdoms and empires.

Professional doomwatchers, as opposed to everyday astrologers or fortune tellers, have a tendency to see only the darker sides of life and death. Often eccentric, their strange powers of looking through a glass darkly have been rewarded and reviled depending upon the fortune of their future glimpses.

The reputation of some soothsayers appears to be especially macabre. In the last century an Englishman named John Worsdale was noted for his remarkably accurate analysis of horoscopes, into which he invariably included the date of his client's death – whether requested or not. Far from being worried over the distress that this caused, Worsdale, who must have been a singularly unpleasant individual, took great pleasure in informing those who paid him of their impending doom, especially if their end was not too distant. Occasionally his cruelty could be merciless. When, for instance, a young girl approached him to enquire as to her prospects for marriage, Worsdale replied curtly that the question was pointless since she would be dead within a month. The poor girl left in tears and her outraged father remonstrated furiously with the seer. Yet Worsdale had not lied. Three weeks later the young woman was drowned in a boating accident. To add insult to injury, the heartless astrologer turned up at his client's funeral to boast to mourners of his successful prediction.

Soothsaying can be a risky business. Historical records show how, in the last decade of the fourteenth century, an Italian palmist named Andreas Carvas made a tidy living in his home town of Bologna simply through correctly predicting the births and deaths of well-known citizens. However, when he foresaw in 1393 that the town's mayor was going to commit a detestable murder the following week, he bit off more than he could chew. The mayor did indeed stab a man to death the following week – Carvas himself, a crime motivated entirely by the slander attached to his name.

Coincidentally, Carvas's successor, a palmist called

Tibertus Antiochus, also fell foul of the local authorities through an insensitive prevision. Antiochus infuriated the local military commander, one General Guerva, when he told him that he was destined to die shortly by an assassin's blade. Guerva angrily threw him out of his house but the story spread throughout Bologna. Exactly one year later the garrison commander did indeed die as predicted – stabbed in the back by an unknown attacker. However, if Tibertus Antiochus felt any satisfaction at being vindicated, the feeling must have been short lived. The day following the murder he was arrested and charged with conspiracy and – though a preposterous accusation and lacking in any hard evidence – was tried, found guilty and hanged. In successfully predicting the death of the general he had also signed his own death warrant.

Today's professional seers may be fewer than in the Middle Ages, but the rewards are far greater and the business is distinctly less hazardous.

Probably the greatest living doomwatcher is the American clairvoyant Jeanne Dixon, who has successfully predicted the deaths of many statesmen, politicians and show-business figures. Today her column is syndicated in almost three hundred newspapers and magazines across the USA and Canada, earning her a fortune. Born in 1918 Dixon began to receive spiritualistic impressions at the age of eight after her mother was told by a gypsy of her remarkable powers. With her ESP developing, she began using a crystal ball to foresee the future, and by the time the Second World War broke out her fame had spread across continental North America. It was also around this time that she began to reveal her peculiar gift for divining death. In December 1944 Dixon visited the White House. The then President, Franklin D. Roosevelt, was an ill man and desired to know how much time he had left. Dixon told him that she honestly believed that he had no more than six months. Roosevelt died on 12 April 1945. Two years later she was to make a similar prediction for Indian spiritual leader Mohandas Gandhi who was duly assassinated.

Another American president to die in office was John F. Kennedy. As early as 1952 Dixon had foreseen Kennedy's death after receiving a vision of the White House with the year 1960 printed on the front, and an ominous dark cloud looming overhead. President Kennedy, who was murdered in 1963, had been elected to office in 1960. Other deaths correctly predicted by Jeanne Dixon during the height of her psychic powers included the human rights activist Martin Luther King and actress Marilyn Monroe. In each case she correctly stated not only the year of their demise but the manner of their exit – murder and suicide respectively.

Perhaps her most striking prediction was the death of Senator Robert Kennedy in June 1968 whilst campaigning for the Democratic nomination. A week before the fateful event Jeanne Dixon had vividly seen the contender gunned down in the lobby of the Ambassador Hotel, Los Angeles. So certain was the prophetess of this eventuality that she repeatedly attempted to contact the politician's family. Despite finally reaching Kennedy's mother, no heed was paid to her warning. Bobby Kennedy continued his scheduled campaign route and was duly shot dead in the Ambassador's lobby.

If Jeanne Dixon is the most successful scryer when it comes to foretelling the deaths of the famous, then another American, Joseph Delouise, seems to have an equally remarkable ability for predicting general disasters. Formerly a hairdresser, Delouise demonstrated his powers to millions of TV viewers and radio listeners during the late 1960s and the 1970s. Much of his doomwatching has proven to be uncannily accurate. For instance, speaking on a radio show on 14 December 1968, Delouise stated that there would be a major rail collision early in the New Year. On 16 January 1969, he was even more specific, saying that the accident would occur the following day in or around the Chicago area. At one o'clock that morning two trains collided head-on in fog, killing and injuring forty-seven people. The location was some forty miles south of

Chicago city. It was by no means the doomwatcher's only spectacular hit. On 25 November 1967 he had predicted the collapse of a bridge within a month, an event which he insisted would 'kill over forty'. On 16 December the same year, the bridge spanning the Ohio river did collapse. Thirty-six died and another ten were listed as missing. Most astonishing of all Delouise's predictions concerned the crash of an Allegheny DC-9 jet liner over Indianapolis in the fall of 1968. Earlier in the year Delouise had suggested that a mid-air collision over Indianapolis would kill a total of seventy-nine persons, but added that a larger figure – 330 – would be in some way involved in the incident. The time of the Allegheny jet's impact with a private plane was given as three thirty p.m. The overall death toll was seventy-eight passengers and crew, plus the light aircraft's pilot, thus exactly matching Delouise's prediction from the previous spring.

Not all predictions come true and even so-called experts often end up with red faces when their prophecies fail to materialise. Edgar Cayce, known as the sleeping prophet, gave many astonishing trance-induced predictions before his death in 1945. Yet he was quite wrong to assume that the formation of an Israeli state in 1948 would coincide with the re-emergence of the lost Island of Atlantis. Equally erroneous was the rash promise of Irenee Hughes, currently America's self-proclaimed First Lady of parascience, who spoke in 1982 of a new ice age beginning the following year. Even Jeanne Dixon has been known to be spectacularly wrong on occasions. Her least successful prediction of death came in 1966 when she confidently asserted on US television that Fidel Castro of Cuba was 'already dead'. Twenty-five years later the bearded dictator remains stubbornly alive.

No prophet can claim a hundred per cent success, and amusing though it is to see those reputations humbled, examples of misplaced predictions should not detract from the extraordinary evidence amassed by professional doom-watchers over the years. Why these walking antennae for psychic impressions occasionally fail is not clear, yet the mere fact that they do in no way serves to invalidate the true predictions they astonishingly make. Jeanne Dixon herself feels that she occasionally misinterprets signs in much the same way that mediums sometimes misinterpret messages from the other side. This may not be an adequate explanation for sceptics, but the fact remains that inspired guess-work cannot reasonably be held up as the reason for the many detailed predictions correctly produced by this select band of gifted individuals.

The phenomenon of prediction has only rarely been studied on a serious scientific basis and whilst this sad state of affairs continues premonitions will remain a faculty of the human mind that is mysterious. Up until very recently scientists have not begun to consider the possibility of precognition, since the very mention of the word places traditional concepts of time and space under threat. If predictions can be proved to exist (and enough evidence would seem to have been compiled to put forward a strong case) then the world we live in is a quite different one from that which the scientists would have us believe we inhabit. Ironically, whilst most of the scientific world refuses to countenance the idea of precognition long after the evidence has become overwhelming, there is one area of study – subatomic physics – where old concepts of time and space are being rapidly revaluated. Since Einstein's theory of general relativity it has become accepted amongst micro-physicists that there can be no absolute sequence of events on a subatomic level, nor any objective way of ordering them. In the invisible world of the nuclear interior time itself becomes a distinctly illusive concept. As Einstein himself said, 'For physicists, the separation between past, present and future has the value of mere illusion.'

Yet even the reputation of the century's greatest mind cannot influence those who oppose the concept of prevision as applied to the human world. For the vast majority of our scientists, the idea that we can see tomorrow remains a nonsense.

If we accepted Einstein's premise and applied it to our own existence, can the knowledge that the future is not entirely separate be of any practical use? If the future remains fixed and inevitable then the answer is surely 'no'. On the other hand if a forewarning can avert future accidents from occurring, then the importance of prediction research becomes incalculable. At present we are no nearer to finding an answer to these questions. Some doomwatchers believe that the story is twofold: that some future events are preordained, fixed and inevitable ... destined to occur long before they do; other events – of less vital importance – are more likely to carry a potential for alteration before they happen.

The truth behind these theories, like prevision itself, remains a long way from being understood. All we can say with certainty is that as long as concepts of time exist, predictions will be around to contradict them.

UNLUCKY FOR SOME

On the night of 20 January 1989 fate descended like the angel of death upon a small area of the English countryside in the county of Surrey. As darkness fell babies began inexplicably to die in villages whose distance was never more than seven miles from each other. By morning ambulancemen had recovered the bodies of six infants from distraught households. In the absence of a causal link between the deaths – which were put down to 'sudden infant death syndrome', a rare mystery illness for which there is no explanation and no cure – paediatricians investigating the bizarre series of tragedies put their odd conjunction down to simple coincidence.

From a medical standpoint the doctors may be right; but is coincidence itself as simple and straightforward as most of us believe it to be?

Certainly, my research for this book has led me to doubt it very seriously. Two instances from among many will serve to make the point. In October 1987 I investigated the fire death of an Essex man surnamed Ashton, the circumstances of which led me to suspect it might be a case of spontaneous combustion. My hunch turned out to be false; the fire in a bedsit in Southend-on-Sea had started naturally. However, a few months later I learned of the genuine SHC death of one Alfred Ashton of Southampton, another coastal town in the south of England. Did my initial interest in the first Mr Ashton trigger a similar though much stranger fate in the second – a man of whose existence I knew nothing? I hope and pray that the two events were unconnected and, rationally, there is no reason to suppose otherwise. And yet ...

Another mystery involving spontaneous human combustion gave me similar pause for thought the following year. The day after I finished writing the introduction to *Unnatural Causes*, containing the details of the three girls who died whilst dancing, I went into a local library to return a book entitled *The Executioner's Song* by Norman Mailer. Mailer's work is a complex study of Gary Gilmour, the American prisoner whose controversial fight for the right to end his death-row limbo life led to the reintroduction of the death penalty in the US judicial system. I returned my copy and whilst I was in the library I spent a little time browsing through the section on mysteries. There I noticed for the first time the combustion of another woman who burst into flames in a Darlington discotheque in November 1980; her name: Vicky Gilmour. I left the library wondering whether someone was trying to tell me something – but if so, what?

Few would disagree that coincidences provide an endlessly fascinating topic of conversation. Everyone has their bizarre experience to relate and even the most trivial of examples can sometimes make us stop and wonder whether some unknown force is at work behind the scenes of our everyday lives. We all like to feel lucky and even the least superstitious of persons will occasionally avoid walking under a ladder. Even so, most modern-thinking Westerners would scoff at the idea that chance could of itself have a direct influence upon their lives. In a world of scientific certainties and materialistic values the sceptical viewpoint is perfectly logical; yet my researches have led me to believe that it is also entirely wrong. For during my investigations I have found too many examples where fate has appeared suddenly and terrifyingly in the form of a macabre cosmic joker intent on making sad fools of his human victims. Some of these sinister coincidences concern famous deaths, such as the assassination of statesmen; others involve the passing of individuals whose demise would otherwise have gone unreported. Many involve the deaths of a few people; some concern the slaughter of thousands. Taken altogether they compile a body of evidence so remarkable that it offers us little alternative but to accept the startling probability that the physical universe as we know it is controlled by underlying forces, forces the significance of which humanity has yet to recognise.

According to the dictionary definition coincidences occur when two or more unrelated happenings in everyday life share eccentric correlations of time, place or circumstance. In my own studies I have discovered that the most intriguing examples are often the ones where all three factors are woven together in a sinister tapestry of doom. The following true story, which came to my attention soon after I began my initial research, is an excellent demonstration of just how bewildering these sequences can be.

The coincidence concerns the deaths, in separate road accidents, of two brothers from Merseyside, England, a full report of which was carried by the *Liverpool Echo* on 21 July 1975. Entitled 'The Cruellest Twist of Fate', the newspaper article began by describing how the two men, both in their twenties, had been killed whilst driving mopeds in the same street; in each case the other vehicle involved in the fatal collision was the same taxi. The report went on to explain that not only was the taxi driver the same on both occasions but that the cab was carrying the same fare-paying passenger en route to the same destination each time. This last detail seems especially strange, since that particular passenger was not a regular cab user and had not travelled along that road in between times. Finally, to complete the oddity, the *Echo* reported how both brothers had met their respective demise at approximately the same time of the day and exactly twelve months apart.

A cruel twist of fate it certainly was, and faced with such an appalling procession of chance the bereaved family of these luckless Liverpudlians must have surely wondered whether we are truly 'as flies to wanton boys' in the hands of Shakespeare's malevolent gods. Yet when the Liverpool paper went on to describe the tragedy as probably being unique in the annals of coincidental death, it could have hardly been more wrong. For, as we shall see, when fate turns to fatality weird sequences like the ones detailed above are far from unique ... and they are not always accidents.

A case of delayed-action murder might be the best way to describe the curious fate of Henry Ziegland, a farmer from Honey Grove, Texas who was shot and wounded by a vengeful neighbour in 1893. The bullet which was intended to kill Ziegland merely grazed his body and embedded itself in a tree on his property. Yet the bullet must have had his name on it for twenty years later when Ziegland decided to remove the same tree from his land using explosives, he was struck in the head and killed instantly by the very bullet fired all those years before.

Often it is similarities between apparently unconnected incidents which raise the hairs on the back of one's neck. A few years ago a high-ranking member of the West Midlands Constabulary noticed a marked resemblance between the circumstances surrounding two violent murders. The crimes, which had taken place on the detective's own patch, were in many respects identical. Both had been carried out in the same manner – strangulation – and for the same motive: to satisfy a depraved and sadistic sexual appetite. Yet despite these facts and a further series of overlapping details, the West Midlands Police did not consider it likely that the same man might be responsible, or that the crimes could be linked in any way. Their certainty was perfectly logical: the two identical murders were committed over one hundred and fifty years apart.

In the first killing, twenty-year-old Mary Ashford was found dead on Tuesday 27 May 1817. The location was Erdington, then a village five miles outside the city of Birmingham. The body of the other victim, Barbara Forrest, also twenty, was discovered on the morning of

Tuesday 27 May 1974. She lay in precisely the same spot as her predecessor, though the area by that time had been swallowed up by the metropolis. Further grim similarities were apparent in each assault. Both women had died at roughly the same time the night before; each had been raped; after they were strangled, a hurried but unsuccessful attempt had been made to hide their corpses. A further likeness involved each girl's movements prior to her murder. Both Mary Ashford and Barbara Forrest were on their way to Whit Monday dances when they met their respective killers. Neither had returned home after work since both had changed into party dresses at the houses of friends.

The strangest of all duplications concerned not the crimes themselves but subsequent events. For in the weeks following the two killings a man was arrested and charged with the murder – each with a surname of Thornton. Both men stood trial, pleaded innocent and were acquitted on the grounds of insufficient evidence. Neither homicide was ever solved. Officers of the West Midlands Constabulary became uneasy over the similarities between the two events, yet as a newspaper report pointed out they simply *had* to be coincidence. There could be no other explanation.

Not all coincidental killings are separated by such a long period of time. Consider the details of a little-remembered political assassination which took place at the beginning of the present century. In 1900 King Umberto I of Italy was dining with an aide in a restaurant in Monza, when during the meal the restaurant proprietor, also called Umberto, visited the royal table to enquire as to His Majesty's satisfaction. Whilst the two men were talking it became evident to the King that certain key events in the host's life mirrored those of his own. Not only did they share the same birthday, 14 March, but both men had married women named Margherita on the same date and sired sons named Vittorio. Even their careers had begun at the same time, since the restaurateur had opened his premises on the day of his namesake's coronation.

Although not a naturally superstitious man, Umberto I was fascinated by these common bonds of fate and promised to return to the restaurant again on his next visit to the city. It was never to be. The following day, as he was preparing to leave for Rome, the monarch was informed that the man he had met the previous night was dead. In an attack apparently without motive, Umberto the restaurant proprietor had been gunned down in the street. By all accounts the Italian monarch was shaken by the news, yet we cannot tell whether he viewed it as portentous. He certainly should have done, for the two men whose lives had been intertwined so closely met their deaths in like fashion. On that very afternoon, as King Umberto I stepped on to the streets of Monza to greet the crowds of cheering subjects, he was cut down by a single anarchist's bullet.

The tale of the Italians, strange though it is, pales into insignificance beside the most famous of coincidental assassinations – the deaths of American Presidents Lincoln and Kennedy. The links surrounding the lives and deaths of both victim and gunman stand as a definitive testament to the extent to which coincidence can run on and on and on ... For the historian, it is their achievements in office which make the deaths of these two American statesmen momentous; for the student of the inexplicable, the relevant details concern the deaths themselves.

Abraham Lincoln, Emancipator of the Slaves and Leader of the Union, was shot in the back of the head at point-blank range whilst watching a play in Ford's Theatre, Washington DC. His killer, John Wilkes Booth, used a pistol for his crime which took place in 1865, a few days after the end of the American Civil War. John F. Kennedy, Democratic President and champion of civil rights legislation, was shot in the head whilst travelling by motorcade along a Dallas thoroughfare. His murderer, Lee Harvey Oswald, chose a high-powered rifle with a telescopic sight as his weapon. The date, as everyone knows, was November 1963.

So what are the supposedly strange connections between the two crimes? Both took place on a Friday, but that is a minor coincidence, as is the fact that both assassins were Southerners. Of much greater interest is the birthday of the two killers, for Lee Harvey Oswald was born exactly one hundred years after Lincoln's killer. This century time span, a small point in itself, will be seen to recur with ominous regularity as we examine the life histories of other men involved in the drama. It is interesting to note, for example, that John Kennedy was elected to Congressional office exactly one hundred years after his illustrious predecessor, and that their respective elections to the office of President also share the same century-wide margin. Both Lincoln and Kennedy were succeeded by Southern Democrats named Johnson, and the birth dates of each of these is also separated by exactly one century: Andrew Johnson born in 1808; Lyndon Johnson in 1908.

There were further coincidences of name apparent in the murders. JFK's personal private secretary was surnamed Lincoln; Abe Lincoln's secretary had the Christian name of John. Abraham Lincoln died in Ford's Theatre in Washington, whilst Kennedy was riding in a Ford-manufactured automobile on the day of his eclipse. The limousine in which the President rode along with his wife Jackie was a Lincoln Continental. Perhaps we now might be forgiven for redefining our view of the universe on this evidence alone. Yet even this is not the end of the eerie parallels between the two murders. It is well recalled that neither Booth nor Oswald lived to stand trial; what is less well known is the similarity between the way each man had attempted to escape justice. Booth, having committed his terrible deed in a theatre, ran to a warehouse to hide. Oswald, on the other hand, having aimed his deadly salvo from a warehouse window, ran into a theatre in order to make good his escape; neither, of course, succeeded.

Perhaps the most intriguing among all the many presidential parallels concerns the first public proposals for

Lincoln's nomination. In a letter printed in the *Cincinnati Gazette*, 6 November 1858, came a call for Lincoln to run for president alongside a long-since-forgotten vice presidential running mate, then Secretary to the Navy. The Secretary's name? John Kennedy.

The above details, scarcely believable in their complexity of chance correlation, defy all concepts of randomness. During the last forty years many researchers into the paranormal have come to believe that such irrational convergences cannot be explained without taking into account the possibility of underlying forces – forces which 'at all times and in all places seek to create order from disorder', in the words of one writer.

If one wished to find evidence for such forces one need look no further than the published works of Arthur Koestler. A highly respected philosopher in the humanist tradition, Koestler became intrigued in his middle years by the new science of parapsychology and the possibilities of latent powers in the minds of men. As his interest developed, he began to conduct his own research into the subject, encompassing not only the more sensational aspects of psychic phenomena such as hauntings and clairvoyance, but also those everyday occurrences, the often minor anomalies of chance that we commonly label 'coincidence'. It was this branch of his inquiry which proved most fruitful and eventually took shape in two books, *The Drinkers of Infinity* and *The Roots of Coincidence*. Koestler was particularly fascinated by instances where fact and fiction intermingled, and in the second of these works he considered the startling connections between stories previously written and real-life events that subsequently took place.

One notable example was 'The Narrative of Gordon Pym', a short story by the master of terror, Edgar Allan Poe. In Poe's tale, written during the early 1840s, the hero is shipwrecked and cast adrift in an open boat along with three other survivors. As weeks go by, hunger turns to starvation and the men agree that one of their number should be eaten. Lots are drawn to decide who should provide the necessary sustenance, and a cabin boy named Richard Parker proves the unlucky member of the crew. He is then killed and eaten as planned. The real-life events which horrifically paralleled this goulish tale took place in 1884 when a cargo vessel named the *Mignotte* sank in mid-Atlantic following a storm. Four seamen survived and spent some time drifting in a lifeboat. Eventually, driven mad by hunger and thirst, the three older sailors attacked and ate the youngest member, who, as in the Poe story, had been the ship's cabin boy. His name was Richard Parker. There is only one striking coincidence in this case – the name of the cannibalised seaman. Yet it is surely difficult to imagine a more astonishing one. Can Edgar Allan Poe have unconsciously predicted the future when he chose the name of his unfortunate character? Or could his story have been somehow responsible for the real Parker's grisly end?

Another example of the fact-following-fiction variety of coincidence discovered by Arthur Koestler surrounds events which took place on the maiden voyage of the now infamous SS *Titanic*. In one terrible night in 1912 more than thirteen hundred men, women and children lost their lives as the great ship, pride of the White Star Line and considered unsinkable by its designers, slipped beneath the icy waters of the North Atlantic. The maritime disaster was on a scale unprecedented in peacetime. Yet the events had been described by a writer in quite meticulous detail over fourteen years earlier.

In 1898, British novelist Morgan Robertson published a novel entitled *Futility*. In the book, a great liner strikes an iceberg on its maiden voyage, and despite a reputation of unsinkability, goes down with huge loss of life. The author called his fictional vessel *Titan*. The similarity in name would be connection enough for most people to suspect the hand of fate, yet further details bear out the eerie comparison to an incredible degree. Like her fictional predecessor, the *Titanic* carried too few lifeboats; as with the *Titanic*, the *Titan* was reckoned to be the largest vessel afloat. Even the dimensions of the two vessels bore an uncanny likeness: the berth capacity, number of funnels, of turbines, of propeller screws were all exactly the same. Indeed, in almost every imaginable sense the two ships were identical. More importantly, so was their dark destiny.

In discussing 'The Narrative of Gordon Pym', and *Futility*, Koestler formed an opinion that a causal link must exist between mankind's collective imagination and the objective world of matter. Fictional representations, he felt, must operate on a level of thought which can, under certain uncertified conditions, directly affect real happenings across time and space. The framework of possibilities might then be seen as a three-dimensional spider's web across which thoughts and events interact through a system of telepathic communications too deep to be detected. Only when coincidence occurs do we notice this influence at work. Over the past two decades this hypothesis has gained some ground academically, yet there remains a clear majority of scientists and mathematicians who prefer to avoid the question altogether. There are a few more who refuse even to discuss the possibility that the human brain can affect the working out of events elsewhere. However, there have been exceptions even among the academic establishment.

The first person to study the laws of coincidence scientifically was Dr Paul Kammerer. An Austrian by birth and a biologist by discipline, Kammerer was a director of the Vienna Institute of Experimental Medicine when in 1919 he published a formidable paper on the subject of chance. He called it 'Das Gesetz der Serie' – the Law of Seriality. Through this conceptual law, Kammerer sought to bring the phenomenon of coincidence within the area of conventional scientific reference, thus making it a fit subject for serious experimental study. Coincidences, he believed, came in series, 'a recurrence of clustering in time and space whereby the individual members in the sequence are not connected by the same active'. The first part of the Austrian's study was concerned with the classification of experiences into groups or categories. These were largely personal since, prior to the writing of his work, Kammerer had kept a logbook of his own experiences, and it is from this diary that his observations were made. In the second, more theoretical study the author developed his central idea that there is an a-causal principle which at all times and in all places tends towards unity.

In some respects this force might be comparable to a universal gravity – yet it is distinct from gravity in the sense that it does not act upon all mass (in this case events) indiscriminately. In contrast, wrote Kammerer, seriality acts selectively upon form and function to produce configurations in time and space, like a multi-dimensional jigsaw puzzle being assembled. It becomes active initially through a correlation between like and like.

Seen in this light, the laws governing coincidences become nothing less than the manifestations of a universal principle as fundamental as the laws of physics. Without a material form themselves, and more subtle than magnetism, they were compared by the Austrian to those illusive particles of subatomic matter which exist in a space-time continuum beyond man's capacity to comprehend. The only time we become aware of them is when a particular pattern affects us as individuals – when a coincidence occurs in our own lives. This recognisable part is merely the tip of a very large iceberg. In reality, argued the author, seriality was nothing less than the umbilical cord by which thought and feeling were connected in the visible world.

If Paul Kammerer had been hoping to change the course of modern scientific thought with his novel theory he was quickly disappointed. Initially, the paper was ill-received by the academic establishment, though some notable figures, including Einstein, gave favourable reviews. More damaging to the biologist's reputation, however, was a scandal in which it was proved that he had deliberately falsified evidence during an experiment. Thrown out of his prestigious post at the university, and with his promising career in ruins, Kammerer committed suicide.

Today, over seventy years after its publication, 'Das Gesetz der Serie' looks like a singularly unsatisfactory piece of speculation. Indeed, many of its most controversial assertions concerning physics have long since been disproved. Nevertheless the Austrian's efforts were not altogether wasted, for whatever drawbacks seriality may have had as a workable theory, it did open up fields of thought previously unexplored. It also led to the development of some more interesting research. This came nearly forty years after Kammerer's death when, in the late 1950s, Nobel Prize-winning physicist Wolfgang Pauli joined forces with the distinguished Swiss psychologist Carl Gustav Jung to produce the concept of synchronicity.

In the book they wrote jointly on the subject of co-incidence, these two eminent figures modified and extended Kammerer's seriality, yet the basic framework remained the same – since both agreed that coincidences must be 'visible traces of invisible principles'. Like the Austrian biologist, the physicist Pauli felt that he could detect non-causal, non-physical factors operating in nature. In the middle of the twentieth century this was still a highly unusual position for a respectable scientist to hold.

Jung, on the other hand, had experimented with parapsychology and spiritualism during his early days in medicine. Unlike Kammerer, who rejected ESP out of hand as a possible contributory factor, Jung saw it as having a central role in coincidences and other strange phenomena. Indeed, the psychologist went to the opposite extreme by interpreting all events which could not otherwise be accounted for as being manifestations of this same principle; the collective mind, as he called it, working on the deepest strata of the human psyche. Summing up their position, Pauli and Jung wrote that precognition, coincidences and other preternatural happenings were all evidence of a single force field which is – as Kammerer had previously suggested – trying to impose its own form of discipline in the general confusion of everyday events. This force field was labelled 'synchronicity' and the bringing together of events it created were 'synchronisms'.

Given the formidable reputation each enjoyed in his respective field, the combination of Wolfgang Pauli and C.G. Jung might have been expected to have produced a powerful argument for their theories. In fact, the reverse proved true. Hampered by Jung's confusing literary style, rich in verbiage and short on hard facts, the book was considered unreadable by all but a few. Another serious limitation, in scientific terms, was that synchronicity was completely untestable. Thus, whilst the term synchronicity is now part of the language, the theory it describes has remained largely ignored outside the rarefied realms of parapsychology.

By considering coincidence as a fit subject for serious scientific research, Professors Kammerer, Jung and Pauli were attempting something unfashionable in the academic world. The majority of their learned colleagues preferred to work within orthodox fields of study, leaving the border-lands of supernature to the spiritualists and other 'cranks'. To many scientists a willingness to explore the world of the unknown was considered to be at the very least unwise, and at the very worst heretical. Little has changed in the years since *Synchronicity* was published. Physicists today are just as quick to ridicule any hypothesis which includes the possibility of mental control of normal physical laws. Once exposed, their so-called logical opposition is usually found to be a subtle form of bigotry – an intellectual bigotry entrenched in a quagmire of dogma and laid firmly upon a bedrock of hardened scepticism. In the case of coincidences this blinkered prejudice has a powerful ally: the Law of Probability. Conventional mathematicians always argue that coincidences are both natural and predictable; as one logician put it: 'Since there are millions of people in the world doing billions of things, it must be obvious that some totally unconnected similarities will come together. Even the million-to-one chance is really unremarkable.'

Viewed from this perspective coincidences become little more than naturally inevitable occurrences. Despite the mathematicians' bland assurances, those caught in the middle of genuinely sinister coincidences remain stubbornly unconvinced, as do writers like myself who have made it their business to study the phenomenon of irrational convergences.

Perhaps the strongest evidence for the existence of an underlying force behind coincidences comes when we consider the manifestation of jinxes. This specialised form of ongoing coincidences occurs when one factor – the person or object (or even a name or a number) – is surrounded by apparently interweaving variables which amount to rather more than chance groupings. Generally speaking, these coincidences tend to do more harm than good.

On an everyday scale jinxes are quite commonplace and most of us are probably already aware of one example. Usually, as in most cases of coincidence, jinx stories tend to be of a trivial nature. For instance we have all heard of a car which is constantly needing repair, and commiserate with our unfortunate friend or neighbour who owns it. Another case might surround a household item which seems unlucky – a knife, perhaps, with which every member of the family seems singularly determined to cut themselves. All of us have had experiences of these and even the most rational minds can at length be driven to talk in terms of 'that bloody thing', as if the offending article had a vindictive personality of its own. Even so, with hindsight, we inevitably cool down and accept that the luckless item was not to blame, reassuring ourselves that the ill fortune surrounding it was no more nor less than coincidence. Jinxes, like curses, do not form part of the modern man's frame of reference. However, unhappily for some, not all illogical runs of bad luck remain on a minor scale. Sometimes jinxes not only bring about death, disease and ruin, but do so with such a single-minded malevolence that it would appear to rule out any mathematical laws of probability. At this point the active force behind the pattern of coincidence becomes stronger and more menacing.

Paranormal investigators have long since established that the jinx force appears able to attach itself to anything: an individual, or group of individuals; works of art and literature; houses; precious diamonds or other sacred relics; even particular stretches of road or railway line. Two of the most frequently inhabited objects would seem to be ships and automobiles. In some cases it is possible to date, albeit tentatively, the beginnings of a jinx, whilst in others it is too difficult.

Why an object or place should acquire a jinx is an even more difficult question to answer, though very often an initial tragedy appears to have set a whole series of further misfortunes into motion. The only factor universal to all those numerous examples that I have investigated is that the jinx itself invariably leaves both misery and death in its wake.

The most remarkable jinxes I have come across involve those which have attached themselves to human beings. These peculiar runs of ill fortune can appear to envelop whole groups of people as well as individuals. Family jinxes, for instance, are extremely commonplace and I could not begin to list even a fraction of those that I have discovered. In America it is the most famous political clan – the Kennedys – which provides the best known modern example.

For decades tragedy haunted the destiny of America's first political family. Naturally everyone remembers the sensational assassinations of Jack and Bobby, but it is curious how many of the clan met their deaths or had a close shave in incidents whilst travelling. John F.

Kennedy's elder brother and sister both died in mid-air plane explosions in the 1940s and, of course, the President himself died whilst travelling in a motorcade. His younger brother Edward nearly died in another plane crash in which several Democratic party workers were killed; Edward again had a brush with death when his car plunged from Chappaquiddick Bridge, drowning his companion Mary Jo Kopechne. The Senator survived but his reputation lay in ruins. In 1968 J.F.K.'s younger brother Bobby Kennedy Snr, talked of his family's misfortunes being a tangible reality: 'Good luck is something you make and bad luck is something you endure,' he said. Two weeks later Bobby was shot dead. Although in this case the Kennedy's killing did not involve motion, the family's travel jinx returned with a vengeance only a few days later when the train carrying the statesman's coffin hit some mourners, cutting one man in half.

In the 1970s the next generation of Kennedys was plagued by drug addiction, scandal or severe ill health; there were also a number of automobile accidents. In one of these, Pam Kelly, a granddaughter of Joseph Kennedy, was paralysed for life. In another, a car driven by Bobby Kennedy Jr ran down and killed a Mexican peasant boy on a trip to Central America. As the decade progressed the family's misfortunes continued to be mysteriously linked with travel. In 1976 David, another son of the deceased Bobby Kennedy Snr, was stabbed by a black drug dealer in the public toilet of a railway station. He survived but two years later was found dead in a Palm Beach motel room whilst on a touring holiday in Florida.

Sometimes people from the same professional grouping become the centre of a jinx – at least for a period of time. In a fifteen-week period between March and June 1987 the British press reported a string of mysterious deaths among scientists working in the defence industry. The incidents included eight apparent suicides, one accident and a disappearance. Five of the deaths involved men working for the Marconi firm, yet these, like all the others, seemed unrelated. Neither colleagues nor family could offer a reason why these men should have ended their lives and police investigating the suicides were perplexed by the curious similarities between their violent methods of destruction. Typically the scientists would use a car to effect their death, either by exhaust fumes or crashing their vehicle. One man loaded his saloon with cans of petrol and drove headlong into a row of shops; another decapitated himself by tying a rope to a tree and looping it around his neck before driving away. Inquests into each of these deaths failed to find any connection between them – apart from their common occupation. (Or were these deaths in fact engineered by the powers-that-be in a sinister conspiracy to quash certain sensitive scientific findings?)

When people think of thirteen as an unlucky number they are probably right. In West Germany, road traffic statistics for a ten-year period up to 1987 suggested a regular increase in accidents across the country on every Friday 13th. Personally, I have collected so many cases of individuals claiming an unfortunate association with the number that I have little doubt that it is jinxed. In contrast seven seems almost everyone's lucky number. Almost, but not quite. Certainly not for Captain Hugh Donald McLeod, an American merchant skipper, born 7 July 1877 the seventh son of a seafaring family. The McLeod jinx first struck on 7 December 1909 when two of his brothers were lost as the steamer *Marguerite* sank en route to Port Stanley, Ontario. Their bodies were washed up separately on the seventh day of the next month – the same day Hugh McLeod received his first Captain's commission. On 7 April 1914 another of Hugh's brothers drowned after falling overboard from a barge that Hugh's own steamer was towing across Lake Huron. The rest of the seafarer's career was thankfully devoid of tragedy although his last voyage before retiring ended at Pearl Harbor on 6 December 1941 some seven hours before the Japanese aerial bombardment began on the seventh.

Captain McLeod seems to have demonstrated the Jonah

syndrome, a particularly odd type of jinx in which luckless individuals become the focus of tragic events whilst personally remaining immune. Quite unaffected themselves, they inexplicably trigger accidents, illness and death in those they live and work with. People with this unwanted gift of promoting misery have sometimes been labelled 'Jonahs'. By far the most infamous Jonah, and probably the most prodigious in the number of others she affected, was Typhoid Mary, a young American servant girl who solely may have been responsible for the epidemic which claimed the lives of some forty thousand people in the early part of this century. Her history of contamination began in 1906 when members of several wealthy New York households were stricken down with typhoid. A girl cook named Mary was discovered to have worked in the kitchens of all the affected residences, and whilst they could not explain her own immunity to the disease, health inspectors considered her to be the cause of the outbreak. She was imprisoned in an isolation cell for three years.

During her incarceration all tests to justify the health inspectors' opinions proved negative, and Mary was eventually released on the condition that she avoid domestic service in future. Sadly she did not take the advice. Five years later a number of people suddenly became ill in the city's Sloane Maternity Hospital. Typhoid was diagnosed and the luckless Mary was discovered to be working in the kitchens, under an assumed identity. Once more she was detained, this time without reprieve. Typhoid Mary ended her days in solitary confinement, reviled as one of the most prolific killers of all time.

Many people would still today consider hers a just punishment for the blatant disregard she held for the wellbeing of her fellow men and women. Yet recently medical figures have begun to doubt that Typhoid Mary was the cause of the outbreaks. Why, for instance, had no one been infected in the intervening years when she had worked in jobs handling food? Why also was typhoid never detected in her body in all the tests carried out over a period of many years? The mystery was never solved, but the indisputable fact remains that Typhoid Mary was at the epicentre of all the outbreaks. Could she have been the unknowing victim of a force every bit as deadly as typhoid – yet far more subtle?

We will never know whether Typhoid Mary really was a Jonah or not. Few, however, could doubt that her contemporary Jeanne Weber truly deserved the title. Weber, a French woman from the lower classes, was labelled 'The Ogress' for her apparently unconscious ability to bring about the deaths of children in the years following the turn of the century. In 1906 she was accused of murdering a total of four infants, two of whom were her own sons. Each child had expired in her custody, yet medical evidence supported her plea of innocence since the individual inquests recorded the deaths to have been the result of separate and unrelated natural causes.

However, her acquittal in 1906 was not the end of the story. In the year following her release from prison, Jeanne Weber was staying at the house of a friend who had a small boy. On only the second day of her visit the child choked to death whilst sitting on Weber's lap. Once more suspicion fell upon her and she was charged with infanticide. After two trials failed to produce a shred of evidence linking her with the cause of death she was freed.

A similar talent for promoting sudden illness and death in the young was displayed by Miss Christine Fallings, an eighteen-year-old epileptic from Blounstown, Florida. In February 1980, Fallings, who earned spare-time money as a babysitter, telephoned the state police to report the death of a baby in her care. The cause of the infant's death was found to be encephalitis, a brain inflamation. One year and one day on, having moved to Lakehand, Christine Fallings watched in astonishment as two young brothers went into convulsions the moment they were introduced to her for the first time. These two recovered in hospital, yet within a

271

week another boy she was sitting for had died of myocarditis, a heart condition. The next week another of her charges ended its life the same way. Finally, on 12 July 1981, a little girl died in Christine Fallings' arms moments after being given an inoculation for whooping cough. Following this last disaster, a distraught Fallings gave up the idea of working with children for good. Extensive medical tests were subsequently carried out upon the teenager, proving conclusively that she was not carrying any known communicable disease.

Occasionally jinxes attach themselves to a particular book or story. In these cases, the jinx does not always become active, or at least apparent, immediately the work is published or first performed. It may quite possibly begin to become jinxed only when the story is translated into another medium, or perhaps a different language. One famous twentieth-century work of literature which for many years seemed dogged with more than its fair share of ill luck was the *I Claudius* saga, written initially in the form of two novels by the late Robert Graves. Graves, a distinguished British author of both prose and poetry, originally published his Roman chronicles in the early 1930s, when they were justly acclaimed. However, though successful in its written form, attempts by Hollywood to turn the Claudius myth into a movie met with a series of unprecedented financial and physical disasters. After years of unsuccessful and costly mistakes and not a few mysterious fires on Hollywood studio sets, the whole project was dropped. *I Claudius* became a byword for bad luck in the movie capital. Strangely the Roman story was not the only piece by Graves to become jinxed. In 1947, whilst researching his book *The White Goddess*, a treatise on ritual magic, the Englishman became disturbed by a series of odd misfortuntes in his own life.

These experiences led Graves to believe that his project had become the centre of strange forces – and unlikely to bring him the fortune he had hoped. Nevertheless, Graves was a brave man, having survived the horrors of the

Somme, and went ahead with his planned study regardless of these preternatural warnings.

On completion of his script, Graves sent the text by mail to his usual publisher. Two days later the author received a phone message informing him that his publisher had suddenly died. In fact he had suffered a heart attack reading *The White Goddess*. Undeterred, Graves then sent his manuscript to a second publisher, who returned it abruptly together with a curt and decidedly uncomplimentary reply. This same man was found the next day hanging from an apple tree in his orchard. Eventually, having found no recognised publisher or agent prepared to touch it, Graves showed his manuscript to his friend, the poet T.S. Eliot. The great man not only liked it but published it at his own expense, whereupon the book became a success.

Believers in the occult, and I count myself among those people, might argue that the subject of *The White Goddess* had much to do with its pre-publication difficulties. True or not, it cannot be denied that fictional representations concerning the Devil and all his works do seem to have an increased likelihood of acquiring a jinx. Take, for example, *The Omen*, a 1975 film which described the coming of the Antichrist. The production of the film, which went on to become a box-office blockbuster, was positively plagued by odd accidents, illness and death. The author of the original script, David Seltzer, narrowly escaped death when the passenger plane in which he was flying was struck by lightning; meanwhile, on the same night, Gregory Peck, the film's star, suffered a similar experience on a separate flight. Director Dick Donner was knocked down and seriously hurt in an accident on location, whilst chief special effects man John Richardson was injured in another car accident in which his passenger was killed. In the worst incident of all, two stuntmen were badly savaged and a keeper killed when lions ran berserk during filming at a zoo. By the time the movie was completed the majority of the cast and crew were reportedly convinced that the Devil himself was involved in their string of misfortunes. John Richardson, the special effects expert who had narrowly survived the car crash, felt particularly certain, since his accident had taken place outside a small Dutch down called Ommen.

Britain is traditionally considered to be the home of haunted houses; it also has its fair share of jinxed ones. One particularly unhappy residence was acquired by a widow, Mrs Penelope Gallencault, in the spring of 1972. The house, a picturesque cottage set in the village of Bray in Berkshire, was meant to be Mrs Gallencault's dream home. It turned out to be a nightmare.

The first people to feel that something was wrong with the cottage were a couple of friends who stayed for a weekend.

They could not sleep in their room which, they said, seemed spooky and unnaturally cold. Certainly, the place had atmosphere – so much so that it had been once used as a location shot for a cheaply made British horror film. As it turned out the real horror was about to begin, for during the next two years tragedy would strike repeatedly in the life of Penelope Gallencault. In the first instance a neighbour was found dead in her garden, his body lying undiscovered for a full week. Then, incredibly, her two adult sons both drowned in separate incidents within a space of a month. The first, Charles, was found in the house's bath, whilst the younger, Richard, fell into a river which ran along the back of his mother's property. On this very same spot another man's body was found the following week – he too had drowned. The gruesome round of coincidence was further compounded when on 30 September 1973 a visitor to Mrs Gallencault's home inexplicably fell in the river and was drowned in the same stretch of water as the two men. The distraught widow promptly sold her dream home for a song.

Mrs Gallencault was not the only person to be convinced that something strange was taking place.

Following the last fatality the Berkshire Constabulary conducted a lengthy investigation into the string of co-incidences. Perhaps not surprisingly they drew a complete blank. Nevertheless, it was suggested that their own men noticed an eeriness about the cottage and, in summing up their findings to reporters, a police spokesman concluded by saying that the detectives working on the case were convinced that the deaths were more than just a bizarre series of unconnected incidents, even though no admissible evidence existed to support the hypothesis.

Another house which has regularly brought misery to its owners is Kelvedon Hall, a sixteenth-century mansion in the Essex countryside. The Hall, which is currently owned by a former British Cabinet Minister, The Rt. Hon. Paul Channon MP, began its legacy of doom in 1932 when it was converted briefly into a convent school. In the first year after the Sisters of St Michael took over the building, a number of inexplicable accidents and fires occurred. Then, in 1934, a chain of deaths rocked the establishment. First to die was a child who contracted tetanus poisoning after a playground fall. Within weeks another pupil died of a cerebral haemorrhage. The tragedies continued the following term: in September a Sister Premauesi was found drowned in the mansion's pond; a fortnight later another child died after a bout of pneumonia picked up during a spell of mild weather. The nuns who ran the school prayed hard for a change of luck yet their run of ill fortune was not over, for in late October a paying guest at the house, Mrs Margaret Gallivan, fell to her death from a third-floor window.

An inquest returned an open verdict on the unfortunate Mrs Gallivan, but the Sisters of St Michael were certain that sinister powers were to blame. Within a week of the woman's accident the Mother Superior closed the school and moved her nuns out. She was quoted in the local paper at the time as believing that there was something evil and terrible about the place, adding that her companions felt the same way. A spokesman for the local diocese meanwhile was reported as saying that the whole matter was 'uncanny to the last degree'.

Exorcists from the Roman Catholic church subsequently visited the Hall before it was sold in 1937 to the Channon family. Clearly its new occupier, Sir Henry Channon MP, immediately felt the same vague unease about his acquisition, and he asked the bishop of nearby Brentwood to bless the property. The blessing may have done the trick, for Sir Henry lived to a rich and prosperous old age and saw his son Paul also enter the Palace of Westminster. However, the jinx returned with a vengeance in 1986 when Paul Channon's daughter Olivia was found dying in her student flat at Oxford. An autopsy confirmed that she had swallowed a lethal cocktail of alcohol and heroin. In the resultant scandal, Channon lost not only his child but the chances of Cabinet promotion. Subsequent events suggested that the jinx of Kelvedon Hall was spreading somewhat wider, into the area of Paul Channon's ministerial responsibility. After becoming Secretary of State for Transport Channon was dogged with an unprecedented series of transport disasters throughout the United Kingdom, culminating in three major train crashes in the winter of 1988/89. With his political reputation coming under pressure Channon used a Parliamentary debate on 6 March 1989 to restore confidence in the public transport system. Yet at the precise moment that the Minister rose in the House of Commons to begin his speech another two trains collided in Glasgow killing and injuring more than fifty people. The following July Channon's misery was complete, when, upon the publication of an independent report critical of his role in the Lockerbie 747 disaster inquiry, he was sacked unceremoniously by Margaret Thatcher.

If houses are among the most common hosts for a jinx, then ships must surely be the outright favourite. Hoodoo vessels have been part of seafaring folklore ever since the Vikings. Whilst the early mariners relied so heavily upon luck and a fair wind this was not surprising, yet even in the relative safety of modern-day sea travel tales of jinxed ships continue to chill the spine of the most level-headed and experienced sailor.

During the last century the most famous liner to earn itself the unenviable reputation of a hoodoo was the *Great Eastern*. Built by Isambard Kingdom Brunel in the years between 1854 and 1857 the *Great Eastern* was meant to be the British engineer's finest achievement – a Victorian eighth wonder of the world. It was a true colossus: five times bigger than any other vessel afloat and designed to carry four thousand passenger across the Atlantic in a luxury previously undreamt of. With a double hull measuring more than seven hundred feet from bow to stern and divided for safety reasons into sixteen watertight compartments, Brunel's monstrosity was hailed as the greatest vessel to be constructed since the Ark. In reality it proved to be a floating danger area.

Initially the construction of the mighty iron-clad vessel progressed smoothly, taking just under the scheduled three years and involving no more than the usual number of industrial accidents which might be expected during such an undertaking. Yet towards the end of that time a mystery emerged when two workers – a riveter and his boy apprentice – went missing. It was known that they had been working upon a section of the hull prior to their disappearance and rumours spread suggesting that they may have been inadvertently sealed inside the thick double-layered sheets of metal. For his part Brunel remained blissfully ignorant of the speculation surrounding the fate of his two unfortunate employees. Nevertheless, for the famous designer all was far from well. The economic calculations of the ship's creator had been seriously wide of the mark, and the construction of the *Great Eastern* had become like a dinosaur greedily gobbling up Brunel's vast personal wealth. Even the launch proved unexpectedly costly since the great hull had to be painstakingly moved four hundred yards to the water's edge, a manoeuvre which took three months. Finally, even when the ship was in position, the ceremony had to be delayed once more when it became clear that the swell from its entry into the Thames would swamp onlookers. By the time it had finally been set afloat the *Great Eastern* had cost over one million pounds – two-thirds over budget. Even then, the ship's interior was not fully furbished.

The strain of the *Great Eastern* project led to a deterioration in the health of its creator. One afternoon, whilst inspecting his giant ship, Isambard Kingdom Brunel suffered a stroke. A week later, having just heard that one of the *Great Eastern*'s funnels had exploded, the famous engineer died. Soon afterwards another accident in the boiler room of the ship scalded five men to their deaths, and in an entirely separate incident on the very same day a painter fell into one of the great paddle wheels. His body was never found.

These early accidents were an inauspicious enough start to the liner's career; as it turned out they were the first in a whole parade of misfortunes. Three months after Brunel's death and with the *Great Eastern* still to begin her maiden voyage, the ship's captain was lost when a sudden squall upset the gig in which he was being rowed ashore. His coxswain also died along with the purser's nine-year-old son. On hearing of this latest tragedy, the entire board of the ship's managing company resigned.

Months went by and as prospective sailing dates passed with depressing regularity, people began to wonder if the giant of the seas would ever leave the Thames. In the end, when it finally set sail for America nearly a year behind schedule, the ship designed to carry four thousand passengers began its maiden voyage with just thirty-five. Nor did New Yorkers trust the hoodoo vessel any more than Londoners. On its return there were only nine paying customers. To make matters worse the jinx was about to strike again. Approaching Milford Haven the *Great Eastern* ran down a small boat, killing its two occupants. Later that same day it collided with a Royal Navy frigate, the *Blenheim*.

When news of this twin disaster broke the hoodoo story was reinforced and any hopes of improved financial returns were lost. In desperation the owners hired a new captain and senior crew but to no avail. In September 1861, a hurricane caused £60,000 worth of damage; once repaired the *Great Eastern* hit a rock on its very next voyage, tearing a gaping hole of fifty feet long in its side. Miraculously it stayed afloat but the new repair bill was even more expensive than the first and the ship's owners went bankrupt.

In 1872, only fifteen years after it was originally constructed, the *Great Eastern* was scrapped for a sum of £20,000. During its disassembly workers discovered the skeletons of the two riveters entombed between the twin layers of the giant's hull.

It is impossible to say for certain that the deaths of the two workers which took place early in the life of the *Great Eastern* played any part in the creation of its jinx. However, we can say that many ships acquired jinxes only after a tragedy occurred during their construction.

Another similarly ill-starred ship was the *Scharnhorst*, a German World War II battle cruiser which began her unhappy career by rolling on her side in dry dock, crushing some sixty construction workers in the process. At her ill-fated launch another death occurred when, watched by Hitler himself, she broke away from her seven-inch steel cable moorings. Once afloat the battle cruiser seemed to be in the way of every Allied shell, bomb or torpedo fired in her direction and on two occasions her own gun turrets exploded causing carnage amongst her crew. By the time she rammed and sank her sister ship the *Bremen* in 1942 the name *Scharnhorst* became a term of abuse in the German Navy and the following year she sank, taking more than nineteen hundred seamen with her to the bottom.

If hoodoo ships usually curse all who sail in them, then some are more particular. An outstanding example of this variety was the *Hinemoa*, a British tramp steamer which jinxed its captains after the first one decided to use gravel from a graveyard as ballast. That skipper went mad, and of his successors two were murdered, one committed suicide and another drank himself to death. The *Hinemoa* descended beneath the waves in 1908, taking her last skipper with her.

Jinxed ships which damn their crews to a watery grave are a legendary part of sailors' folklore. Jinxed automobiles are less well known, yet the case histories of two vehicles provide an eerie sequence of ill luck to match the tales of any ocean going vessel.

In 1955 film star James Dean ended his life on a lonely California highway. A notoriously reckless driver, a heavy drinker and womaniser, Dean died as he had lived – at full throttle. So when his body was pulled from the mangled wreckage of his silver Porsche, most people assumed that the actor's love affair with speed had been to blame and not the car itself. However, the vehicle's subsequent history was to cause some to think again. In the week following the star's death the Porsche was towed to a nearby garage. Apparently damaged beyond repair, it was initially decided that the car should be broken for spare parts. For the garage proprietor it proved to be a costly decision, for during disassembly the engine fell from its mountings and crushed him as he worked underneath. A little while afterwards, the work having been completed by another mechanic, parts from the same engine were bought by an amateur racing enthusiast who installed them in a hot-rod he was building. He was killed in his first race. Also killed in the same event was another amateur racing driver, a doctor by profession, who had likewise bought some spare parts from Dean's cannibalised Porsche.

Meanwhile back at the garage, someone had the bright idea of restoring the shell of the original car and exhibiting it as James Dean's death carriage. This ghoulish idea was soon put into practice and the car towed on the back of a trailer across the Southern States of America where it proved to be a great attraction. However, unlike its former owner, the jinx was far from dead and the truck pulling the sideshow was involved in several crashes. Moreover, the car itself had an uncanny habit of falling off its display mountings. In Memphis a teenager's hip was broken after just such an incident, whilst in Oregon three viewers were seriously injured when the vehicle slipped down its ramp. Finally in 1959 the sideshow came to an ignominious close when the fated Porsche fell once more from its display vehicle and disintegrated into eleven pieces.

Odd though it is, the jinx which dogged the cult hero's convertible for four years pales into insignificance when compared to the murderous history of the Mercedes-Benz limousine which was originally owned by the Austrian aristocrat Archduke Franz Ferdinand. The double killing of the Archduke and his wife in Sarajevo whilst travelling in the car proved to be the spark that lit the fuse of World War I, yet it also began a separate and quite astonishing legacy of destruction in which the vehicle itself remained firmly at the centre. Immediately following the outbreak of hostilities in Europe, the Mercedes passed into the hands of a distinguished senior officer in the Austrian Cavalry, one General Potiovek. Used as the General's staff car the Mercedes proved an unlucky omen since its owner's fortunes in battle went sour. Disgraced as an incompetent, Potiovek resigned his commission and retired to his country retreat where he quickly went insane. The car meanwhile was passed on to a subordinate officer in the same regiment, for whom it was to prove an equally unlucky possession. Early in 1915 the captain who had acquired the car drove into the back of a truck; he was killed along with his driver and two other soldiers.

After the Armistice was signed the Mercedes passed out of the armed service into civilian hands. Its first owner following the war was the Governor of Yugoslavia. Despite being used only rarely, the car still managed to become involved in several accidents during its official duties, the most serious of which occurred in the autumn of 1919 when it overturned on a bend, killing its chauffeur and causing the Governor himself to lose an arm. Having been auctioned by the authorities the car then became the property of a prosperous doctor. After two years of apparently trouble-free motoring, he too met his death at the wheel. And so the bloody saga continued ... Of the automobile's last four civilian owners, only one did not die in a fatal accident whilst driving it. The single exception, a wealthy jeweller, took his own life. The car's final owner, a Serbian farmer, died in a head-on collision with a bus; in the same accident his four passengers also perished. All in all, a staggering twenty-two people ended their lives in accidents involving the Mercedes-Benz of the murdered Franz Ferdinand. Happily for the world's motorists the car is now safely installed in a Vienna museum.

Of all the different varieties of coincidence, the jinx syndrome is by far the most troubling to the self-confident rationalist. A career of mayhem like the one the Archduke's car enjoyed can hardly be put down to the workings-out of pure chance. Probably such jinxes occur more frequently than we think, yet remain unnoticed because the original events which began the catalogue of disasters are in themselves of minor importance to all but a few bereaved relatives and friends. Had Franz Ferdinand and James Dean themselves not been famous the histories of their vehicles would likewise have probably gone unrecorded.

Is it really possible that bad luck can attract more bad luck like a series of magnets laid end to end? It is not hard to conceive of a law of attraction in the psychical universe. In fact, in the physical universe evidence exists all around us. Through gravity, subatomic particles join to form atoms, and these link together to become molecules; from these tiny invisible beginnings, continents, oceans, planets and solar systems evolve along with the billions of life forms which inhabit them. Is it so unlikely that a pattern of events can draw the tides of life and death towards itself? As C.G. Jung stated, there may well be a huge synchronistic iceberg which reaches to unfathomable depths, an iceberg upon which our own personal *Titanic*s may flounder at some future predestined date.

Writing on the subject of coincidences, the Austrian psychologist contended that the phenomenon must surely be like a coin which has both positive and negative sides. The question is, who spins the coin? Is it ourselves, both individually and as a race, or can it be some higher principle or law separate from our own personal and collective minds? Jung himself thought it was a blend of the two. In science, he pointed out, there is a law that states that to every action there is an equal and an opposite reaction; so why should not the same be true of para-science?

Looking at the same problem from a religious perspective, it is perhaps worth remembering the beliefs of Eastern mystics which hold that every thought and action a man creates in his life will eventually affect that man's soul to an equal and proportionate degree. In the same way the Bible tells us that 'those who live by the sword shall die by the sword' and 'as ye reap so shall ye sow'. Could the words of Christ and Buddha have held a far more literal truth than we have so far imagined? Perhaps in synchronicity there is a measure of divine retribution after all. Nevertheless there are drawbacks to this theory. For, however attractive this concept may be to those who wish to see good rewarded and evil punished, the phenomenon of jinxes would appear to undermine its very foundations. Jinxes, whatever else they do, act as amoral agents, bringing death and unhappiness to saint and sinner alike, scything down indiscriminately all those who happen to be in their path. Frankly, one would need to be an extremely credulous person to believe God creates jinxes as a clumsy tool for his administration of justice. However, even if we take jinxes into account, the whole idea for cause and effect need not be thrown aside totally. For if we accept Jung's theory that coincidences are controlled and ordered on a super-conscious level of mankind's collective mind, it does not mean that the system which has evolved is necessarily perfect – just as Man himself is not yet perfect. Indeed, being created by human minds synchronicity may suffer a malaise in exactly the same way that a single person's mind may suffer a depression or mental illness. Seen in this light, jinxes might be considered to be merely an aberration or psychic tumour in an otherwise smoothly running system of mentalistic impulses.

Like cancer cells, which remain dormant and harmless in a human body until activated into their unnatural growth, the potentialities contained in all objects for acquiring a jinx could remain hidden until put into motion by some special set of circumstances. Precisely what these special conditions are is not clear, yet they might well include a high intensity of negative emotions: grief, hate, depression etc., centred upon the object. Once begun, the unhappiness goes on to reproduce similar circumstances, attracting or entrapping more and more unfortunate events like a terrible psychic net.

Of course, this theory still leaves us with several problems unsolved. For instance, it does nothing to explain why some tragedies produce jinxes and others do not. Nor does it reveal how some jinxes run their course before the focus of their ill fortune is destroyed. The truth is that I have no idea and, as far as I am aware, neither does anyone else. As long as coincidence remains forbidden territory for serious scientific study I have little doubt that the situation will stay that way.

One man who was less interested than most in any such metaphysical speculations was Charles Hoy Fort, veteran compiler of enigmas and the father of modern-day paranormal research. Fort's view of the universe, a highly unusual one, was formed upon life as it was experienced rather than life as the scientists conceived it to be. Thus the reported existence of anything – whether a common everyday object or a vision of the Virgin Mary – was all that mattered; its reasons for being there were unimportant. The world view of science, which rejected all that it did not immediately comprehend, Charles Fort deplored. For, in noting so many anomalous impossibilities, he was forced to accept that the impossible could happen and therefore he detested those who sought to deny this fundamental truth. For myself, although I do not believe Charles Fort's philosophy to be either complete or satisfactory, I must nevertheless respect his efforts in assembling a body of paranormal evidence to confound the most hardened sceptic. Like my long-since deceased American counterpart I too have looked over the edge of the dark abyss we label the supernatural and, like Fort, I have come to realise that there are more questions than answers. Moreover, as a researcher, I owe him a debt of gratitude. Many of the multifarious examples of strange happenings and weird phenomena contained in the chapters of this book were first noted and collected by Fort. So it is as something of a tribute that I end this chapter with an example of a deadly parallelism which Fort first discovered and afterwards counted among his favourites.

The story surrounds the arrest, conviction and subsequent hanging of three men convicted of the crime of murder in 1926. According to a report published at the time in the New York *Herald Tribune*, the murders had taken place in the London home of Sir Edmund Godfrey in the district of Greenbury Hill. Three men had been arrested the next day, charged with the homicides, and were subsequently tried at the Old Bailey and found to be guilty. Still protesting their innocence, all three men were executed on the morning of 26 November.

And the coincidence? In this case it was simply one of name. For the three men who stepped on to the gallows on that dull November day were Messr Green, Berry and Hill. A malicious joke by the cruel master of ceremonies, or evidence of a judgement by a higher authority? Who can say – yet the same question remains for us all.

There but for the grace of *what* go we?

AFTERTHOUGHTS

Charles Fort once wrote that 'mysteries come in an infinite variety of forms'. He might well have been thinking of unnatural deaths. Ghostly creatures that haunt the death chambers of aristocrats; demonic entities that possess and destroy men's minds; energies beyond the knowledge of science which have the powers to incinerate human bodies in seconds or transport them into another dimension, lost for ever. These are just a few of the dangers which lurk menacingly behind the veil of the unknown. For some readers, the evidence contained in the previous chapters will have come as a shocking revelation. Others may prefer to dismiss it all as a mixture of distortion, fabrication and plain old-fashioned lies. To those people I can do no more than to repeat my assertion to the contrary. Yet there is another group of individuals whose scepticism needs addressing more vigorously. These are the committed rationalists, who, whilst accepting odd things sometimes happen, persist in believing that a simple, logical answer has been consistently overlooked. It is my contention that such objections cannot be upheld for very long. A brief consideration of a couple of specific examples should be enough to demonstrate why.

In the chapter entitled 'Sinister Encounters' we saw how in 1948 Lieutenant Thomas Mantell's USAF fighter crashed moments after making visual contact with a huge silvery coloured mechanical object over the skies of Kentucky. Could it not be possible, we must ask ourselves, that his target was misidentified? That he hallucinated? That his fighter simply malfunctioned ...? Need there have been an alien ship at all? These are questions that require serious consideration, yet inevitably we are drawn back to the UFO version of events. Remember that Mantell's visual description of a large saucer was corroborated not only by his fellow pilots but by Godman Base ground staff, civilians and state highway patrolmen. More importantly, the Godman Base incident was just one of a series of encounters in which USAF aircraft were lost after making contact with flying saucers over American airspace. Under the United States Freedom of Information legislation, the true versions of all these and other disturbing events are now being declassified with the passing of time. The truth behind Project Blue Book's systematic debunking of the UFO menace is at last becoming available for public scrutiny in Washington DC. Can we really believe that Chiefs of Staff of the world's greatest military power were asking the CIA and the FBI to restrict the flow of information about a phenomenon they all knew to be harmless?

If flying saucers really were misidentified planes, balloons, planets or satellites why would the British Ministry of Defence spend hundreds of man hours every year attempting to suppress evidence of them? The question remains unanswered, as reports of UFO activity are once more on the increase ...

Take another entirely different phenomenon – disappearing people. Twenty-five years after the event took place, what can we make of the Cleghorn brothers' testimony in which they claim to have seen their young relative vanish before their eyes whilst walking along a Glasgow street in 1966? Is it not more likely that they were simply drunk, or perhaps lying? Might they not have murdered their brother and disposed of his body? These possibilities must be taken into consideration yet, as before, they fail to stand up to close examination. Firstly, the Cleghorns were not drunk, but perfectly sober at the moment the event took place (in truth they were on their way to a public house at the time). Secondly, there was no motive for killing their brother, nor were the Glasgow police ever suspicious that they had done so. Indeed, a less plausible story could hardly be imagined for an alibi. The blunt truth is that, whilst the fate of young Martin Cleghorn remains enigmatic, it is perfectly consistent with eye-witness accounts of similar disappearances which surface sporadically from around the globe.

Examples of death falling from the skies remains equally impervious to the rationalists' argument. The unfortunate Dusseldorf carpenter impaled by an ice spear might just conceivably have been the recipient of a freak accident, since ice is known to build up on the undersides of aircraft. Such a scenario cannot, however, account for the massacre of over a thousand Chinese slaughtered in an ice bombardment in 1986, nor can the 'aircraft theory' be helpful in explaining the numerous ice falls recorded in the days before the advent of powered flight. Whatever the mystery we choose to consider, it is invariably the repetition of events which belies the natural explanation. Thus, whilst the nightmare prevision of little Eryl Mai Jones of Aberfan might possibly have been a single coincidence, the same argument collapses when one places it in the context of the two hundred other premonitions reported to have been received prior to the Welsh disaster. 'If prevision be a fact,' said one scientist, 'then it undermines our whole theoretical framework of the universe'. But prevision is real, no matter how uncomfortable it may seem to be and it is our concept of linear time that would appear to be at fault.

As we have seen, scientists determined to protect their entrenched beliefs have remained unwilling to embrace the challenge of the supernatural. Largely this is because it is easier to deny that which will not conform, rather than disprove it. The hostility of mainstream science is compounded by the abject failure of parascience to construct a meaningful alternative model of the universe. In over a century of psychic research, no one has come up with anything approaching a comprehensive explanation for the paranormal. It could hardly be called a success story. Yet to be fair, we should recognise the difficulties involved in psychic investigation. Preternatural manifestations cannot be created under laboratory conditions. They happen in the outside world spontaneously, without warning. Moreover, what evidence does remain is often frustratingly inconclusive and contradictory. A strange tale ... a blurred photograph ... an odd paw print ... a mutilated corpse. This may be the perfect recipe for a good piece of horror fiction but is profoundly dissatisfying as a basis for serious study. Since the bulk of documentary evidence for all paranormal occurrences comes in the form of eyewitness accounts it is all too easy to dismiss it as unreliable, even though the same quality of human testimony might be enough to send a murderer to the gallows. Small wonder, then, that parascientists have failed to convince their counterparts in mainstream disciplines.

Nevertheless, there is some light on the horizon, for despite the inherent limitations of paranormal research the evidence supporting preternatural forces grows daily. Indeed, the case is now virtually unanswerable. 'Impossible' phenomena such as ice falls, lightning balls and spontaneous combustion are now proven fact, whilst UFOs, poltergeists and other visionary creatures appear to millions around the globe. The experiences of so many cannot be exclusively the product of fraud or fantasy. Nor can we reasonably discard the evidence simply because it does not fit into our established jigsaw pattern. If science is to remain credible it must take into account what has happened, not simply what it believes can happen. Logically, the first consideration should modify the second, not vice versa.

Some parascientists studying the latent powers of the human mind have recently become convinced that a single source of energy is responsible for such diverse psychic gifts as faith healing, extrasensory perception and divination. These observable mental faculties are – we are told – the result of development of hitherto unused parts of the brain. The force which is brought to bear upon physical objects, such as that which bends metal spoons, is termed telekinetic energy. However, whilst we can create a label for this force, no one has been able to explain it satisfactorily.

Much the same can be said of the energies responsible for the unnatural deaths described in this book. Could a single force lie behind these individual and quite different mysteries? Interestingly, parallels do exist between incidents that seem totally unrelated. Take three phenomena at random: omens, lightning and spontaneous combusion. Preternatural animals, when they are not haunting the deathbeds of aristocrats, appear to spend their time taking the lives of large numbers of their mortal counterparts. How this force might influence, or be influenced by, the energies involved in spontaneous human combustion remains obscure, yet researchers have identified several reports where a series of livestock mutilations coincided with an outbreak of the unnatural flames. Likewise, lightning and SHC might seem to share little in common, yet it is interesting to note that an unaccountably high proportion of women are the victim of both (a ratio of approximately three to one). The similarities between the three phenomena become even more apparent if we look closely at eyewitness accounts. For instance the hellish canine visions which terrorised the Suffolk churches of Blythburgh and Bungay in the seventeenth century, scorching men like leather, caused much the same devastation as the lightning balls which tore through congregations at Widecombe and Châteauneuf. The black dogs of Suffolk appeared during a thunderstorm. Remember, too, the black omen which challenged a wagoner near Hatfield Peverel, Essex, more than two hundred years later. The man was reduced to ashes, a fate reminiscent of contemporary descriptions of spontaneous combustion.

To carry this line of argument a stage further, it should be remembered that certain physical locations appear to attract (or produce?) a plethora of psychic manifestations. In Great Britain, black dogs, UFOs and ghosts habitually frequent areas that have a history of occult practices. These areas include countryside marked by stone circles, ley lines or ancient burial mounds. In America, Indian burial grounds appear to have attracted a similarly disproportionate degree of unnatural visitation. If occult lore is right in believing that black magicians have the power to create objective manifestations of evil from the etheric substance it becomes far easier to imagine why such unearthly visions should be so concentrated. However, these are no vaporous images from the past. They have the power not only to unhinge the minds of the living but to destroy their flesh, blood and bones as well. Whatever dimension they come from their purpose can hardly be for the benefit of mankind.

How likely is it that any of us would die unnaturally? On first examination the chances seem reassuringly slight. Even given the likelihood that thousands of unnatural deaths go unreported every year, their proportion of the total number of deaths can only be tiny. However, this ignores the possibilities raised in the chapter entitled 'Unlucky For Some', which suggested that coincidence might itself be the outpicturing of an unseen force. Coincidences affect us all whether we like it or not. All that remains to be seen is the level of their influence on the overall pattern of deaths. In order to do this I decided to look at official government figures for death rates across the United Kingdom over the last few years. Examining the figures on a region-by-region basis I wondered whether any inexplicable anomalies could be identified. Sure enough aberrations did exist that had no conventional explanation. Taken as a whole it was clear that these were not minor fluctuations in an otherwise logical pattern, but widespread inconsistencies that involved thousands of people and appeared to indicate the influence of a hidden factor.

Has the Grim Reaper really got our postcodes? It may

seem hard to believe that the area you live in should decide how long you live or what you will eventually die of, yet remarkably this would seem to be the case. Without doubt the angel of death visits some places more frequently than others. In these places – black spots indeed – people die far more often and much younger than can be explained through any medical hypothesis. One glaring example is the town of Kirby, Merseyside; compared with a similarly sized community to the south, Chipping Norton in Oxfordshire, people in Kirby die at a rate of three to one. Could these figures be the result of environmental factors? Certainly it seems likely that poverty – poor housing, diet and hygiene – plays a part. Differences in climate and even the distribution of hard and soft water may mirror the mortality map to a degree. Still, not all the anomalies can be readily explained by these socio-medical factors. If income were the chief cause of life expectancy, how is it that men in the worst social class categories in East Anglia live longer than those in the upper and professional classes in Scotland?

Fatalities due to illness was the first category to gain my attention, with particular diseases having their own individual black spots. Many of these examples confound the medical authorities. Why, for example, should a woman in Brighton be six times more likely to die of breast cancer than a woman from Teeside? Or a Glaswegian male to be twice as likely to suffer a fatal stroke than a man from London? Such enormous variations are highly significant of something ... yet we do not know what that something is. Bronchitis, sometimes called the English Disease because it kills so many in the British Isles, follows a particularly strange regional pattern. It is an established medical fact that chronic lung ailments account for the deaths of more men than women (a ratio of roughly three to one across the UK), yet in 1984 the highest number of deaths in any one area in Britain – the north-west of England – actually killed more women than men (ratio four to three).

The reason behind this contradiction? After speaking to the British Medical Association a spokesman admitted they were baffled. Heart disease – the greatest medical killer of all – has its chosen area of concentration: a rural area in the Cumbrian peninsula where the death rate for men is fifty per cent above comparable areas in Britain. Another peculiarity surrounds lung cancer. The fact that men smoke more than women might be enough to explain why more males die of lung cancer than do females. Yet no one has been able to understand how urban British males are seven times more likely to contract lung cancer than women living in the countryside. A further conundrum appears when we isolate six neighbouring districts in the West Midlands: Birmingham, Dudley, Wolverhampton, Walsall, West Bromwich, and Warley. All have extraordinary high incidences of lung cancer in males, yet women enjoy very low rates – thirty per cent below the UK average.

However, it is not only illness that follows illogical patterns. The decision to take one's own life might appear to be a highly subjective one, based probably on a number of personal factors. It is puzzling, then, to see how nationality plays a significant part in the process. British government statistics (per head of population) demonstrate that five men kill themselves in England for every six north of the border. Relative affluence in the south seems to make little difference, since Scottish women are much less likely to commit suicide than their English counterparts. Indeed a Glaswegian female is fifty per cent less inclined to take her life than her counterpart in either Liverpool or Manchester, two English cities which are socio-economically comparable. A further oddity is suggested by the fact that the lowest English rates of suicide are found in Essex and Kent, commuter belt counties where the so-called rat race is at its most stressful, whilst the highest are to be found in Devon and Cornwall, counties where the pace of life is far more relaxed. Most arresting of all is the fact that Northern Ireland has by far the lowest suicide rate for either sex of all the regions. The troubled province, with its desperate poverty, religious intolerance and sectarian violence is, at least on this evidence, the happiest place in the United Kingdom – although statistics do show that suicides always diminish drastically during wartime.

Most striking of all the statistical anomalies between regional death rates concerned fatal road accidents. Ministry of Transport figures calculating risk per hundred thousand head of population demonstrate that the most dangerous roads in Britain are those in the south-western corner of England. Here annual deaths per hundred thousand average 197 as against the national average of 156. Scotland also has a very high total, 193, whilst Greater London is actually the safest place to drive, despite its high density of motorists.

Since over 350.000 people have died on British roads since World War II, regional variations must have played a part in reducing the population of some rural areas, where accident figures seem worse. Is there a hidden cause behind the imbalances, or can they be explained more rationally? At first glance, rural areas simply seem more dangerous than metropolitan districts. But the truth is rather more ambiguous. Wales, for instance, has an extremely low accident death rate, yet it is a predominantly rural country. For every three persons to meet their death in vehicles in Wales, four will end their lives in the same way in Scotland. If the Welsh had a significantly lower proportion of car ownership than their northern counterparts it might make some sense. But they do not – indeed the very opposite is true. Scotland, with its appalling level of accident casualties, has the lowest level of car ownership of any region in the United Kingdom. As with illness and suicide, statistics for death through motor accidents are hard to comprehend.

What conclusions can be drawn from these curious statistical irregularities? Here the traditional concept of chance is hardly worth considering given the prodigious size of the figures involved. By accepting that major variations in the pattern of deaths across a nation of fifty million exist – and that these variations cannot be explained through socio-economic or geo-climatic factors – we necessarily find ourselves facing a hidden, or at least hitherto unrecognised, factor: what some people have labelled the X-factor. After all, something has to be responsible. Seen in this new light, familiar killers like disease, accident or suicide begin to look like the out-picturing of an underlying tendency. Fate, if you prefer, in its weakest form.

Perhaps there is no such thing as a death due to wholly natural causes. The conspicuously unnatural deaths like spontaneous combustion may turn out to be only the tip of the iceberg which affects us all to a greater or lesser degree. It is interesting that in 1987 a London based UFO group claimed to have established a link between flying saucer activity and a high incidence of cancer in a parti-cular area. Meanwhile, in a recent British publication entitled *Subtle Energy* British author John Davidson suggests it may be possible to predict a whole range of natural and preternatural phenomena – from mental illness to the outbreak of spontaneous fires – through a close study of the earth's electromagnetic field. Much more research must be carried out before we can con-fidently begin to predict causal links of this kind. Never-theless, it remains a fascinating direction of enquiry and I have little doubt that time and patient investigation will afford us some unexpected results in the years to come.

Meanwhile the catalogue of sinister events continues. At the time of writing, a radio news broadcast has described the death by fire of a Middlesborough invalid who burst into flames while sitting in her wheelchair. In the same week a man obsessed by black magic has smashed the skulls of his wife and family before hanging himself in Essex. In Warrington, a thirty-nine-year-old secretary has vanished without trace the day after she reported an encounter with aliens. As always reasons will be found to explain these enigmas in safe, conventional terms. The woman who spontaneously combusted will doubtless be seen to have dropped a lighted cigarette on her clothing, whilst the Essex killer will be post-humously certified insane, whether or not he had a history of mental illness. As for the secretary who vanished, she will soon be forgotten and her name will be placed in the missing persons file along with thousands of others every year.

The world remains blissfully unaware of the unnatural forces of destruction in our midst. Some might feel it is better that it should remain so. But I am not of that opinion. This book is dedicated to those who have seen the hand of the unnatural in our world, have recognised it for what it is, and have had the courage to tell the truth as they know it to be.

FOR THOSE WHO WISH TO INVESTIGATE FURTHER ...

Throughout *Unnatural Causes* many books have been cited as containing evidence of particular mysteries. Readers who wish to look more deeply into the realm of the paranormal may also find the following titles interesting:

Bord, Janet and Colin, *Modern Mysteries of the World*, (London, Grafton Books, 1989).

Coleman, Loren, *Mysterious America*, (Boston and London, Faber & Faber, 1983).

Evans, Hilary, *Gods, Spirits, Cosmic Guardians*, (London, Aquarian Press, 1987).

Fort, Charles, *The Complete Books of Charles Fort*, (New York, Dover Publications, 1974).

Keel, John, *Strange Creatures from Time and Space*, (London, Spearman, 1975).

MacKenzie, Andrew, *The Seen and the Unseen*, (London, Weidenfeld & Nicolson, 1987).

Probably the most literate and thought provoking studies of all supernatural phenomena remain the various books by British writers Lyall Watson and Colin Wilson.

Futura now offers an exciting range of quality titles by both established and new authors. All of the books in this series are available from:

Futura Books,
Cash Sales Department,
P.O. Box 11,
Falmouth,
Cornwall TR10 9EN.

Alternatively you may fax your order to the above address. Fax No. 0326 376423.

Payments can be made as follows: Cheque, postal order (payable to Macdonald & Co (Publishers) Ltd) or by credit cards, Visa/Access. Do not send cash or currency. UK customers and B.F.P.O.: please send a cheque or postal order (no currency) and allow £1.00 for postage and packing for the first book, plus 50p for the second book, plus 30p for each additional book up to a maximum charge of £3.00 (7 books plus).

Overseas customers including Ireland, please allow £2.00 for postage and packing for the first book, plus £1.00 for the second book, plus 50p for each additional book.

NAME (Block Letters) ....

ADDRESS ....

....

☐ I enclose my remittance for _____

☐ I wish to pay by Access/Visa Card

Number ⬜⬜⬜⬜⬜⬜⬜⬜⬜⬜⬜⬜⬜⬜⬜⬜⬜⬜

Card Expiry Date ⬜⬜⬜⬜